D1564495

In a Materialist Way

In a Materialist Way

Selected Essays by Pierre Macherey

EDITED BY WARREN MONTAG

Translated by Ted Stolze

VERSO

London • New York

First published by Verso 1998
This edition © Verso 1998
Translation © Ted Stolze 1998
Introduction © Warren Montag 1998

The rights of Pierre Macherey, Warren Montag and Ted Stolze to be identified
respectively as the author, editor and translator of this work have been asserted by
them in accordance with the Copyright, Designs and Patents Act 1988

Verso
UK: 6 Meard Street, London W1V 3HR
USA: 180 Varick Street, New York NY 10014–4606

Verso is the imprint of New Left Books

ISBN 1–85984–949–0

British Library Cataloguing in Publication Data
A catalogue record for this book is available from the British Library

Library of Congress Cataloging-in-Publication Data
A catalog record for this book is available from the Library of Congress

Typeset by SetSystems, Saffron Walden, Essex
Printed by Biddles Ltd, King's Lynn and Guildford

Contents

Acknowledgments

I would like to thank Michael Sprinker for his tireless advocacy of this project and for his useful advice, and Steve Cox and Jane Hindle for careful editorial work. I owe a debt to all those with whom I have discussed this project over the years: Peter Wissokur, Geoffrey Goshgarian, Etienne Balibar, Ted Stolze and Gregory Elliott. Without the generosity of M. Olivier Corpet and the informed assistance of François Matheron, both of the Institut Mémoires de l'Édition Contemporaine in which the Fonds Althusser are held, I could never have written the preface I did. Finally, of course, I must thank Pierre Macherey himself for sharing so much in so many ways.

Warren Montag

Notes on Abbreviations and Original Sources

Throughout this collection we have used the following standard abbreviations for Spinoza's writings:

CM   *Metaphysical Thoughts* (*Cogitata metaphysica*)

E   *Ethics* (*Ethica*)
  App   Appendix
  Ax   Axiom
  C   Corollary
  Def   Definition
  Def. Aff. Definition of Affect
  D   Demonstration
  Exp   Explanation
  Lem   Lemma
  P   Proposition
  Post   Postulate
  Pref   Preface
  S   Scholium

  Note: A comma within a citation from the *Ethics* means "and"; for instance, the abbreviation E VP20D, S indicates that both the Demonstration and the Scholium of Proposition 20 of *Ethics*, part V are being cited.

Ep   Letter (*Epistola*)

KV   *Short Treatise on God, Man, and His Well-Being* (*Korte Verhandeling*)

PPC   *Descartes's "Principles of Philosophy"* (*Principia Philosophiae Cartesianae*)

TdIE   *Treatise on the Emmendation of the Intellect* (*Tractatus de Intellectus Emendatione*)

TP   *Political Treatise* (*Tractatus Politicus*)

TTP   *Theologico-Political Treatise* (*Tractatus Theologico-Politicus*)

Quotations from Spinoza's writings are based on (but usually modify) the following translations: Curley (TdIE, KV, CM, E, EpI–28); Shirley (TTP); Wernham (TTP, TP); and Wolf (Ep 29–84). For longer quotations we cite as well Gebhardt's standard Latin edition, which we abbreviate as, for example, G II/153 (= volume two, page 153).

We have taken the articles in this collection from the following sources, and gratefully acknowledge the publishers for their co-operation in the preparation of this volume:

"Soutenance" was Pierre Macherey's "defense" of his entire corpus presented to an academic jury on 25 May 1991.

"Philosophy as Operation" first appeared as "La philosophie comme opération" in *Digraphe* 42, December 1987, 69–81.

"For a Theory of Literary Reproduction" is previously unpublished.

"The Hegelian Lure: Lacan as Reader of Hegel" first appeared as "Le leurre hégélien" in *Le bloc-note de la psychanalyse* 5, 1985, 27–50.

"At the Sources of *Histoire de la folie*: a Rectification and its Limits" first appeared as "Aux sources de 'L'histoire de la folie': Une rectification et ses limites" in *Critique* 471–2, August–September 1986, 753–74.

"Foucault: Ethics and Subjectivity" first appeared as "Foucault: Éthique et subjectivité" in *Autrement* 102, November 1988, 92–103.

"From Canguilhem to Canguilhem by Way of Foucault" first appeared as "De Canguilhem à Canguilhem en passant par Foucault" in *Georges Canguilhem: Philosophe, historien des sciences*, 286–94 (Paris: Albin Michel, 1993).

"Deleuze in Spinoza" most recently appeared as "Deleuze dans Spinoza" in *Avec Spinoza: études sur la doctrine et l'histoire du spinozisme*, 237–44 (Paris: Presses Universitaires de France, 1992).

"Spinoza's Philosophical Actuality (Heidegger, Adorno, Foucault)" most recently appeared as "L'actualité philosophique de Spinoza (Heidegger, Adorno, Foucault" in *Avec Spinoza: études sur la doctrine et l'histoire du spinozisme*, 222–36 (Paris: Presses Universitaires de France, 1992).

"Spinoza, the End of History, and the Ruse of Reason" most recently appeared as "Spinoza, fin de l'histoire et la ruse de la raison" in *Avec Spinoza: études sur la doctrine et l'histoire du spinozisme*, 111–40 (Paris: Presses Universitaires de France, 1992).

"Georges Canguilhem's Philosophy of Science: Epistemology and History of Science" first appeared as "La philosophie de la science de Georges Canguilhem: Épistemologie et histoire des sciences" in *La pensée* 113, January–February 1964, 50–74.

I
Introduction by
Warren Montag

Several years ago, Pierre Macherey wrote a column for the journal *Futur Antérieur* entitled "Chronicles of a Dinosaur." It is not difficult to guess why he would choose such a title. Known primarily as a student or "disciple" of Louis Althusser, whose text, *A Theory of Literary Production*, represented, in the words of many commentators, the doctrine of an "Althusserian literary criticism," it is no wonder that thirty years after the publication of his first book, and at least twenty years after the "Althusserian" moment passed, Macherey could refer to himself as a dinosaur. After all, is he not a survivor of the "structuralist" epoch, the textual monuments of which are regarded by contemporary readers as curiosities, as puzzling in their complexity as the simultaneously strange and familiar skeletons exhibited in a museum of natural history? And if the label of structuralist were not enough to qualify his work for a place in the museum of extinct theories, theories that could no longer lead any other than a posthumous existence as embalmed corpses whose spirit had long since fled, there is, of course, the matter of his Marxism, or rather his "structural Marxism" the rise and fall of which was recounted years ago. If Macherey could describe himself as a dinosaur in France, where he has published seven books and more than fifty essays since *Pour une théorie de la production littéraire* appeared in 1966, what might we expect in the Anglophone world where, until last year, *A Theory of Literary Production* was his only translated work (apart from a few essays, all of which dated from the Sixties and Seventies)?

Of course, no matter how we may protest the inaccuracy of the reception of Macherey's work, in particular, the routine reduction of his writing to "structuralism," "structural Marxism"or even "Althusserian-ism," categories which function less as taxonomic markers than as forms of denunciation, it cannot be ignored. This reception is neither purely subjective, consisting of inadequate ideas in the minds of readers, nor mere "error," which might be dissipated through a confrontation with historical reality. The reception of Macherey's work, formed by the commentaries that his work provoked, some hostile, others sympathetic, a reception therefore quite variegated and complex, is fully material, in the sense of the materiality not only of words, but also of the institutions in which Macherey's work is "consumed." Moreover, it will determine how Macherey's later work, the work represented in this volume, will itself be received. There is no reason to be fatalistic about this, however, for it is possible that, by analysing this reception, we can diminish the power and frequency of its repetitions, and allow the texts included in this volume to speak in a new and previously unheard voice which might in turn contribute to a transformation of what is understood to be denoted by the proper name "Macherey."

Let us begin with the well-known "fact" that Macherey was an "Althusserian" and therefore a "structuralist." Macherey was indeed a student of Althusser's: he attended the Ecole Normale Supérieure from 1958 to 1963, and after completing his *Maîtrise* (roughly the equivalent of a Master's Thesis), "Philosophie et politique chez Spinoza," under the supervision of Georges Canguilhem in 1961, began to work closely with Althusser. At first, as Althusser helped Macherey prepare for the *agrégation* (a standardized, national version of what, in the US, is called the qualifying examination), the relations between the two men were those of a student to his professor; Althusser read and corrected Macherey's written exercises, often reproving him for faults in style and argumentation. It was around this time that Macherey, together with other students, approached Althusser for guidance in studying the texts of Marx and Engels.

Beginning in the academic year 1962–3, their relation became more collaborative. Althusser organized a seminar on structuralism in which Macherey participated, along with other students (among them Michel Pêcheux, Jacques Rancière, Etienne Balibar). The participants presented papers on a range of topics, from what Althusser called the "prehistory of structuralism; from Montesquieu to Dilthey" to the work of such figures as Lévi-Strauss, Foucault, Lacan and Canguilhem. Macherey's first publication in 1964 grew out of his contribution to the seminar "La philosophie de la science de Georges Canguilhem: épistémologie et histoire des sciences" which appeared in *La Pensée* (the theoretical journal of the French Communist Party) with a preface by Althusser himself (a translation of the essay appears in the present volume). The notes taken by Althusser during the seminar, together with fragments of the texts of his own presentations, indicate very clearly that the participants regarded structuralism not as a unified theory or ideology but as the site of "real disorder," as Macherey later put it, and philosophical divergence. In particular, if the theoretical anti-humanism of the structuralist enterprise was welcome, its field also contained the blind spots of its own "unthought": for while structuralist texts subverted the concept of the human subject, the individual endowed with consciousness, they often did so in the name of an anonymous subject called structure, a subject that, like any other, employed means to realize the ends that it "desired." Hence the need to draw lines of demarcation, dividing lines that would make visible in the field of "structuralism" itself the distinction between a tendency that was nothing more than "humanism with a structural face" and a theoretical tendency that was both anti-subjective and anti-teleological. It was precisely for this reason that Althusser later wrote that "history is a process without a subject *or goals*" (emphasis added), opposing any functionalism or teleology (although nothing prevented his critics from suppressing the phrase "or goals" in order to charge Althusser with functionalism: there can be no functionalism without goals).

The decision to devote a year-long seminar to structuralism, many of whose seminal works had yet to be produced in 1962, was also exemplary of the way this group, consisting of Althusser and a number of fledgling philosophers, had already begun to think about the activity of philosophy. Precisely because they were Marxists and materialists, they granted philosophy what few others would: an objective, historical existence, a fact that paradoxically earned them the label of "idealist." Paradoxically, because they began by refusing the myth of the independence of philosophy, a myth that has its positive and negative variants. In the positive variant of this myth, philosophy transcends any particular time or place, a fact that renders it timeless and universal, according it a freedom to speak not to particular classes, genders, or nations at particular moments but to all people at all times. According to the negative variant, philosophy is properly speaking nothing, or rather a dim reflection of the reality that is its cause but which it cannot affect in return; once social relations were made transparent, philosophy even in its phantom, spiritual existence would simply disappear: the death of philosophy. Such, of course, was the view of philosophy presented by Marx and Engels in *The German Ideology*, or rather one of the views, the other being precisely its contrary, namely the idea that no philosophy was without a connection to the social reality that made it possible. Pursuing the latter idea to its conclusion, these philosophers argued that philosophy could itself only be understood as a practice, specifically a theoretical practice, inescapably endowed with a material existence and linked to other practices. As such, philosophy was not read, interpreted or misinterpreted; rather, it produced effects, some of which escaped the intentions of the philosopher, no matter how coherent the arguments with which they were validated. Philosophy understood as practice was compelled constantly to confront its own effects and to readjust itself to produce new effects in an ever-changing historical situation whose variability and complexity it could never master. Only by reflecting critically and historically on the philosophical present, the "theoretical conjuncture," and by staking out a position on and in the moment to which they inescapably belonged, did these philosophers believe they could practise philosophy in an effective way. There was thus no possibility of doing philosophy *ex nihilo*, in a void, free of historical and social determinations. In philosophy, as Althusser wrote, every space is always already occupied and one takes a position only against the adversary who already occupies that position.

It also marked their own sense of distance from the organizing principles that dominated the field called structuralism, that is, the fact that, despite the protestations of several generations of commentators, they were not structuralists and had already begun what would be a rather sustained critique of "structuralist ideology." The emergent "community of thought" formed by Althusser and his comrades was of course no more homogeneous than any other; each philosopher even as he participated in this community developed singular interests and positions. It was Macherey, more than any of the others, who in his earliest publications, and therefore prior to some of the most seminal structuralist documents, elaborated a critique of structuralism. Particularly instructive in this regard was Macherey's essay "Literary Analysis, the Tomb of Structures," which appeared in a special issue of *Les Temps Modernes* devoted to structuralism in 1966 (the essay appeared the same year as a chapter in *Pour une théorie de la production littéraire*). Althusser, consulted by the editors as the contributions to the issue were solicited, urged Macherey to write "an article on the structuralism of Barthes and Foucault. . . . It is important that we enter this issue in force for now decisive political and theoretical reasons" (Louis Althusser to Pierre Macherey, 23 June 1965). The article Macherey wrote (dated November 1965) was an extraordinary critique of the dominant themes of structuralist approaches to literature which, he argued, shared with traditional methods of literary analysis the search for the "rationality, the secret coherence of the object" (*Theory* 142). Literary analysis would no longer discover hidden structures but rather the radical absence of such structures, precisely the place of a lack of the rationality that would totalize its parts or elements. Where there was assumed to be depth, there was only surface, what was sought was discovered not to be hidden (the text offers no refuge of concealment), but missing and missed: the tomb of structures.

If it would thus appear that Macherey simply carried out an intervention for Althusser by proxy, a series of letters, themselves part of a larger exchange that was probably carried on mainly in direct conversation between the two men, shows exactly the opposite. It was the 27-year-old Macherey who subjected the published work of his former teacher to some very rigorous criticism, which was characteristically welcomed and productively assimilated by its recipient. In an exchange of letters in May 1965, a month before Althusser secured a place for Macherey in the Structuralism issue of *Les Temps Modernes*, Macherey confessed to a certain distrust of the "idea of a *structured whole*" and wondered if the notion of the whole was not "precisely the spiritualist conception of structure" (Pierre Macherey to Louis Althusser, 10 May 1965). In a letter dated four days later, Macherey counterposes to Althusser's concept Spinoza's notion of the infinity of attributes, referring specifically to Spinoza's letter to Oldenburg of November 1665. The particular reference is significant apart from the fact that it reveals Macherey's rather detailed knowledge of and interest in Spinoza, an interest that he shared with, but did not owe to, Althusser (and others in their circle, a number of whom, not coincidentally, have since become prominent Spinoza scholars). In the letter Macherey cites, Spinoza argues (against any notion of a whole or a totality) that every individual thing is composed of individual things, themselves composed of individual things, *ad infinitum*. In the same way, "since the nature of the universe ... is absolutely infinite, its parts are controlled by the nature of this infinite potency in infinite ways, and are compelled to undergo infinite variations" (Spinoza, *Letters* 194). Macherey's recommendation that Althusser consult Spinoza's text is immediately followed by another reference to a work that Macherey clearly considers to be related: Deleuze's commentary on Lucretius (first published in 1961 and later, in 1969, incorporated into *The Logic of Sense*), a part of which refers explicitly to the problem Macherey raises in relation to Althusser's text: "nature as the production of the diverse can only be an infinite sum, that is, a sum which does not totalize its own elements. There is no combination capable of encompassing all the elements of nature at once, there is no unique world or total universe" (*Logic* 267).

Then, in an undated letter written after receiving a copy of the essay destined for *Les Temps Modernes* (and therefore probably in the late summer or early autumn of 1965), Althusser refers to critical remarks directed by Macherey against the notion of a "latent structure" employed by the former in his essay "The Piccolo Teatro: Bertolazzi and Brecht" (published in 1962 in *Esprit* and again in 1965 as a chapter in *For Marx*), and especially in the conclusion to his contribution to *Reading Capital*. After reading "The Tomb of Structures," Althusser writes: "I have understood what you indicated to me one day, when you told me that the concept of 'latent structure' appeared to you dubious.... I now see clearly what you meant.... It is that the concept is ambiguous, divided between a conception of structure as interiority, therefore as the correlate of an *intention*, or at least of a unity, and another conception, very close to yours, in which structure is thought as an absent *exteriority*." Thus was the educator educated.

Althusser's words to Macherey, or rather his interpretation of Macherey's own words, capture with admirable lucidity the contradiction proper to structuralism. On the one hand, the notion that every human endeavour resembled language conceived as a finite set of elements whose combination into units of significance was governed by rules or laws (a notion that dominated structuralist inquiry even in its diversity) undoubtedly "subverted the subject," and called into question every individualist theory of society or culture and every philosophy of consciousness. It did so, however, only by positing an ultimate order, system or structure of which a given individual or a given event was merely a function. Thus theoretical humanism or anthropology was displaced but in a way that left its form intact: there was still an origin and a centre of a given field, the principle of its order, but instead of man, endowed with an invariant nature (whether this nature was rational or irrational, competitive or sociable matters little), there was structure, a new, more rigorous, and even superhuman form of intention and unity.

While Althusser clearly resisted the model of language and the image of the combinatory that it offered to critical reflection, and, further, argued that structuralism was at heart a formalism, he did not entirely escape its effects. Macherey pointed to certain formulations in the first edition of *Reading Capital* (all of which Althusser removed from subsequent editions) in which structure was precisely "latent" in the field it defined, the hidden order, and thus simultaneously immanent and transcendent, of a manifest disorder. This was still a "spiritual whole," even if it did not take the form of what Althusser called the expressive totality. Of course, the meaning of these formulations was entirely at odds with the statements within which they were interspersed. Althusser elsewhere imagines structural causality, in directly Spinozist terms, as the cause that exists solely in its effects, immanent or, perhaps more accurately, absent, any possibility of a principle of unity disappearing into the diversity and complexity of the real (which diversity and complexity Althusser tried to capture with the concept of the overdetermined contradiction). It was during this time, the summer of 1966, that Althusser formulated one of his virulent critiques of structuralism, in this case, the structural anthropology of Lévi-Strauss, which Althusser found to be functionalist. For Lévi-Strauss, "if there are given rules of marriage, etc. in primitive societies it is *in order* to permit them to live or to survive etc. (a biologistic functionalist subjectivism: there is a 'social unconscious' that assures, as would any acute intelligence, the appropriate *means* to allow 'primitive society' to live and survive . . . it is necessary to criticize this functionalism that, theoretically is a form of subjectivism, that endows society with the form of existence of a subject having intentions and objectives" (*Ecrits* 424–5).

These were the problems that defined the field in which *A Theory of*

Literary Production constituted an intervention. In the revised version of "The Tomb of Structures" that appears as chapter 20 of *Theory*, Macherey states most directly an argument found throughout the text: if the term structure is to be used at all, it is only to be used in a sense diametrically opposed to the meaning given to it in structuralist discourse. As if to continue the dialogue with Althusser, Macherey writes: "If there is a structure, it is not in the book, concealed in its depths: the work pertains to it but does not contain it. Thus the fact that the work can be related to a structure does not imply that it is itself unified; structure governs the work in so far as it is diverse, scattered and irregular" (*Theory* 151, translation modified). Of all the concepts available to literary analysis, that of structure alone would appear to allow us to escape the illusions of manifest or latent order, harmony and coherence; structure alone "can think irregularity" (151). Finally, the two sentences in the concluding paragraph have exhibited, in the interval of thirty years that separates us from the moment of their appearance, an extraordinary fecundity which is very likely not yet exhausted: "The concealed order of the work is thus less significant than its real determinate disorder (its disarray). The order which it professes is merely an imagined order, projected on to disorder, the fictive resolution of ideological conflicts, a resolution so precarious that it is obvious in the very letter of the text where incoherence and incompleteness burst forth" (155).

Among the most serious difficulties encountered by the structuralist enterprise was its apparent inability to understand the historical determination of the fields it examined. History, to the extent it figured at all in structural analyses, appeared as pure exteriority, enveloping but never penetrating the objects that it carried along. Thus structuralism produced such notorious dilemmas as structure versus process, or, to use the preferred terminology, the synchronic versus the diachronic. In the realm of literary analysis, the more rigorous the analysis of the text, the more it assumed the characteristics of a closed system in which, no matter what the level of analysis, there was no element, however small, that did not have a systemic function. History had no place in this order which was, strictly speaking, timeless. At most, history could fill the places already defined by the structure, the names and costumes to decorate a narrative that, as a structure of possibility, had always existed. Of course it was Althusser who advanced the most productive critique of what he called in *Reading Capital*:

> the currently widespread distinction between synchrony and diachrony. This distinction is based on a conception of historical time as continuous and homogeneous and contemporaneous with itself. The synchronic is contemporaneity itself, the co-presence of the essence with its determinations, the present being readable as a structure in an "essential section" because the present is the very existence of the essential structure.... It follows that the diachronic

is merely the development of this present in the sequence of a temporal continuity in which the "events" to which "history" in the strict sense can be reduced (cf. Lévi-Strauss) are merely successive contingent presents in the time continuum. (*Reading* 96)

Just as the structuralist approach to the study of history proper could not but fail to grasp the unevenness, heterogeneity, the irreducible divergence of what is better described as a "conjuncture" than as a moment, the moment of the present, so the structural analysis of "narratives" could only ignore or deny that which, in the system of the text "does not work," its faults, gaps and conflicts. Once the text is no longer either a system or closed, its opposition to history disappears. It is no longer external to history, or history to it; the work is itself fully real and historical, no longer a mere representation or reflection of that which is outside of it. On the contrary, if the work is necessarily disordered, it is because the social reality of which it is fashioned (and of which the work thus represents a continuation) is itself traversed with conflicts, so unevenly developed that this reality cannot be summarized in the simplicity of a "present."

Thus the charge, echoed by Terry Eagleton among others, that Macherey's first work is "formalist" cannot be sustained ("Macherey" 152–3). The point is not that form creates or even makes visible "ideological contradictions"; it is rather that no matter how coherent or unified a work appears, it cannot escape the social, historical conflicts that traverse the field in which it emerged. Nor, at the same time, is there anything subversive about a literature that explicitly rejects formal unity, given that its lack of closure, its refusal to reconcile its conflicts, its apparent abjuration of literary norms is nothing more than a dissimulation of disorder in the service of a unifying intention (which is, of course, itself doubled by the unthought and the unintentional, the loci of its own historical truth).

Further, if there is anything "Hegelian" about the positions proper to *A Theory of Literary Production* , as another critic has charged (Gallagher, "Marxism" 43), it is not Macherey's supposed privileging of "art," but rather his refusal of the distinction between form and content, and, perforce, his rejection of any notion that the former could be "imposed" upon the latter indifferently, from the space of an indeterminate outside, without any meaningful connection to a content which is nothing more than a brute material to be shaped, offering itself as a nature to be ordered through art(ifice). The conflicts that Macherey speaks of pertain neither to the form nor to the content of a work, they are the conflicts that precisely reveal the complicity between form and content, an inseparability determined by the struggles in which the work necessarily participates, if only by means of a denial that they exist at all. The most important inspiration for *A Theory of Literary Production* was, of course, Spinoza, whose analysis of Scripture in the *Tractatus Theologico-Politicus* revealed that in place of the perfection and harmony that were thought to characterize the holy word, there was only a faulty, mutilated patchwork, a composite deprived of any unity or order whatever and which could be explained only on the basis of this, its material existence, as a historical artifact. Spinoza's influence on Macherey went unnoticed; as Althusser once remarked "to recognize him you must at least have heard of him" (*Essays* 132).

Do these positions, now familiar at least in part to a fairly broad audience, not constitute the doctrine of an "Althusserian" or even "Machereyan" literary theory? Obviously not, given that Macherey's concern in *A Theory of Literary Production* is to dismantle, one by one, the theoretical obstacles that have so far blocked the emergence of a theory capable of doing more than reaffirming the ideological givens that govern our thinking about what we rather simplistically and quite ahistorically call "literature." Instead of crediting Macherey (if only then to blame him) with a theory that he never formulated, we might much more accurately take him at his word in the final sentence of the theoretical section of the work, "Some Elementary Concepts": "Decentred, displayed, determinate, complex: recognized as such, the work runs the risk of receiving its theory" (101).

After *A Theory of Literary Production* (which by 1980 had gone through six printings, and had been translated into eight foreign languages) a few essays appeared and then a relatively long period of silence ensued, unbroken until the publication of *Hegel ou Spinoza* in 1979, one of the last works to appear in Althusser's *Théorie* series with the publishing house Maspero. The collective project that had produced *Reading Capital* foundered even before 1968, torn by political, theoretical and personal conflicts. 1968 brought in its wake an entirely new and unforeseen theoretical and political conjuncture that required a readjustment of perspective and line. Neither the enemies nor the allies were entirely the same as before, and it was therefore impossible to go on speaking in precisely the same way. The fortunes of academic Marxism followed the general shift in the balance of social forces; demobilization and fragmentation in theory as well as practice reigned. To speak of Marx's texts became increasingly difficult; audiences dwindled as the practical forms of Marxism appeared one by one headed for extinction, leaving behind only its "spirit," as Derrida has recently argued.

But what would come to be called the crisis of Marxism had another dimension for the fragile community of thought to which Macherey belonged: the philosophers who participated in the colloquium on *Capital* were all in their twenties when they published their first works in Althusser's *Théorie* collection. The contributions to *Reading Capital*, as well as Macherey's *A Theory of Literary Production*, were precocious and very ambitious, perhaps even naïvely so, but whatever the criticisms we (and above all their authors) would make of them today, no one can deny their extraordinary force, their power, if we define power with Spinoza as the capacity to produce effects. These works were explosive; the effects showered down upon their authors with an unforeseeable violence, altering the terrain to such an extent that the authors were left disoriented, unsure of how to proceed to confront the consequences of their "intervention." It is no wonder then that these philosophers turned to the question of the practice of philosophy, the struggle of which it was the site, the stakes of this struggle and the means with which one affects its outcome. Hence, also, the repeated efforts at "self-criticism," that is, the specification and readjustment of their initial theses.

In a letter to Macherey, dated 21 February 1973, Althusser writes:

> Given the objective "myth" that we became, that "I" became, given that this "myth" has given rise to a quantity of questions and interpretations (as well as a number of stupidities from people invoking our name) *what should we do*? 1) Is it better to leave things as they are and act through the intimidation of silence, offer some *new* productions that without speaking of the past nevertheless displace its elements? (Which obviously presupposes that we are *capable* of producing new books bearing on new things: for my part, this is not the case—and as it is not the case—this would simply mean administering silence...) 2) Would it not be better to speak of the past as clearly and precisely as possible, an act rare, if not unthinkable, among philosophers, saying what happened and in what ways we went wrong? There are several advantages to such an action: first, it is nearly without precedent; second, it will really help people of good will to understand what was in question, what was done and why; finally, to take the initiative and therefore the leadership of the critique (in the form of self-criticism) by taking it out of the hands of our adversaries and helping our friends orient themselves.... Let us make no mistake: we are in a situation comparable to the analytic situation of "transference" in relation to our readers, friends–enemies etc. We must take into account their own reading, their own reaction, their utterly singular (and extremely powerful) relation to our "myth" and calculate the terms of our self-criticism in the light of this overdetermined situation.

Perhaps we can say without too great an oversimplification that in this extraordinary letter Althusser describes to Macherey the crossroads to which their philosophical and political adventure led them, and thus, the terms of their separation, their dispersion along very different paths. For while Althusser chose to return to the early texts, their problems and stakes, and to formulate a more rigorous critique of his work (and the work of his colleagues) than any critic had heretofore succeeded in producing, his choice was clearly predicated on the sense that he could no longer write books, at least books that could match *For Marx*. Such was not the case with Macherey, who precisely chose to write new books on new things. While it is doubtful that Macherey shared Althusser's rather grandiose fantasy of an intimidating silence, it is nevertheless useful to regard the phase of his work that begins in 1979 with *Hegel or Spinoza* in Althusser's terms as a displacement, neither a rejection of nor a return to the past, but instead an attempt to discover new points of application from which one might speak about certain problems and questions without being drowned out by a chorus of commentators or without one's words automatically falling on deaf ears. Thus, while his second book might appear austerely narrow in its focus relative to the programmatic character of the first, the choice of subject matter ensured the elimination of all but the most serious readers, even as the opposition inscribed in the title of the book, Hegel or Spinoza, recalled the earlier attempt to demonstrate the specific difference that defined Marx in relation to Hegel. Not that Spinoza was for Macherey a stand-in for Marx, but rather that the very problems in Marx that occupied the attention of Macherey, Althusser and others could be found in even more highly elaborated forms in the works of Spinoza, including, as Macherey argues in the stunning conclusion to the work, the possibility of conceiving a dialectic free of any teleology or of the negativity that teleology requires.

Such a possibility, of course, suggests that it is less a matter of opposing Spinoza to Hegel than perhaps of applying Spinoza to Hegel, as if in the light of Spinoza's philosophical project the contradictions internal to Hegel's development, its paradoxical incompleteness and openness despite (or perhaps because of) all the efforts at closure, become visible and intelligible. Why bother with Hegel at all? Because, as Macherey argues, it is through the mediation of Hegel's philosophy, which acts like a mirror that simultaneously reflects and magnifies, that what is most powerful and actual in Spinoza's thought is made to appear. The encounter between the two produces something new—not, to be sure, a synthesis, but rather the opposite: a line of divergence and a common limit. Far from our having crossed or passed beyond this limit, we cannot even acknowledge it as a limit until Macherey confronts us with our inability even to imagine what the Hegel–Spinoza encounter produces: a dialectic of the positive. If Macherey appears to privilege Spinoza's philosophy, the conditions of this privilege are purely histori-cal. Spinoza's philosophy is strangely actual, present in the ruminations of our time, even (especially) when he is not cited or named. It does not so much consist of a body of theories to be reproduced and verified or refuted but is, rather, as Hegel might have said of his own philosophy, a philosophy "in perpetual becoming, as if it were itself in search of its own true meaning."

"In search of its own true meaning": perhaps this phrase is as true of

Macherey's practice of philosophy as of Spinoza's and accounts for his sustained interest in his contemporaries, i.e., his fellow dinosaurs whose names even in the US and Britain, not to speak of France, appear to denote a way of thinking whose day has come and gone: Lacan, Foucault and Deleuze, to name only them. In opposition to the crude historicism common to a certain "postmodern" sensibility and its most bitter adversary, liberalism, Macherey rejects the implicit comparison of philosophy to the human individual whose life has a beginning, a middle and an end. On the contrary, the meaning of a philosophy, to borrow a phrase from Derrida, is originally deferred, activated only later, even much later, by an encounter with other philosophies, as well scientific theories, literary works etc. No philosophy is closed upon itself, immured in a fortress built from its dogmas, logical or anthropological; it must think by means of other philosophies, it becomes what it is through them. Macherey is among the few to recognize that thought is dependent on a dialogue that necessarily exists, in which it participates whether it wants to or not, and often without knowing it. He has thus never ceased to attempt to understand the historical conditions of possibility of his own thought, the place it occupies in the disposition of social forces external as well as internal to philosophy. And, as Macherey suggests in his extraordinary *Soutenance* (the formal "defence" of his *oeuvre* with which we have chosen to begin this collection), nothing less is required of one who would practise philosophy in a materialist way.

II
In a Materialist Way

1

Soutenance
(25 May 1991)

How should one present a group—we might even say a jumble—of
divergent works so as to replace them in the framework of a course of
study truly deserving the name—and here the singular should carry all
its weight—of a work? To begin, I must say that this dispersion really
testifies to the way in which a process of investigation has unfolded,
through an accumulation of incidents rather than with a spirit of
continuity, without any truly premeditated idea at the beginning, without an already traced plan which would have conferred on its outcome
the equilibrium of an organized architecture, in the manner of the
methodical staging of a polyptych, with its central subject, organized
harmony, frontal arrangement, the composed and measured putting into
perspective of its elements. I must admit it, then: the works I present
here I did not pursue systematically but obliquely and in isolation,
uncertain of what would have been required to unite them, and even, for
a time, relatively indifferent to the possibility of such a connection.

However, it seems to me that given the point of development at which
they have arrived today, these works can be defended, "sustained," by
arguments permitting a kind of order to be derived from them. An order
that, without having been precisely formulated from the beginning,
might finally be sketched, according to a necessity whose movement,
more objective than subjective, would thus have partly escaped me. Isn't
true order always a hidden order? It is on the basis of this interpretation
that I now justify proposing a presentation of it which should itself have
only a provisional value, corresponding not only to the state of the
questions I have tackled, with their relative degree of development, but
also their delays, their lacunae, indeed their inconsistencies or obscuri-
ties, in which I would hope to show, at the same time as symptoms of
incompleteness, the necessity of new investigations.

Three series of questions have successively preoccupied me, without
any one of them replacing or preventing me from returning to the others;

and this is how these studies have been pursued, intersected, broken off again, so as finally to come together, under conditions of opposition and complementarity. These questions are those of Spinozism, of the relations of literature and philosophy, and of the history of philosophy in France. The simple fact of stating these themes of study dramatically reveals what separates them and renders their connection more than improbable, incongruous. It would obviously be tempting to turn them into the panels of a triptych, with its central painting onto which are folded, by adjusting them closely, two lateral shutters: but this would presuppose an ultimately arbitrary distribution of their subjects of interest, causing one of these three questions to stand out as primary, the other two falling back onto it and having only to set it off, so as to prepare its exposition while differentiating it. I therefore prefer to abandon such effects of symmetry, which would evoke only the shadow of a system, divided and undone as soon as it is deployed. And consequently it only remains for me to bring out the retrospective logic of an investigation, provided that the latter has reached the point that it offers itself to a reconstruction, the moment that the threads are tied, features emerge, and a figure of totality begins to be drawn. This figure is irregular and unequal, essentially dissymmetrical, because it has not been traced by the spirit of a system.

In order to carry out this reconstruction, here I would start with the question I have taken up last, in the course of the last six years. I make this choice because it is the consideration of this question that, in fact, has allowed me to establish the connection between the other two. It concerns the history of philosophy in France, to which are devoted a collection of studies and a short book published in 1989 which comments on some well-known passages of August Comte's *Cours de philosophie positive*. Before explaining briefly how I have carried out this work, I would like to say a few words about the reasons why I have undertaken it. In doing so, I will not evade a question which is sometimes put to me, undoubtedly not without various ulterior motives, and within the framework of a trial, one of those examinations of intentions which cannot be heard before a tribunal of reason: Are you still a Marxist? In response, I must state, and specify to myself, what Marxism did not need to become because it had always been it. More seriously, I have never been able to regard Marxism as an already completely formed knowledge, a finished theory, with its system of prepared responses and its fossilized concepts. Instead, Marxism seems more and more to be a knot of simple and concrete problems, of the kind from which Marx himself set out, suggested, for example, by the following polemical reflection from *The German Ideology*: "It has not occurred to any of these philosophers to inquire into the connection of German philosophy with German reality, the connection of their criticism with their own material surroundings."[1] Hence this notion that Marxism was the first to explore: philosophy is not an independent speculative activity, as would be a pure speculation, but is tied to "real" conditions, which are its historical conditions; and this is why, let it be said in passing, there is a history of philosophy, which can be retraced and understood.

It is from such a perspective that I have asked myself: What does this have to do with philosophy in France today? To what type of historical practice does it correspond? In what social context is this practice inscribed? In my eyes, these questions are really, and profoundly, philosophical. They correspond to the very spirit of the philosophical procedure, which leads to asking oneself about the conditions of an activity while it is in the process of occurring, according to the dimension of what Spinoza calls the "idea of the idea," which is known to offer its true content to reflection by the intellect. Having to do with philosophy in France today: here there is something which does not proceed on its own, which is not simply given, but poses a problem, precisely because this activity is limited by its conditions, which do not immediately and directly appear as it unfolds. In order to emphasize the urgency of this questioning, I must therefore set out from the following negative premiss: there is no French philosophy, in the sense of a natural datum completely determined by belonging to the land and by the filiation of the people or the race. There is rather what I have proposed to call "philosophy *à la française*," resulting from an institution which has had to be socially elaborated, in relation to the transformations of society considered in the totality of its economic, political and ideological structures. This French institution of philosophy, which still governs our current practice of philosophical thought, seems to me to have been produced in the very last years of the eighteenth century; it coincides, then, with the event of the French Revolution and with what this event testifies to, the establishment of a completely new system of society, even if it was a long time in gestation: let us say, for the sake of brevity, democratic society in the specific form that the latter has gradually assumed in France.

Under the determinate conditions that have produced this democratic society, philosophical activity was confronted with certain pressures which it had never experienced before. According to the fundamental principle of communication that defines democracy, it has had to establish a new relationship with language, from the moment that language became national, and by the same token adopt a completely different mode of exposition, adapted to the conditions of its transmission and its reception, the means of which have been given to it essentially by the State School. Then the fact that philosophy is taught has become a distinctive feature, and has necessitated a comprehensive reform of its procedures: philosophical investigation has assumed the form of "research" associated with certain tasks of teaching through which it has been progressively integrated into the functioning of the State and its apparatuses: one must go back to the Ideologues and to Victor Cousin to understand how this assimilation has been carried out. In particular, its consequence has been that the elaboration of philosophical discourse has been pervaded by directly political stakes: it is one of the essential characteristics of philosophy *à la française* that, within the framework where a teaching society has placed it, it has only rarely separated pure speculation from the concerns of conjunctural interventions. Simultaneously, philosophy has become a "subject" of teaching: a "discipline" with programme and tests which sanction its assimilation; in order to carry out its social integration, it has had to be exposed to the test of such a codification.

In this way the forms of philosophical activity have been inflected, if only through the alignment of the status of the philosopher with the function of the professor of philosophy. But this transformation has also concerned the mechanisms for producing speculative thought, and has thus helped to modify its doctrinal content. By formulating such a hypothesis, I do not intend to lump together the various philosophical positions to the restrictive, and completely premeditated, system of a philosophy of State, which would have administered its orientations by maintaining them all in the same sense, without risk of blunders and conflicts, hence, by eliminating every possibility of resistance. But I have sought to understand how philosophical discourse, by slipping into the complex network of the social fabric, has equally developed a theoretical reflection on this practice from which it has made itself inseparable. In other words, it has appeared to me that the direct politicization of its procedures which singularizes the case of philosophy *à la française* has, rather than sterilizing or denaturing it, stimulated the movement of thought, providing both its object, and at the same time the means to reflect on this object.

On this basis, it seems to me that it is possible to present a reading of the philosophical works produced in such a context which, while taking into account the differences and oppositions between the doctrinal and philosophical options, would detect, on this side of those conflicts of opinions or convictions, effects of resonance and echo, establishing silent and secret systems between what appears to be the most distant and disparate systems of thought, in relation to the fact that these systems reflect the structures and evolutions of the same social formation that has given its content to their speculations, and in relation to which their alternation cannot be that of paths which are completely isolated, indifferent to one another. On this point, I have been particularly stimulated by the reflections presented by Foucault around the notion of epistemology, which I have reinterpreted, perhaps abusively, in the sense of a social and political thought determined by its historical rooting.

What makes this conception fruitful for me is less the outline of causal explanation that it might suggest than the fact that it authorizes a new putting into perspective of doctrinal positions, which are transversal to the different currents of thought that their labels make autonomous only in appearance. Thus, between Destutt de Tracy and Bergson, by way of Cousin, it would be possible to reestablish the connection of a mysterious filiation, around the thematic of spontaneity and the relations of consciousness and time, from a perspective which is phenomenological before the letter. Another particularly significant example: the philosophical genesis of the concept of sociality which led Comte after Saint-Simon to associate, if not to confuse, the competing inspirations coming from Condorcet and Bonald, on a terrain which was already that of a "critique of dialectical reason": then, in an unforeseen way, the three irreconcilable references of conservatism, liberalism and socialism have also intersected. Now the connection of the two themes I have just evoked is itself illuminating: it allows us to restore to the theoretical space inside which are pursued the debates of philosophy *à la française* all of its openness, its true breadth. It is perhaps Maine de Biran who was early on most clearly aware of the stakes of these debates when, around 1820, in the margin of a reading of Bonald, he identified, in the context of the anthropological project associated with the advent of what could not yet be called the human sciences, the two extreme poles represented by the "internal human being," the subject in the sense of consciousness, and the "external human being," the subject in the sense of society. Indeed it is in fact these two competing models opened up by a psychology and by a sociology which in France from the beginning have divided the field offered to philosophical reflection, and exposed the latter to a contradiction that even today has perhaps not been overcome.

Another figure of these debates: the alternative of the scientific and the literary, which has assumed a particularly sharp form when philosophy has had to find its place inside an academic programme which is by regulation compartmentalized and normalized. Victor Cousin had wanted to turn it into a sovereign discipline overhanging the entire field of studies and realizing its final synthesis: which in fact amounts to drawing philosophy to the side of the traditional "humanities," revitalized in appearance by means of the illusory programme of a "science of mind," and tendentiously reinterpreted in the sense of a general rhetoric. But what remained of this project at the moment when in the middle of the nineteenth century the bifurcation between literary and scientific paths was established? As Durkheim later explained in a report on the teaching of philosophy, the literary stamp impressed in a unilateral and exclusive manner on philosophy has assimilated philosophy to a rival cultural inculcation of the constituted sciences: the idea of a "defence of philosophy," which one knows is not exhausted today, here finds one of its sources. The permanent dialogue that philosophy *à la française* carries on with literature is explained by these objective conditions. Yet this dialogue is not simply formal and institutional; but it interferes, on the level of thought itself, with the content of works: at exactly the same moment Balzac and Comte wanted to apply the conceptual scheme of the "unity of composition" to the study of society; Zola and Schopenhauer developed the same terrifying vision of the world as blind will; with the same irony Queneau and Kojève exploited the theme of the end of history. What is striking is to see the relation of philosophy and literature turned around here: instead of taking literature as a model of reference, philosophy intervenes on its own terrain by becoming an instrument of writing, or a literary subject matter, in a completely different sense of the term "matter" than that conferred on it within academic space.

All this has led me to present in broad strokes the second of the questions on which I have worked, that of the relations between philosophy and literature, which I have constantly found by studying the history of philosophy in France in the nineteenth and twentieth centuries. On this question, I propose two works published at an interval of twenty-five years: *A Theory of Literary Production*, which appeared in 1966, and *The Object of Literature*, published a few months ago. These two books cannot be separated from their contents, which are quite different. The first was inscribed within the framework of a discussion with structuralism: it was a question, in opposition to a formalism very much in vogue, of providing a context for literary discourse, without however falling into the pitfalls of "realism." The rereading of such texts as Balzac's *The Peasants* or Verne's *The Mysterious Island* had allowed me to restore to the labour of literary production its true subject matter: ideology, or the social thought of an age, whose analyser literature had thus seemed to me to be. I had then been led to insist on the conflicts which divided these discourses from inside, going so far as to sort out competing frameworks of writing in them. In *The Object of Literature*,[2] composed in a completely different intellectual conjuncture, these considerations have been simultaneously reprised and displaced: I have sought to show that a kind of thought, in the philosophical sense of the word, is present in literary texts, under very varied forms, none of which can be reduced to the philosophical model of interpretation. In other words, the philosophy at work in Sade's *The Hundred and Twenty Days of Sodom*, Flaubert's *The Temptation of Saint Anthony* or Queneau's *The Sunday of Life* is a properly literary philosophy, whose content coincides with the very composition of these texts, which do not constitute for it simply an envelope or a surface, on the order of effects produced by a literature of ideas.

All this leads me to return to the formula "literary philosophy" which

I have just used and to specify its meaning. I have entitled the book in which it is explored: "What Does Literature Think About?" and not "What Does Literature Think?" In fact, I have rejected the conception according to which literature contains an already completely formed philosophy, to which it only has to own up. But I have attempted to show that literature, with its own means, also produces thought, in a way which constantly interferes with the procedures of philosophy. What does literature think about? could therefore also be extended as follows: "What does Literature Make it Possible to Think About?" What does it enable to be thought about, provided that one pays attention to it, that is, when one makes the attempt, as I have sought to do through a philosophical reading of its productions. In speaking of literary philosophy, I have not meant, then, that philosophy "is" literary, in the sense of a definition of an essence which would have reduced all philosophy to literature, by absorbing it and thereby erasing the reference it also maintains to scientific discourse. In fact, my intention was not to restrict the perspective of philosophical labour but to enlarge it: the philosophical reading of literary texts makes it clear that philosophical ideas do not exist only through the efforts of systematization offered to them by professional philosophers but also circulate, more or less freely, in literature which, by presenting these ideas in its own way, for example by recounting them, directs them at a distance.

It thereby becomes possible to draw from literature an essential philosophical lesson, which concerns philosophical thought itself: the latter is not a subjective, artificial construction, subordinated to the good will of philosophers alone and delimited by their stated intentions, but depends on the objective preexistence of what I would be tempted to call philosophy as such. In this spirit, to restore the broken, or loosened, connection of literature and philosophy is to proceed in a direction which, far from reducing all of philosophy to literature, by taking the risk of annulling its specificity, in an inverse direction draws literature toward philosophy, in order to reestablish the common relation to truth that governs their respective approaches.

For I am convinced that literature and philosophy tell the truth, even if they don't, strictly speaking, speak the truth. But doesn't this supposition rest on a re-employment of the notion of truth that displaces it toward an allegorical usage? It is to this attempt that every reductionist approach would be finally exposed. Likewise, there is no question of identifying the literary with the philosophical and the philosophical with the social, by following a simple causal chain that, in order to substitute explanation for interpretation, would be no less deprived of a real theoretical foundation. I have found this theoretical foundation my work required by reading Spinoza, and precisely in the conception of truth that specifically emerges from him: truth no longer thought of as *conventia* of the idea with an object that remains external to it, but as *adaequatio* of the idea with itself and with all the effects it can produce, the idea being transformed into the idea of the idea by the fact of this complete adherence to itself. With Spinoza I have learned that ideas have a force precisely in so far as they are ideas, and that truth is the manifestation of this force, itself in communication with the universal *conatus* that constitutes the very nature of things. And philosophy is at base only the detailed realization of this power. Therefore I had to set out from the study of Spinoza, because this study gave a support, a basis, and also a meaning, to the totality of my other inquiries.

On the subject of Spinozism, I am presenting a collection of studies presented at different colloquia during the last ten years and a book, *Hegel ou Spinoza*, published for the first time in 1979. In realizing these works, I have pursued two objectives. On the one hand, I have attempted to restore certain articulations of doctrine, as is done within the framework of the traditional study of philosophical systems, and this has led me to tackle primarily the following points: the status of immediate consciousness in the *Short Treatise*, in relation to the question of intuitive science; the ethical dimension of the *De Deo*, in relation to the question of the order of things, as it is clarified by the distinction between *actio* and *operatio*; the philosophy of history underlying Spinoza's political philosophy. On the other hand, I have attempted to situate the Spinozist doctrine in the context of its own history: that of its successive readings, which have in some sense reproduced it by adapting it to theoretical and ideological configurations sometimes very far removed from the conditions in which it was initially produced. What does Spinoza's thought become when it is resituated from perspectives as heterogeneous as those according to which it has been approached by Condillac, Hegel, Russell or Deleuze? How far does it maintain its own identity while being reflected through such an interpretive prism?

This question could also be formulated as follows: what exactly is the relation between the internal organization of the system, which is supposedly coherent and univocal, and these broken images, which are necessarily divergent, and produced away from their native ground? One would at first be tempted to present the latter in terms of truth or error: there would be the truth of what Spinoza himself thought and once and for all inscribed in the obviously untouchable letter of his text, provided that this letter be definitively established; and then, in addition to and independent of this unsurpassable reference, there would also be, this time on the side of the inauthentic, the approximations, deviations, and perhaps the errors or faults, diverse attempts of recomposition effected with apologetic or critical intentions. And it seems that these attempts, necessarily conducted at a distance, situate Spinoza's discourse in a space of constantly evolving variations, as if it were itself in search of its own true meaning. However, shouldn't one also see in the dynamic of this reproduction a manifestation of the power characteristic of Spinoza's thought itself, which would finally be revealed as carrying more than a single philosophy? And then, from the fact that doctrine is no longer presented as independent of the history of its interpretations, what at first glance appeared to be on the order of planned or involuntary falsification turns into forms of expression which, by virtue of being deviant, are no less authentic in their own way, and in any case are necessary: these are, if I may put it this way, "true errors," which reveal meanings that no one can claim to be radically foreign to the work itself, since the latter deploys through them speculative effects which testify to its intrinsic fruitfulness.

It is in this spirit that I have studied in particular the relation of Spinoza to Hegel, relying on the passages of the Hegelian *oeuvre* devoted to a critical reading of Spinoza. By examining this relation, I have not wanted to oppose, as has sometimes been attributed to me, the "good" Spinoza to the "bad" Hegel. But I have tried to show how an insurmountable philosophical divergence arises between Hegel and Spinoza—let us say, by simplifying in the extreme, the divergence that opposes a providentialism, based on the presupposition of a rational teleology, and a necessitarianism that rejects in principle every explanation by final causes. Yet this divergence makes the misunderstanding between these two forms of thought inevitable when they confront one another. And so, when Hegel reads Spinoza, which he does with great care, it is as if he were prevented by the appearance of his philosophical problematic from seeing—even before setting himself the question of understanding it—what Spinoza had actually been able to say: Hegel is then obliged to set up an imaginary form of thought, or that which is, at the very least, a product, indeed a figure, of his own doctrine. What is particularly interesting here is that Spinoza's philosophy, projected outside its own theoretical frontiers, thus plays the role of an indicator or a mirror, on whose surface conceptions which are apparently the most foreign to his own by contrast trace their contours.

But what then entitles one to state that these reflections do not specifically concern Spinoza's philosophy? Do they not on the contrary belong to it, in the sense of this strange, and perhaps disturbing, familiarity which, beyond their manifest differences, secretly resembles all the figures of thought in the unique—if also tortuous, broken and contrasted—discourse of philosophy, which from then on can reject none of them? "Hegel or Spinoza" could be rendered just as well by "Hegel *sive* Spinoza" as by "*aut* Spinoza *aut* Hegel"; thus it is that this ultimately very dialectical formula—and in this way the last word of this confrontation could revert to Hegel—states the simultaneity and the tension of an alternative and of an equivalence, from which the very essence of the philosophical, which does not allow itself be enclosed in any particular philosophy, would not be absent.

Ten years later, I returned to this question of the relation of Hegel to Spinoza in a short study devoted to "Hegel's Idealist Spinoza," which corrects certain failings in my previous book. In that book, I must admit, Spinoza interested me more than Hegel, the latter in this regard then playing the role of a kind of medium: as a result, I had thought myself justified in situating on the same level the various interpretations of Spinoza's philosophy proposed in Hegel's successive works, as if the latter had constituted a homogeneous totality. But later I realized that these interpretations had undergone a significant shift as the elaboration of the Hegelian system continued: the Spinoza of the *Science of Logic*, a primitive and oriental thinker of the *Abgrund*, is not entirely that of the *Lectures on the History of Philosophy*, who is essentially a post-Cartesian philosopher, a "modern" marked by the categories of analysis and reflection characteristic of a logic of essence. With the realization of this fact, it was as if I had come full circle: Hegel had made me reread Spinoza, Spinoza led me back to Hegel, by offering a new light on the development of his thought.

One may thus glimpse how the theoretical preoccupations corresponding to the three domains of studies I have just evoked are associated. In every case, it is a question of opening up the field of philosophical inquiry, by extending it beyond the limits of a speculative domain identified once and for all by its doctrinal frontiers. Philosophy, after all, is only made up of ideas which have a history: by following and by making known the shifts, breaches and conflicts of these ideas, this history also reveals their productivity, their fruitfulness. Philosophically this has the meaning of constituting the history of these ideas, for they are not reducible to formal and settled opinions but are the vectors and schemas of a thought which is actually engaged in the movements that transform, make, unmake and remake reality. The projection of a system of thought into foreign figures (the case of Spinozism), the philosophical rereading of texts classified as literary, which reveals their effects of truth, the establishment of the institutional and speculative network that conditions the philosophical activities and interests of a historical society (the case of philosophy *à la française*): these three examples testify to the fact that philosophy always thinks more than it says and seems to be saying, and its processes, thus escaping the subjective initiatives of its "authors," possess an objective—and one might say material—import and significance, which turn it into something completely different from, and much more than, just a premeditated and concerted discourse on reality. For me philosophy is first of all, along the lines of what Hegel called the "truth of the thing," the complex discourse of reality itself.

I don't want to end this exposition without mentioning two names, to say what I owe to two persons I came to know at almost the same moment, when, more than thirty years ago, I set about studying philosophy, and without whom I would have worked differently. First, Althusser who, with what others might call blindness but which I would call fearlessness, opened so many paths, certain of which proved to be scarcely negotiable, while others have retained an inexhaustible fecundity. Next, I want to thank Monsieur Canguilhem, to whom I owe a certain idea of the rigour of the concept and of its possible reconciliation with a historical perspective, and whose teaching and *oeuvre* have constituted for me, and indeed for others, a model all the more unsurpassable as it seemed unattainable.

Notes

1. Marx and Engels 1976, 30.
2. The French title of Macherey's book is *À quoi pense la littérature?*, i.e., *What Does Literature Think About?* (Trans.)

2

Philosophy as Operation

To present philosophy as operation is to affirm its practical orientation, by detaching it from purely theoretical speculation; but it is also to connect it with a determinate mode of practice. For all practices are not of the same kind or value. To recognize this, it suffices to consider the opposite, completely classical, conception of an inoperative philosophy, which takes place by means of a disinterested inquiry, aiming exclusively at ideal values of the true and good outside of every technical consideration: wisdom without works, literally "disworked" (*désoeuvrée*), idle, inoperative but not at all inactive, all the more active because it puts into play, if not to work, this kind of practice of leisure, eternally dissident because it is severed from every connection to objective realizations, is realized in an absolute activity which takes itself for an end, because it avoids a confrontation with external results which would limit its scope.

Under the heading of a "praxis" opposed more to a "poiesis"—that is, precisely to an operation—than a "theory," Aristotle established the concept of this inoperative activity. One must return to it, in order to bring out the opposite characteristics of operation, and thus to discover the issues raised by a presentation of philosophy as operation. Operation, "poiesis," amounts to a production of a work, that is, it is a technical activity exercised with a view to a goal external to the procedure that it pursues, and hence without intrinsic or immanent finality, because "its origin is in the producer and not in the product."[1] In this case, action, considered in itself, because it depends on the decision of its artisan, is only an arbitrary, artificial intrigue; it remains foreign to the elements it utilizes and which for it are only means to be exploited, outside of its characteristic ends; it consists in an artificial production, which is essentially distinct from a natural genesis, the latter proceeding, on the contrary, through the internal development of a principle or power which is actualized, without external break or intervention, in its completed form. Let us take some classical examples from Aristotle to illustrate this distinction. To build a house—this is the very model of a "poietic" operation—is a finite activity which is accomplished in the goal that limits it: the "finished" house, that is, the terminated house, apart from which it would remain deprived of meaning, because it would be useless. What would be the art of a builder who endlessly pursued his manipulations and did not lead to the production of any actual construction? Here activity is exhausted, disappears, one might say it is "reified" in its result, with a view to which alone it has taken place. To live, on the contrary, is *par excellence* the form of a "praxis," because this activity completely finds its end in itself, without having produced an external effect capable of being isolated from the process that accomplishes it, and responding to a motivation which would be foreign to it: the significance of this activity is natural, irreducible to any kind of artifice, because its subject coincides with its object, and it finds its sole justification in this identity. Thus, if health cures, and not the doctor, it is because the art of treating does not amount to a technical procedure but consists in a way of living based on nature, in a "regime" based on a correct apprehension of causes and ends.

This conception of "praxis," as its very name indicates, belongs to classical antiquity; and Aristotle only systematized its expression. It is to the "divine Plato" that Freud traced back the discovery of the fact that the erotic drive has value in itself and exists independently of its objects and its goals, a thesis he takes up in his turn in order to place it at the foundation of his own theory of sexuality; and, in a general way, Freud credited ancient civilization for thus having practised the drive for itself, in its unlimited movement, before submitting it to a final destination.[2] Yet what characterizes this "use of pleasures" and makes it a privileged example of practice is that it displaces the interest of the object toward the subject, whose diverse activities only reveal the intimate power, the intention. To live one's practice in this way is to make it depend on a relationship to the self whose purity must not be altered and whose depth must not be limited by anything. If Socrates, through the myth given to him by Plato, discovers in the art of questions, and not in that of answers, the form *par excellence* of amorous provocation and the perfect image of philosophy, it is indeed because the intention is what matters most of all, along with the appeal it makes to the soul to fold back onto itself in order to discover in itself the infinity of the idea. The ancient Greeks did not, as the standard version would have it, establish an exclusive relation between practice and theory which separates and opposes them: on the contrary, they invented the concept of a practice whose vocation is primarily theoretical, since it guarantees a relation to the truth which is also the foundation of every authentic knowledge.

This invention was to have a great future. Let us offer only one example: what one finds at the basis of the Kantian notion of practical reason, entirely opposed to that of a pragmatic reason, that is, a technical reason which "acts" by adjusting means to ends, the latter remaining independent of one another. From this perspective, an operative reason, which privileges content over form, must necessarily remain impure: it is pathologically affected by the material interests that become its functioning. Practical reason, on the contrary, tries to realize itself in a form of activity which is pure, free in relation to every determination imposed from the outside. Here again, it is a question of an objectless practice, because it finds its complete destination in its subject, with which it is completely identified. And this is why it is also an intentional activity: it takes place in the fact of being willed, without being connected to the conditions that would be required for its execution. For if reason not only *can* but *must* act, it can do so only provided that it frees itself from every hypothetical imperative which would subject it to other interests, under the pretext of ensuring the success of its undertakings: establishing itself from a truly anti-Machiavellian perspective, it renounces every search for mediations, every ruse of reason.

If the question of practice is the occasion of a crucial choice for philosophy, this choice does not amount to an elementary decision that would make it opt for or against practice, but depends on an investigation bearing on practice itself, and trying to dissociate the diverse forms that the latter assumes, in relation to the stakes that qualify it. Thus, there would be an essentially philosophical practice, centred on the subject and showing the latter its destination, which would have to be privileged in relation to the degenerated forms of material practices inscribed in a world of necessity where no freedom is even possible. The philosopher, a practitioner who is spontaneous and conscious of himself, whom no objective determination separates from his intimate vocation, is then in a position to decide sovereignly on all things, at least in a negative way: without attachments, his attitude is that of universal critique, which carries out an unlimited requestioning of the ordinary forms of obligation and belief. His function is one of interrogation, of provocation: through his presence alone, he calls forth scandalous evidence of the state of facts, whose right he denies in his name alone, completely exposing himself in this defiance. Here philosophy unconditionally devotes itself to practice; one might even say that it frees itself from every theoretical obligation, its primary concern being not to know but to act, in the name of principles so absolute that they do not even have to be put to the test of a speculative examination which would scrutinize them and technically delimit their content.

This figure of philosophy is the one Hegel precisely included under the rubric of the "spiritual animal kingdom": this ironic formula he himself implicitly applied to those intellectual circles which had begun to proliferate in Germany, and particularly at Jena, at the beginning of the nineteenth century, and which appear quite similar to those Marx would himself cruelly mock in *The German Ideology* by also placing them within the context of a degenerated Hegelian filiation. It is worth while to take the trouble to linger over this description, for it has lost nothing of its topicality. What is an intellectual animal? And first of all what is animal in this form of intellectuality? It is the conviction of having naturally its value in itself, all the rest existing only according to the necessity of supporting it and putting it to good use as its "element."

> The original determinateness of the nature is, therefore, only a simple principle, a transparent universal element, in which the individuality remains as free and self-identical as it is unimpeded in unfolding its different moments, and in its realization is simply in a reciprocal relation with itself; just as in the case of indeterminate animal life, which breathes the breath of life, let us say, into the element of water, or air or earth, and within these again into more specific principles, steeping its entire nature in them, and yet keeping that nature under its own control, and preserving itself as a unity, in spite of the limitation imposed by the element, and remaining in the form of this particular organization the same general animal life.[3]

Just as fish flap their fins or birds display their feathers, in conformity with their essential nature that they seek only to make appear, the intellectual animal is devoted to the pure practice of his capacities, his talents, which he removes from the test of external conditions because they would ruin his appearance. "In this way, the entire action does not go outside itself, either as circumstances, or as End, or means, or as a work done."[4] For this figure is precisely that of the inoperative intellectual, and here we find our point of departure.

The intellectuals Hegel is talking about, and whose image remains for us quite present, are all the more interrogative, questioning and critical because they remain without works. Their non-productive practice completely draws its certainty from the end with which it is so identified that it refuses to be separated from it: although they are without works, they are not at all without causes, or rather with a Cause to which they are devoted with impunity. Exclusive defenders of a right, they claim its universal nature to the point that they do not consent to determine its concept, nor differentiate the domains of its application, nor rank its levels of validity. Specialists of amalgamation, if one may put it that way, spiritual animals are rather cool and without commitments: to the extent that they shy away from the limitation of a point of view, of a position, they do not at all aim at a certain result, depending on concrete occasions and perspectives that the latter lead to reality, but rather at an abstract totality and global ends, whose fiction would be annulled by being subordinated to effective arguments, or to the simple consideration of facts. Here we have the representation of a perfect "engagement": so perfect that no concrete approach nor any concrete content has really engaged it. And the freedom thus offered for our admiration is the freedom of the void, which vanishes in the myth of an indeterminate, inaugural Action, claiming only a value of spontaneity, innocent of all knowledge. As a fable puts it: in the beginning was the action.

Yet to this ineffective conception of practice Hegel opposes another conception, which is that of practice as labour and as process: the latter is not that absolute action which finds its end in itself, pure "praxis" in the original sense of the word, but an operation which produces objective effects and works. If there is an activity of reason, being exercised within the very limits of reality, it consists in such an operation, for it finds its realization, its *Wirklichkeit*, in it. One knows that in this last instance, Hegel intends another word: *wirklich* is only that which results from the movement of a *wirken*, that is, literally, from a production of works. Thus, is something actual only if it is operative? One can say: everything rational is operative, everything operative is rational. We find here literally the idea that philosophy is to be considered as an operation.

What distinguishes this operation from an action in general? It is the fact that it is inserted into a process, that it proceeds from an intervention that, as such, presupposes intermediaries and a point of view: in order to produce works, one must adopt the point of view of a position, one must take a position, for without doing so it is not possible to enter into a relation with a determinate content. To the unlimited form of an objectless—but not subjectless—praxis, the point of view of operation opposes the necessity of submitting to the conditions of an actual and no longer fictitious engagement. Yet these conditions are limitative: *determinatio negatio est*—which means not that the productivity of a point of view is tied to the restrictive choices on which it relies, by virtue of a kind of law of compensation, but that the share of negativity it includes constitutes it in its very order, inside and not outside the unfolding of the "operations" whose linkage it authorizes. The result is that between the agent and the end that it pursues one must interpose a third element—Hegel speaks of a third term—in order to indicate, as in a syllogism, the rationality intrinsically characteristic of every operative process. The fictitious action of which we previously spoke is spontaneous: it is immediate and without mediations. Actual operation, which depends on a determinate taking of a position, is, on the contrary, necessarily mediated.

The Aristotelian conception of activity, which brought back activity to the transition from power to action, or from the virtual to the real according to a dual schema, formed the economy of such a mediating element. By considering activity as foreign to the nature of movement, to which it does violence and deviates in the sense of something artificial and arbitary, the Aristotelian conception excluded activity from its internal rationality. Now by substituting for this binary representation a

ternary, properly "dialectical," representation—a substitution that illus-
trates the metaphor of the "labour of the negative"—Hegel not only adds
a term to the enumeration of the moments that constitute practice, but
he completely overturns their internal disposition, so as to establish their
concrete, actual unity, no longer in the form of a succession or adjustment. In fact, if the middle term appears as the practical syllogism's
motor of development, it is because this term is not injected from outside
in its unfolding, through an artificial and abstract violence, but because
it coincides with the necessity of its own operation.

The change thus introduced into the theoretical constitution of practice
is not formal but also modifies the content of practice. The pure activity
of "praxis," as we have seen, amounts to an essentially subjective
practice: its end is to explain the potentialities given in the existence of a
subject-substance, that is, of a subject without process, which in its
action, never has anything but a relation to itself. On the contrary, in so
far as it is thought of within the conceptual field of an immanent
negativity, and no longer that of an extrinsic negation, which disqualifies
it by restricting it to the consideration of strictly technical ends, operation
becomes an objective practice, determined as a process which is no longer
that of the exposition of a subject. What is an objective practice? It is not
a practice subservient to objects, and by the fact of this submission
enclosed within a finite perspective. It is a practice that, in its own
movement—in so far as the latter returns negatively onto itself, and
thereby is inserted into a much vaster movement which includes it, the
latter in its turn growing beyond its apparent limits in order to be
inscribed within a context of still larger development, etc.—ends up
producing its objects. It "produces" them not in the sense of a material
fabrication, carried out completely externally—and from this point of
view it must be said that the usual critiques of Hegelian "idealism" are
off the mark—but in the sense of a manifestation or a revelation, which
emphasize them within their own finite limits, by cutting them off on the
basis of an overall organization, simultaneously natural and historical,
within which all aspects of reality tend to be in play.

One can say that such an objective practice is a "process without a
subject," in the sense that here the process is to itself its own subject: it
produces itself rather than being produced, inside the movement that
determines it, in relation to the totality of its conditions. It is not a
question of a spontaneous production, dependent on some isolated
initiative, but of a labour which is collective in the strongest sense of the
word, since in its own constitution it requires no less than all of reality,
caught up in the differential chain of its moments. This means that
operation, if it refers to an operator, does not rely on it as if on an
autonomous principle, which could be detached, *tamquam imperium in
imperio*, from the activity in which it takes part; it encounters it instead

as a moment in the development of the order to which it itself belongs. Does this imply that operation as such is subordinate to the functioning of a structure? No, if one thinks of this subordination as a subjection and of this structure itself as a finite arrangement of elements, as a system in the mechanistic sense of the word, already constituted prior to the practices in which it takes place: such an account would deprive the concept of operation of its content by removing its internal negativity, that is, the faculty that belongs to a determinate activity: reconsidering onto itself, or transforming itself and modifying its conditions at the same time that it carries out its effects. For an operation is by no means prefigured and somehow preestablished in the system of its conditions, of which it would be only an application or a particular case. But it effectuates itself, in the active sense of this expression, in relation to works whose realization, in return, overturns the objective field inside which they are produced.

To operate is thus to take part, in the sense that making a commitment is to carry out activities which require the limitation of a point of view, so as to displace these limits inside the movement that governs them, instead of accepting them as given, and as such unsurpassable, limits. Basically, one will say: to operate is to take risks, including the risk of making a mistake. In fact, by producing works one exposes oneself to the test of a necessarily antagonistic confrontation through which the meaning of what one does must be intrinsically altered, because it cannot escape a resumption which, connecting it with new presuppositions, modifies its initial constitution. Operation is not finished in its outcomes, for the latter never have a definitive, "finished" form; instead, their accomplishment is inseparable from their contestation, which from particular effects gradually gives rise to the general system of conditions on the basis of which which they have been produced. "And even at the end of each truth we must add that we are bearing the opposite truth in mind."[5] Nothing takes place which does not divide, by the same token splitting up the field of its realization and revealing its internal contradictions.

To consider philosophy as operation, and not as the creation of ideas or the defence and illustration of well-known causes, whatever the nature of those ideas and causes, is to know that neither thought nor action exhausts itself in its manifest content but behind itself pursues a secret destination, a destination that no totality or destiny decrees. While seeking his father and mother Oedipus blinds himself by awaiting them where he believes them to be. One is seized, surprised, deciphered by one's sources instead of inventing or even interpreting them. An operation is simultaneously a diversion and a detour, no *a priori* form of correctness directs it; instead, a ruse of reason is at work in it, a ruse so conducted that one knows neither who leads it nor who is led by it. This indecision, this uncertainty, finally open up, on the basis of a limited point of view at first, a global field of investigation, in which enters into play more than simply its stated pretext, but which is only its factual origin. They pertain to that "knowledge of the union that the thinking mind has with all of nature,"[6] whose possession constitutes, according to Spinoza, the sovereign good. This is why one must set aside a specialized conception of operation which would erase these backgrounds and, enclosing them in the false alternative of intentions and works, would freeze their specificity, by ignoring the fact that the series of determinations in which it is inscribed is, in fact as well as by right, unlimited. No one knows what a body can do, nor what a mind knows.

In order to express its nature as operation, it might be said again that philosophy is a "theoretical practice," provided that this formula does not merely suggest a formal equivalence between a theory and a practice, the latter taking the place of the former and vice versa, so that by being confused they would both lose their own natures. "Theoretical practice" is not the magical formula that would guarantee that the identity of theory and practice could be given initially: rather, it indicates a process in which operations are produced, inside which theory and practice take shape concurrently, against each other, with each other, in the sense that they are reciprocally put to work, in a movement in which it appears that there is never pure theory, whose meaning would be limited to its stated results, nor any pure practice, innocent because it would elude the confrontation of its intentions with its effects. If philosophy is operation, it is because it is penetrated by that contradiction of theory and practice which is also the condition of their concrete unity, the latter consisting in the actual development of their antagonism instead of in their final, ideal reconciliation—the end is after all only another beginning.

To the ritualistic question "What is an intellectual?" the following response will be proposed: an intellectual is one who, whatever might also be the domain of his particular activities, expresses himself in works whose meaning goes beyond their immediate justification and in order to be recognized necessitates not only the effort of an interpretation, by explaining his intentions, but a testing of their immediate results, that is, their transformation. In fact, an authentic theory is one that, rejecting as illusory the criteria of truth guaranteed inside of its own order, takes shape in the form of its own practice, which is not its simple application, since it tends to modify its internal constitution. And a consistent practice is one that, not being limited to imperatives of execution which directly attach to it the norms of its success, encounters, or rather generates, the theory in which it reflects on itself in order to place itself in a new perspective which, at the same time that it indicates other means to it, also changes its orientations. This is why intellectuality does not belong, like private property, to a specialized and talkative caste, assembling in a closed order the holders of true knowledge, the knowers of good language, or the masters of the most just causes: intellectuality is instead found in all domains of activity, provided that they do not give way to mechanistic tasks accomplished without principles, or to the pure illustration of self that transforms every practice into an exhibition, a spectacle.

But if philosophy is, in this sense, operation, one is bound to wonder: what kind of operation is it? What are the materials, means and stakes that distinguish it? Or else must one say that philosophy, belonging to all domains of activity, is based in them and mixed up with them? Doesn't philosophy then risk being diluted in an abstract and unanimous form of activity in general, a form that would only be so enlarged because it would also be deprived of content? If philosophy is everywhere, and if everyone is a philosopher, philosophical operation loses its determination, thus ceasing to be, in the strict sense, an operation. To an operating philosophy, or one claiming this characteristic, one must ask the following question, then: what are its works? Do they consist in a general methodology applied indifferently to all practices so as to govern their functioning by attaching criteria and ends to them? One could then wonder from where philosophy itself would derive the criteria and ends authorizing it to produce such a model. Above all, one would be astonished to see philosophy bring back its relation to practice in the form of an application, that is, of an external and mechanistic relation entirely opposed to the conditions we have recognized as being those of an actual implementation.

But philosophy is not the undifferentiated practice of all practices, a kind of common Operation, which would include all the forms of operation in the field, then purely theoretical, of its observation. Nor is philosophy a single practice defined by the limits of a domain of objects, in which are attached to it the obligations of productivity characteristic of a definite enterprise, and which terminates, more or less, in its immediately noticeable effects. As operation, philosophy is practice itself, in all sectors of its intervention, in so far as it puts back into question the limits inside which its activities are carried out, and thus discovers the tendentially unlimited power of its processes. This can also be said in the following way: every practice is philosophical, or in relation with philosophical ulterior motives, which strives to go beyond the goals that directly inspire it, in order to reflect the global content and universal requisites that inevitably put its simplest procedures into play. In every practice, philosophy is that which incites it to think about itself, not in terms of a preestablished knowledge, but by relying on the development of its own operations, in so far as the latter are all, in their way, images of the absolute.

From this point of view, the traditional project consisting in making all the approaches of philosophy enter into the framework of a Theory which would rigorously systematize their unfolding, by making them enter into the limits of an order, which—by right if not in fact—is finished, appears more derisory than insane. Philosophy, which is this movement of going past limits, of reflecting the immediate in the mediated, a movement all of whose modes of activity can find the incentive in themselves, provided that they strive for it, cannot enclose its pretensions within the boundaries of any domain, or of any discourse, whatever prestige is attached to it. This is why philosophy's universality genuinely arises not from theory but from practice: philosophy is not the universality of a knowledge which would include everything, and would substitute its determinations for reality once and for all; rather, it is the potential universality of an operation which, without being enclosed within the fiction of a general form, pursues inside itself the movement that leads it beyond its given limits, and thus carries out the encounter of its truth.

Philosophy finds its truth in practice, for the latter provides it with the conditions of its actual implementation: thus, this truth is not a separate, exclusive truth, relying only on the authority of its stated principles, in the form of a self-sufficient discourse. Philosophy is, instead, truth as it stands out from the development of a process which, without requiring the guarantee of any external authority, expresses its relation with reality considered in its totality, and thereby, in practice, justifies itself and demonstrates the correctness of its approach. To philosophize is perhaps, according to a very ancient conception, to identify oneself with the totality. But if this formula can be retained, it is with the qualification that it cannot be a question of a given identity, whose models an actual thought must reject. The identity pursued by philosophy takes shape through the movement that tends to connect philosophy with all of reality: it is the identity of philosophy's operation.

Remarks on Practice

1. To think practice is not to think of practice, or to think about practice, from outside, from a point of view not its own, without taking part in practice.

One must instead think practice within practice.

2. Practice, first of all: one must start with practice, one must rest on practice. But what does practice start with? On what does practice rest? Practice starts with practice. Practice rests on practice.

Thus, the primacy of practice is the primacy of practice over itself.

3. Where does practice go? Nowhere but into practice, that is, into other practices. Practice does not constitute its actions as complete

totalities, with clear-cut contours, but continues them into others, then into still others, without ever reaching definitive results.

To begin, practice. To end, still practice. Everywhere and always, there is practice, that is, diverse forms of practice, which are connected with one another and act on one another.

4. If practice is instructive, it is because it is a permanent reconsideration of its own effects: thus, there is always something new to learn from it. Practice is not doomed to the destination of a single meaning which would be its law, its only law.

This is why it is futile to seek guarantees in practice: practice can make all guarantees; it can also break all guarantees.

Practice traces and effaces limits: its element is the limit; and its signification is beyond limits.

5. To be put back into practice: it is always practice that decides. But its criteria do not have a uniform function: practice does not constitute a homogeneous order in which all practices are mixed together because they conform to a single model which is that of Practice.

In practice, within practice: these formulas have an objective value of determination only if they refer to a differentiated content, to a network of articulated practices, which are sustained by opposing one another.

6. There exists no Practice as such. There are only materially, historically, socially determined practices.

7. To think practice is to grasp the infinity of its processes, their complexity, their tendential nature, the necessity of a movement which always continues—in excess, or in default—on itself. Not in order to absorb practice or enclose it within the limits of a complete theory, but in order to accompany it, if possible to inflect its development, and thus, provisionally, to master it.

8. Where do correct ideas come from? From practice. But where do false ideas come from? Also from practice. From practice come, together and concurrently, correct and false ideas.

If practice, in the last instance, distinguishes correct ideas, it is because it is divided in itself, causing several instances, unequal and antagonistic levels of decision, to appear.

Practice develops in the midst of contradiction: it is impossible to think practice without contradiction.

9. "In the beginning was the action." But it does not suffice that an action begin for it really to produce effects. An action must continue beyond from its beginning, it must "leave" its beginning behind. An actual action is not only the positive and continuous deployment of what was given at its point of departure: by being linked to other actions which compete with and complete it, it also enters into a negative relation with itself.

Practice never amounts to a single and simple action: instead, it develops by means of contradiction through a complex ensemble of various actions.

10. Ideas come from practice: let us say instead that they come within practice, from which they emerge without ever truly escaping, for they are also always brought back to it. They are formed at the knots of practice, wherever its different moments intersect, interconnect, and break.

Wherever practice divides, a knowledge appears, which articulates it.

11. "It is necessary to act, not to allow something to be done, but to do something." These formulas, which one often hears, betray an impatience and an embarrassment: they express an indetermination instead of a determination. How to determine oneself to act? How to determine the content of one's action?

To intervene is literally to come between, interpose, or be interposed, that is, also, "to find a means," an intermediary which, by resting on the internal contradictions of a situation, provides practice with its actual impetus.

To know (*savoir*) is to discover those mediations which give every practice the principle of its development: to recognize (*connaître*) is to extract the middle term.

12. One proves movement by walking. One recognizes the taste of a pear by eating it. Our forms of knowledge are submitted to the law of facts. But this law is not external to them, nor are they foreign to it. The law of facts is also the knowledge they carry with them, which is discovered in practice.

A blind practice, which does not generate its forms of reflection and control, is an illusion. A formal knowledge (*connaissance*), which makes its truth foreseen independently of the conditions of its production, is a game.

13. No practice is without knowledge (*savoir*), whether explicit or implicit.

No knowledge (*savoir*) is without practice, whether concerted or involuntary.

14. "The proof of the pudding is in the eating." No: this proves much more that one is tasting something believed to be pudding. What teaches the consumer about his daily experience is that things are not necessarily as they seem to him or as their name indicates to him.

The proof of the pudding is instead that one makes it: only then does one knows what one has put in it. The truth of facts cannot be found by consuming it, but by producing it.

15. We say that something is practice when it seems to agree with our usage: it is as if it were made for us, or us for it. A practical mind, likewise, fits situations or occasions. Practice is a matter of adjustment: correctness is the form of its truth.

But this correctness is not the undifferentiated exactness of an external, mechanistic adaptation: it presupposes an evaluation and the choice of an orientation, the implementation of a perspective, reconsidering itself in such a way as to produce its own transformation. It is the correctness of an engagement. Correctness is also the result of a labour, and this labour is costly.

Nothing is given by practice. Practice does not give without compensation, that is, without a commitment: one must take part in it, that is, expose oneself to the risk of a permanent readjustment, which modifies the subject of the practice as well as its object.

16. To be pragmatic is to recognize the sovereignty of practice, to stick to experience as closely as possible and to embrace detours, to bow to the facts, to adapt oneself to them. But to follow—and only to follow—practice is to yield to the illusion that practice constitutes an autonomous order and is self-sufficient; basically, it is to believe that, full of itself and free of lacunae, proceeding straight ahead toward its goals, practice decrees laws which only remain to be applied, without itself being implicated in them, without discussing or seeking to modify them. It is therefore to remain external to practice, by renouncing participation in its incessant self-transformation.

It is not enough to submit to practice, one must concretely connect oneself with it, by being engaged in it and by reflecting on it. It is not enough to apply the lessons of practice, one must really put them into practice.

17. Can one speak of a practical truth and say: it is correct in practice, hence, it is true in theory? One can, provided that one considers this correctness in the sense of an adjustment, that is, of a tendential movement, which never leads to definitive results. And also provided that one consider this truth as one moment in a process of knowledge (*connaissance*), whose production is carried out without ever escaping practice.

18. To be engaged is to be engaged with or in something, from a point of view which at the beginning is delimited and definite, hence, determinate. To be absolutely engaged, in an unlimited way, is to engage only one's responsibility, by being enclosed in an intimate relationship of self to self, which seems free only because it is indeterminate: it is not to be engaged with nothing, nor in nothing.

To be engaged is thus to adjust oneself to certain conditions so as to be able, in return, to act on and transform them.

19. A practice is first of all a position, going well beyond its stated goals, or certain goals that it admits to itself. The perspective to which practice is tied is imposed on it by the objective conditions of its operation, outside of which it would be ineffective. But those conditions also lead it to go beyond its immediate intention: thus, they open up a

much larger domain of investigation to it, a domain not limited to simple tasks of execution.

No practice is free at the origin: rather, it is inside its process that a practice discovers and produces the forms through which, negatively reconsidering itself, it grows in a new and unforeseen sense.

20. No practice is entirely free or entirely constrained. Tied to a perspective whose limits oblige it, every practice is a reconsideration, reflection, enlargement or reversal of this perspective. One invents one's practice by consciously accepting its conditions so as to go beyond them.

21. A practice which does not question its rootedness in order to transform it would no longer be a practice. Without roots, it could not carry out this modification.

Notes

1. *Nicomachean Ethics* VI/4.
2. *Three Essays on the Theory of Sexuality* (preface to the fourth edition and note added in 1910 to the first essay).
3. Hegel 1977, 238.
4. Ibid., 241.
5. Pascal, *Pensées* 576 p.224.
6. Spinoza, TdIE 5.

For a Theory of
Literary Reproduction

To the question: How does literature act? we respond here simply: By reproducing itself. But what does it mean for literature to "reproduce" itself? And how is the process of literature's reproduction due to its very nature? How does this process help us understand literature better?

In order to respond to these questions, one must first consider the limits of a theory of literature as pure production, and the insurmountable contradictions to which such a theory inevitably leads. Marx's well-known reflections on the subject of Greek literature and art in a fragment of his *Introduction to the Critique of Political Economy* are in this regard symptomatic. "But the difficulty lies not in understanding that the Greek arts and epic are bound up with certain forms of social development. The difficulty is that they still afford us aesthetic pleasure and that in a certain respect they count as a norm and as an unattainable model."[1] How, in other words, can certain works which have been historically produced, in relation to a determinate social and historical conditioning, arouse a transhistorical interest which seems to be independent of this temporal situation? How can one even read the Homeric poems in conditions which no longer have anything to do with the conditions that gave rise to them? For this question to make any sense, literature—and art in general—must be related to the production of works, material expressions of their age, which by this fact seem condemned to disappear with it. We know the solution to this problem sketched out by Marx: it relies on a nostalgic, purely commemorative, interpretation of what he calls "the eternal charm of Greek art," whose reality does not seem capable of being recaptured except in the past, as the memory maintained by a society—our own—having reached the adult stage, from preliminary phases which traversed the entire nineteenth century, making the Greeks, in the global perspective of a historical evolutionism, the representatives *par excellence* of "childish people." But again on this side of this historical paradigm, one would find the following presupposition: in the very constitution of the work of art in general, and of the literary work in particular, there is something which condemns it to become outdated and no longer to exist except in the form of a relic in the absence of the social content in relation to which it was produced. It no longer subsists except through the mediation of its material envelope, as a "work" inscribed in the literal body of its own text, but emptied of its living significance and by definition ephemeral, and testifying enigmatically by means of this alteration that its time is gone forever. Again, which means, in other words, that these "works" have not been produced as such, but precisely have become works in completely different conditions which are those of their reproduction.

Thus it is not a given form of art, a given literature, like those of ancient Greece, which would be doomed to such a commemorative thought; but it is art as such which would find its essential destination in this ghostly existence, characteristic of an artificially preserved monument, regardless of its actual connection with the concrete conditions of its construction. This analysis, which Marx for his part seems to adopt, arises from a Hegelian inspiration, in relation to speculation revolving around the theme of the death of art. In the *Phenomenology of Spirit*, this time again concerning Greek art, which is, however, presented as a spiritual and no longer only material production, we find the following analysis, which heralds Marx's:

> The statues are now only stones from which the living soul has flown, just as the hymns are words from which belief has gone. . . . They have become what they are for us now—beautiful fruit already picked from the tree, which a friendly Fate has offered us, as a girl might set the fruit before us. It cannot give us the actual life in which they existed, not the tree that bore them, not the earth and the elements which constituted their substance, not the climate which gave them their peculiar character, nor the cycle of the changing seasons that governed the process of their growth. So Fate does not restore their world to us along with the works of unique Art, it gives not the spring and summer of the ethical life in which they blossomed and ripened, but only the veiled recollection of that actual world.[2]

In fact, since according to Hegel art is the initial and preparatory phase of the development of Spirit in expectation of its passage to new stages which progressively bring it closer to the complete knowledge and mastery of itself, it must therefore be projected in its totality back into the past of spiritual life, of which it represents only a preliminary stage, at a moment when the latter has been surpassed once and for all.

> A book has its absolute truth within the age. . . . It is an emanation of intersubjectivity, a living bond of rage, hatred or love among those who produce it and those who receive it. . . . I have often been told about dates and

bananas: "You don't know anything about them. In order to know what they are, you have to eat them on the spot, when they've just been picked." And I have always considered bananas as dead fruit whose real, live taste escapes me. Books that are handed down from age to age are dead fruit. They had, in another time, another taste, tart and tangy. *Emile* or *The Persian Letters* should have been read when they were freshly picked.[3]

Quite naturally Sartre rediscovers the Hegelian metaphor of fruits plucked from the tree to explain the engagement—not objective but subjective, or intersubjective—of the literary work in its age, with which it is at one, to the point of losing its living taste if one presumes to export it, in time even more than in space. And in another text, written at almost the same time, Sartre develops this thesis by lending it the vehemence of a manifesto itself historically situated:

> We write for our contemporaries; we want to behold our world not with future eyes—which would be the surest means of killing it—but with our eyes of flesh, our real, perishable eyes. We don't want to win our case on appeal, and we will have nothing to do with any posthumous rehabilitation. Right here in our own lifetime is when and where our cases will be won or lost. . . . It is not by running after immortality that we will make ourselves eternal; we will become absolutes not because we have allowed our writings to reflect a few emaciated principles (which are sufficiently empty and null to make the transition from one century to the next), but because we will have fought passionately within our own era, because we will have loved it passionately and accepted that we would perish entirely along with it.[4]

Such is, in fact, the condition for the literary act to take on an absolute character: its author must sacrifice to his "era" his own desire for immortality, which would also be only an abstract reverie, properly "bourgeois," according to the term used by Sartre himself; and it is by this gift of self that the author plunges to the greatest depths of the dynamic of his time, to that point from which it is propelled ahead of itself, toward other times, for which still other authors must sow and reap new works.[5] To return to the question that interests us here, "How does literature act?", the response proposed by Sartre would thus be the following: by knowing that literature must abandon reproducing itself in conditions other than those which are forever attached to its production, and this so as to be identified itself more closely with the original act that gives it the irreplaceable savour of exotic fruit.

To this sacrifice agreed to by the author, the engagement assumed by the reader responds symmetrically; the reader must agree to go see on the spot, in the sense of an historical position, what taste the works of the past were able to have for their contemporaries, by plunging them back into their original context, in order to restore their authentic significance to them. It would then be a matter of becoming a Greek again in reading Homer, or becoming an Italian of the Middle Ages again in reading Dante, etc.[6] This poetics of identification and adherence, profoundly romantic in its spirit, thus maintains in its own way the Hegelian idea according to which art as such enters into a privileged relationship with times which are long gone, since it is always made for times which are destined to become long gone, the acceptance of this destiny being that which defines what there is that is immediately living, and essentially savoury, in their very present. And this is also why those who, aware of this destination, persist in interesting themselves in what remains of works when their times are historically past, must know how to bow to the necessity of living or thinking, through means which must be fictive, in this past.

To the question "Why write?", Sartre consequently responds: "One of the principal motives of artistic creation is certainly the need of feeling that we are essential in relationship to the world," which implies for Sartre that "the creation becomes inessential in relation to the creative activity"[7] ("the creation" here means the object created through this activity, or its outcome). By projecting himself absolutely into his work, the writer who gives meaning to it by the same token accepts losing for himself the benefits of this gift which, in order to be complete, must also escape him. And here intervenes the reader whose position is in a way the opposite of, and complementary to, the author's:

> The creative act is only an incomplete and abstract moment in the production of a work. If the author existed alone he would be able to write as much as he liked; the work as *object* would never see the light of day and he would either have to put down his pen or despair. But the operation of writing implies that of reading as its dialectical correlative and these two connected acts necessitate two distinct agents. It is the joint effort of author and reader which brings upon the scene that concrete and imaginary object which is the work of the mind. There is no art except for and by others.[8]

But in order to be effective, this collaboration requires a condition: to be of value only for a single time, which marks the work in its constitution, and constitutes its own time, on the basis of which its production (in the sense of writing) and its reproduction (in the sense of reading) must operate simultaneously. To read Homer today is by every possible means to make the attachment that ties him to his age live again, and to make oneself his contemporary. And so, Sartre specifies again, "for the reader all is to do and all is already done."[9] One would not know how better to say that the work, considered as such, carries its entire future in its past, from which it cannot be extracted, except to become "dead fruit." If the act of reading is free and creative, it is to the extent that it occurs by recognizing its identity with the author's creative freedom in which it is grounded:

> Thus, the author writes in order to address himself to the freedom of readers, and he requires it in order to make his work exist. But he does not stop there; he also requires that they return this confidence which he has given them, that they recognize his creative freedom, and that they in turn solicit it by a symmetrical and inverse appeal.[10]

In other words, author and reader participate, by virtue of the very reciprocity of their positions, in the common creative act through which the work exists with its significance, the latter in its turn giving to their union all the weight of reality it can handle.[11]

The best response to Sartre, on this point as on others, would be found in Foucault, who has shown how illusory is this conception of the work as a mirror in which the author and reader reflect and construct at the same time their reciprocal relationship, in such a way as to give to the latter a feigned objectivity, resting on the mirage of a shared common sense.

> A book is produced, a minuscule event, a little manageable object. Henceforth it is caught up in an incessant play of repetitions; its doubles begin to swarm around it and quite far from it; every reading gives it, for a moment, an impalpable and unique body; fragments of it circulate which one puts to good use for it, fragments that proceed so as to contain all of it, and in which finally it manages to find refuge; commentaries divide it, other discourses in which it must finally itself appear, to admit what it has refused to say, to be freed from what it loudly claimed to be.... The temptation is great for whoever writes a book to lay down the law to all this flickering of simulacra, to prescribe a form to them, to stuff them with an identity, to impose on them a mark which would give them all a constant value. "I am the author: look at my face or my profile; here is what all these reduplicated figures which are going to circulate under my name should resemble; the ones that stray from them are worth nothing; and it is by their degree of resemblance that you will be able to judge the others' value. I am the name, the law, the secret, the measure of all these doubles.... I would like this object–event, almost imperceptible among so many others, to be recopied, fragmented, repeated, simulated, divided, finally to disappear without the one who has happened to produce it ever being able to claim the right to be its master, to impose what he wants to say, or say what he should say. In short, I would like a book not to give itself this status of text to which pedagogy or criticism would well know how to reduce it; but to have the offhand manner of being presented as discourse, simultaneously battle and weapon, strategy and clash, struggle and trophy or wound, conjunctures and vestiges, irregular encounter and repeatable scene.[12]

What is remarkable in this conception of discourse as event, which produces itself instead of being produced, is that it literally overturns the traditionally established relationship between production and reproduction: the event, which is everything but the act of a subject who would be its Author, precedes the work, which is itself only the repetition, in a relationship which is not that of massive identity but of insensible difference. Thus, the work, with the effects of meaning attached to it, is not only strictly speaking the result of a production but of a reproduction, the latter resting on the aleatory event of the discourse supporting it. If one takes this hypothesis seriously, one must go so far as to say that works are not at all "produced" as such, but begin to exist only from the moment they are "reproduced," this reproduction having the effect of dividing them within themselves, by tracing the thin line of their discourse in such a way as to make an entire space of gap and play appear in it, into which seeps the indefinite possibility of variations. Instead of being produced only once, in its place and time, the work thus has realities, in the plural, only in this mirroring that constitutes it at the same time that it disperses it.

One might feel that it was reading Borges, among others, that set Foucault on this path. The conception that comes to be sketched recalls the theoretical fable, "Pierre Menard, Author of *Don Quixote*," which is found in the collection *Ficciones*. This fable turns around the theme of the "second hand," that is, of citation: Pierre Menard, whom Borges had made a French symbolist poet, manages, at the cost of a fierce struggle, to rewrite, identically, certain passages of Cervantes's work.

> He did not want to compose another *Don Quixote*—which would be easy—but *the Don Quixote*. It is unnecessary to add that his aim was never to produce a mechanical transcription of the original; he did not propose to copy it. His admirable ambition was to produce pages which would coincide—word for word and line for line—with those of Miguel de Cervantes.[13]

This reproduction opens onto the realization of a literally identical double which is precisely the original work, distanced from its own text through a simultaneously infinitesimal and infinite discrepancy (*décalage*). Pierre Menard, who symbolizes here the absolute author, is just as much the reader, critic, translator, editor, even, despite what Borges says, a simple copyist. Here are the terms in which he explains his intervention:

> My general memory of *Don Quixote*, simplified by forgetfulness and indifference, is much the same as the imprecise, anterior image of a book not yet written. Once this image (which no one can deny me in good faith) has been postulated, my problems are undeniably considerably more difficult than those which Cervantes faced. My affable precursor did not refuse the collaboration of fate; he went along composing his immortal work a little *à la diable*, swept along by inertias of language and invention. I have contracted the mysterious duty of reconstructing literally his spontaneous work.... To compose *Don Quixote* at the beginning of the seventeenth century was a reasonable, necessary and perhaps inevitable undertaking; at the beginning of the twentieth century it is almost impossible. It is not in vain that three hundred years have passed, charged with the most complex happenings—among them, to mention only one, that same *Don Quixote*.[14]

Menard's *Don Quixote* is the same as Cervantes's precisely to the extent that it is other: it reveals its identity through its transformations, by manifesting the part of historicity which works its text in depth, instead of marking only, and once for all, its initial constitution, even if it leaves intact its apparent framework.

The history recounted by Borges exploits a very old idea, arising in the age in which poetry, closer to its oral sources, recognized more freedom of action than today in the creative and performative memory of its reproducer, who was not a simple reader. In his life of Chrysippus, the philosopher of ancient Stoicism, Diogenes Laertius, relates this anecdote, whose content is just as real, just as imaginary, as that of Borges's narrative: "[He] cit[ed] numerous authorities. So much so that in one of his treatises he copied out nearly the whole of Euripides's *Medea*, and someone who had taken up the volume, being asked what he was reading, replied, 'The *Medea* of Chrysippus.'"[15] The specific contribution of Borges to this tradition consists in the fact of having himself used it in order to constitute a poetics of reproduction functioning as a model of writing: with a view to composing his own texts of fiction, which he only undertook rather late, when he already had behind him a career as poet and essayist, he imaginarily referred these texts to other previous writings, of which they were supposed to give only the inventory and review, as if they were produced by being reproduced. This operation is illuminating by the effect of dissociation it induces: far from being recognized in the author's intentions, which are themselves perceived by the reader in the manner of an authentic meaning, works are no longer reflected except by being dispersed, and by evoking their internal distance through this dispersion, through effects of mirroring which seem to have neither beginning nor end. The notion of an original work succumbs to this splitting: the writer appears as nothing more than his own plagiarist, as if all literature were itself composed of forgeries. Every style could be explained by the implementation of such a mimeticism: Victor Hugo would be the author who, already pursued by the phantasm of identification that also haunts his critic and his reader, writes *as* Victor Hugo, that is, in his manner, as if he set about to quote himself.

It is precisely by reason of this conformity to an imaginary model that a work is supposed to belong to its author, who is himself only a projection of this model. But this image of the author is in its turn exhausted in the representation given through his work: from the beginning it is reduced to a plurality of figures, more or less in conformity with that which is supposed to constitute their original. It is on the basis of such a "heteronymy" that Pessoà constructed an entire poetic art. The same principle suggested to Borges a paradoxical technique of reading, based on the "technique of deliberate anachronism and erroneous attributions." The story of Pierre Menard concludes with the following information: "This technique would fill the dullest books with adventure. Would not the attributing of *The Imitation of Christ* to Louis Ferdinand Céline or James Joyce be a sufficient renovation of its tenuous spiritual counsels?"[16]

From all this emerges a certain number of lessons which can be generalized. If a text is always in a relationship of self-citation regarding itself, the same thing applies concerning its relation to other texts. Except in a dream, one never writes on a completely blank page: the execution of a text necessarily relies on the reproduction of prior texts, to which it implicitly or explicitly refers. Every book contains in itself the labyrinth of a library. From this point of view, literature itself, in its totality, could be considered a single text, indefinitely varied, modulated and transformed, without a single one of its states able to be once for all isolated and fixed. One writes on the written, that is, on top of it: the palimpsest must not be considered only a literary genre, allowing the constitution of certain works to be explained; rather, it defines the very essence of the literary, which coincides with the movement of its own reproduction. The article Proust devoted to Flaubert's style introduces this idea in the form of a theory of pastiche: since the only authentic reading of a text is one that relies on the grasping of the text's stylistic anomalies, it inevitably gives way to the execution of other texts developing their new singularities as an echo. Proust thus reveals what gives literary facts their negative principle: there are no universal rules of the beautiful, or of speaking well, anchored in the stable structures of a definitively ordered aesthetic world. As opposed to a nontemporal universalism, stylistic experience, such as it is shared by the writer and his or her reader, relies on this experience of the singular—let us even say the irregular—which opens up within texts the indefinitely open field of their modifications. And this results from the fact that there is no first writing which is not also a rewriting, just as there is perhaps no reading which is not already a rereading.

The literary text thus does not keep its authentic form behind itself as a treasure, or a kind of hidden letter, whose untouchability should be preserved at all costs. Instead, it carries this form ahead of itself, by opening up the field of its own modifications, and of their exuberant proliferation. Seen in this light, its first—what is commonly called its "original"—figure is itself only a rough draft or document, that is, a "before-text" (*avant-texte*). And there is no text except from the moment that the process of its reproduction is initiated, with the appearance of the variants that draw its structure as it goes along by deforming and reforming it anew. And to think that, one cannot do better than evoke the musical model of the variation, and that which constitutes one of the heights of this form: Bach's *Goldberg Variations*, in which an initial aria is absorbed and prolonged, as if to infinity, within a cycle of its transformations, in order to resurge at the end, no longer as it was at the beginning, but as if it resulted from all the internal labour during which it seems to have been slowly elaborated, in such a way as to emerge only when when this labour would have reached its end, and when it would itself be found, known, encountered. But this end is itself only relative, since by ending and closing onto itself the cycle opens anew as if it were relaunched toward other cycles, themselves in resonance with the previous one.

Throughout such analyses, what is in question is the very notion of the literary work. In fact, literature does not consist of a collection of finished works, produced in turn, then once and for all recorded within a repertoire, in order to be offered next to the consumption of readers to whom is entrusted the task of ensuring its reception. Rather, literature is constituted from texts which, within the limits that specify them, bear within them, like operations in variable geometry, within them the mark leading to their reinscription in new texts. One could even say that, from this point of view, Literature does not exist as such, except as an historical fiction, having arisen by means of the literary genre that is Criticism. But what exists, and in a perfectly real way, is *the literary*, in so far as it forms a corpus in a state of permanent reevaluation, which in each age is redefined in different conditions: the literary, that is, not a collection of monuments, or finished things, whose nature would no longer be anything but inventoried as a purely empirical factual reality, but a complex of processes, dynamically articulating among themselves the labour of writing and the labour of its reproduction—and this independently of a normative ideal which would try to substitute for this ceaselessly pursued movement the illusion of an identity, a stability, or a permanence.

Notes

1. Marx 1973, 111.
2. Hegel 1977, 455.
3. Sartre 1988, 242–3.
4. Sartre 1988, 253–5.
5. This extreme will to push one's time has been subtly analysed by Hollier 1986.
6. And Marguerite Duras, commenting, in an appropriately rough way, on the fragments published in *Les Temps Modernes* of the work sketched by Sartre on Tintoretto, has grasped well the mechanisms of this projection: "Nothing, begins Sartre. 'This life is squandered. Some dates, some facts, and then the chatter of the old authors.' And Sartre. With his iron muscles, Sartre stirs up History, performs a miracle, makes the Republic of Venice reemerge from the waters, traverses four hundred years back to front, *becomes Venetian* . . ." ("Le séquestré de Venise: Sartre," an article published in *Le Nouvel Observateur* in 1958, reprinted in Duras 1984, 187.) And, very lucidly, Duras remarks: "Inevitably, one thinks of Michelet." (ibid., 188)
7. Sartre 1988, 48–9.
8. Ibid., 51–2.
9. Ibid., 54.

10. Ibid., 58.
11. Here is an example of the margin of freedom that Sartre thought he could grant his readers. It is a question of his incomplete philosophical texts (the *Notebooks for an Ethics*), which he hoped would be published as they were after his death: "They will represent what I wanted to do at a certain point and what I decided not to finish, and in that respect they will be definitive. Whereas, while I'm alive ... there is still a possibility that I might take them up again, or that I might say in a few words what I wanted to do with them. Published after my death, these texts will remain unfinished and obscure, since they formulate ideas which are not completely developed. It will be up to the reader to decide where they might have led me." (Sartre 1977, 74–5) Thus there would no longer remain anything for the reader to do, the author being definitively absented from the margins of his text, except to reconstitute what he himself would have been able to think if he had had the possibility, or the intention, to fulfil them.
12. Foucault 1972, 7–8. This text is extracted from the preface written at the time of the reedition of this work which had first been published by Plon in 1961, with another preface, very developed, that Foucault decided to omit at the moment of the republication of his book with Gallimard: the new preface, very concise, has for its objective precisely to justify this change of presentation.
13. Borges 1993, 32.
14. Ibid., 34–5.
15. Diogenes Laertius 1958, 289.
16. Borges 1993, 38.

III
Philosophy *à la française*

4

The Hegelian Lure:
Lacan as Reader of Hegel

Hegel is a lure.[1] This formula appears in several places in Lacan and is found, for example, in "Position de l'inconscient," first presented in a conference at Bonneval in 1960, published in 1964 and reprinted in the *Ecrits* in 1966: at that moment it was a question of the claims and prejudices of general psychology, the dominant ideology in which the activity of the training of psychoanalysts was included; the "central error" of this psychology is to "take the phenomenon of consciousness as unitary,"[2] while from the standpoint of the science Freud inaugurated "everything shows on the contrary the distribution of consciousness, heterotopic and erratic at every level, no matter how its texture is ordered."[3] In order to achieve its preventative and demystifying effects, Lacan's teaching calls upon and uses for its own didactic purposes a certain number of philosophical references in its attack on the spontaneous philosophy of the scientists who reduce the psychoanalyst to the ordinary status of a psychologist and thus seek to "depose" the unconscious: among the most important of these references is Hegel. Does this mean that this speculative doctrine is valuable as an introduction to psychoanalysis and that, behind the pedagogical function it has been called on to serve, the doctrine possesses, in a general way, an intrinsically scientific meaning, homogeneous with analysis itself in its dual theoretical and practical dimension in so far as this doctrine, unlike any other mode of investigation, accedes to the "position of the unconscious"? Here, Lacan takes care to formulate a clear reservation:

> Our use of Hegel's phenomenology does not imply any allegiance to his system but uses it to counter the evidences of identification. Further, Hegelian propositions, even taken in context are always conducive to saying something Other [*Autre-chose*]. Something Other that repairs the link in the fantasmatic synthesis even as it preserves the effect of denouncing the lures of identification. It is our own *Aufhebung* that transforms Hegel's, his own lure, in a moment that reveals, not the steps of an ideal progress but the avatars of a lack.[4]

Hegel subverted, subjected literally to the operation of the *Aufhebung*, his discourse is restored to its most authentic meaning, which is to "say something Other" and in particular something other than what is said in his system which preserves in its own way, in the dialectical sequence of a phenomenology inhabited by the presupposition of absolute knowledge, the myth of the unity of consciousness.

For isn't saying something Other the very function of the lure, that invention of ancient falconers who used a piece of red leather in the shape of a bird to which they attached bait in order to bring the falcon back to the falconer's fist, to master the bird's aggressive action and retrieve it for their own profit? A lure is a trap, a decoy, an imposture, an illusion that serves to "snare" not the prey strictly speaking but this intermediary whose activity the hunter appropriates by means of a ruse which turns the bird from the immediate ends it believes it is pursuing and makes it his prize and an instrument of his art.

It is thus necessary to speak of the lure of Hegel in a double sense: Hegel is a lure in that, by the efficacy of a ruse which is not that of reason, he is used, exploited for ends which are not his own, and not merely because they do not belong to philosophy itself, whose field these ends traverse and disturb. But Hegel is also a lure in so far as in this booby-trapped game that is analysis—for it is always something Other that is said there—he serves to deceive or set right those who must be led away from the path on which, without even knowing it, they are travelling and which is taking them far from their true prey which is in fact running behind rather than in front of them: a falconer must direct them back toward their prey. Thus, everything in Hegel's thought is apparently a lie that deceives itself as it deceives us: but it is precisely there that the unalterable relation that ties it to the truth is established— that hidden or veiled truth which comes to us only in the lie in which it is clothed and into which it seems to have disappeared—and this is why Lacan assigns it a didactic function. The path that leads to Hegel and takes us through him is thus not the royal road to an accession or an assumption, that of a "system," but the complicated and oblique itinerary of the hunter who practises a ruse, returning mystification against mystification: it is then the liar who, having been deceived about the meaning of what he says, offers the truth without even knowing it; he himself is made to take the obliging and seductive form of a lure.

It is clear that nothing is simple about the relation that Lacan establishes between Freudian psychoanalysis and Hegelian philosophy: and it is at the cost of this obscure sinuosity that we are able to grasp and understand something in it. We will be confirmed in our suspicions when we examine the content of the session of the seminar devoted to "denegation" (*dénégation*), in which, on the occasion of rereading Freud's 1924 article on *Verneinung*,[5] Lacan (the psychoanalyst) calls upon Hyppolite (the philosopher) to clarify with the light proper to his training and practice a question which does not directly pertain to his area of expertise since it pertains to the order of analytic technique. On this occasion it is precisely the place of Hegelian discourse in relation to Freud's science that is in question (*en question*) and, we might say, under interrogation (*à la question*). In following the exchange of words that takes place at this session we shall find a way of delineating the position assigned to Hegel, that is, of resolving the enigma of this lure that no light clarifies but through which something essential for psychoanalysis and perhaps for philosophy as well appears.

The session of Lacan's seminar devoted to *Verneinung* took place on 10 February 1954: the seminar, which was then held at Sainte-Anne Hospital, was in its third year and its topic was *Freud's Papers on Technique*. A summary appears in the edition edited by Jacques-Alain Miller,[6] who seems to have stayed as close to what was said then as is possible in a transcription. At the same time, there is another "text" of this session, a text composed by Lacan himself and which he published under his own name in the first issue of the review of the *Societé française de la psychanalyse* of which Lacan was president in 1954, *La Psychanalyse*:[7] a text quite different from the one edited by Miller because, according to the note that served as an introduction, Lacan proposed an "expanded" version of its content; it was this version which first appeared in 1956 and was reprinted in the *Ecrits* in 1966, preceded by a new introduction, "D'un dessein", which served as a commentary.[8]

What was said in a few hours on a single day is set down in a group of texts whose strata begin to split apart as soon as they are examined and which fan out through a long chronicle which runs through more than twenty years: first there is the most recent text, published in 1975 with Lacan's authorization but without his (direct) participation, which seems most of all to conform to the literalness of the verbal exchange of 1954; then there is from Lacan's own hand the text of 1956 that in fact constitutes a written representation of what was said two years before, a transposition which is interesting because of the treatment to which it subjects its own content, whose essential articulations it places clearly in relief in order to draw the lesson it contains. This "lesson" will be taken up and definitively authenticated ten years later at the moment that Lacan collects his *Ecrits*, provided with a new commentary which once again marks the event in order to make its significance understood. Lacan himself thus constructed an entire history whose narrative we can scan and whose composition we can interpret by tracing the course of its successive editions: they are finally attempts to make manifest a meaning that cannot be expressed as such immediately, but which requires such work to be made manifest.

The seminar session devoted to *Verneinung* was exceptional in a number of ways. The fact that Lacan never ceased to refer back to it is testimony enough: it seems that there is only one other session that received such treatment, even to the point of Lacan's overseeing its publication himself, and that was "The Purloined Letter," which was accorded the privilege of serving as an overture to the whole of the *Ecrits*.[9] What was going on in the session of 10 February 1954, to give it such a privilege? We may find the beginning of an answer by considering the group of texts in which, in its earliest version, it was published in 1956 in the first issue of *La Psychanalyse*: the issue's table of contents includes an article by Benveniste, "Remarques sur la fonction du langage dans la découverte freudienne," and then, following the interventions of Lacan and Hyppolite on *Verneinung*, Lacan's translation of Heidegger's essay on Heraclitus, "Logos," and finally Lacan's address from the 1953 Rome Congress, "Fonction et champ de la parole et du langage en psychanalyse." Thus, a theoretical configuration is assembled in which psychoanalysis takes its place in relation to the other "sciences"—most importantly linguistics—and philosophy, represented by Hegel and Heidegger. The purpose of such an enterprise seems clear: it is to insert psychoanalysis into this philosophico-theoretical ensemble through Lacan as intermediary so that it may recognize itself and be recognized through the complex play of identifications and differentiations that results from putting such a network into place. What role does the seminar on *Verneinung* play in such a procedure?

The first remarkable characteristic of this session is that a philosopher, Jean Hyppolite, representing the Hegelian studies in which he is a specialist, takes the floor, or rather, the floor is "given" to him. For Lacan speaks first in order to introduce Hyppolite's proposed commentary on an article by Freud devoted to *Verneinung*, and to say what is expected of Hyppolite. Then, following this commentary which has the place and status of an interlude in so far as it assumes the position of a middle term in the Hegelian "syllogism," Lacan again takes the floor to "respond" to Hyppolite, that is, to explain the meaning of his discourse and to situate it from the perspective of analytic discourse, in which it must itself be inscribed through the production of an effect which is all the more effective in that it is thus fixed in the speech of the analyst who having preceded Hyppolite must also succeed him. Let us successively consider the three temporalities of this session as they are articulated in the schema of a kind of dialectical process.[10]

We shall first examine Lacan's *Introduction* to Hyppolite's commentary.[11] It apprises us of what is in question in the rereading of Freud's essay on *Verneinung*: a double stake. First, it is a question of restoring their original and authentic signification to the fundamental concepts of analytic technique: resistance, repression, transference. But to achieve this end it appears that this theoretical significance must be investigated:

and it is here that at a second level the philosophical interpretation Freud suggests throughout his article is necessary. For it is the notion of the dialectic that anchors this interpretation to analysis which Lacan presents to his audience (or rather to his readers) as "a practice in which the dialectic is an immanent effect."[12] Dialectic is understood here in a very primitive sense, a sense anterior to the exercise of philosophy itself: it serves to characterize an activity internal to the structure of dialogue. Thus, in so far as it is not reducible to a defence mechanism formed by the ego as in the inadequate conception formulated by Ego-psychology, but rather arises from a dynamic signification, expressing a content which comes from the unconscious, resistance manifests itself only through a relation of exchange such as that realized paradigmatically in the confrontation between the analyst and analysand in the cure, where all the conditions of the transference are given. From this determination there is a very important practical consequence: it is impossible to treat resistance without touching on the transference, the condition of which is this very "dialectical" situation that places a subject in relation to himself through the intermediary of another subject.

Thus, according to Lacan:

> it is in so far as the subject arrives at the limit of what the moment permits its discourse to effectuate in speech that the phenomenon where Freud shows us the articulation of resistance to the analytic dialectic is produced. For this moment and this limit are balanced in this emergence, outside the discourse of the subject, of the trait that is most particularly addressed to you in what is in the process of being said. And this conjuncture is proposed as a function of the punctuation of its speech. To grasp this effect we have used the image of the subject's speech vacillating to and from the auditor.[13]

This means that resistance is a "dialectical" effect, that is, a product of the unconscious in so far as it traverses the speech of a subject which is not a conscious and autonomous ego, unified and enclosed upon itself as it thinks itself to be in the Cartesian *cogito*, but rather a subject opened upon its own insufficiency to itself, that lack which impels it toward the real or mythical auditor to whom it addresses itself and for whom it speaks. Henceforth the whole question is to know to whom the subject speaks and how it speaks "to it": to identify this subject is first to know what place the one to whom the subject speaks occupies in its own discourse as it is divided within itself, within its own limits, from the perspective of this other for which it holds together and whose meaning it receives.

This dialectical relation which gives rise to the manifestation of resistance in and through the transference is quite close to the form through which Lacan himself was initiated into the Hegelian dialectic through the mediation of Kojève: it is the struggle for recognition on the basis of desire that gives impetus to the movement described in *The Phenomenology of Spirit*, a movement that culminates, at least according to Kojève, in the dialectic of master and slave. Lacan evokes this relation elsewhere without, however, citing the intermediary interpreter who taught him this reference:

> The ego that operates in the analytic experience has nothing in common with the supposed unity of the reality of the subject that so-called general psychology abstracts as instituted in its "synthetic functions." The ego of which we speak is absolutely impossible to distinguish from the imaginary captations that constitute it in its genesis as much as in its system, in its function as much as in its actuality, by an other and for an other. To put it another way, the dialectic that supports our experience is situated on the level that most envelops the efficacy of the subject and obliges us to understand the ego in the movement of the progressive alienation that constitutes self-consciousness in Hegel's *Phenomenology*. Which means that if you are dealing with a subject's ego at a given moment, you are at that moment its alter ego.[14]

If there is a dialectic of the subject, it is in the sense that the subject is only revealed, only avows itself to the extent that it is alienated from itself in the literal sense of the term; that is, that the subject enters into the relation that links it to the other, a relation that requires the intervention of language which is its "cause." It is in this relation alone that the subject strictly speaking exists.

Thus, there is an essential difference between the Cartesian subject, unified and autonomous, which is a pure ego because it is pure thought for which language is merely an instrument, and the Hegelian subject in the sense indicated by the reference to the dialectic, a divided subject that affirms itself only in so far as it encounters its own limit in the relation of dialogue imposed on it by language. It is the difference between a fully conscious ego which is potentially master of itself and the universe, and a subject which only recognizes itself in a relation which is simultaneously that of self and other, conscious and unconscious, because it is caught at the outset in a relation of an inside and an outside that constitutes and limits it by dividing it.

In an address delivered in 1955 to the *Société française de la psychanalyse*, published in the third issue of *La Psychanalyse*, Jean Hyppolite was obliged to reaffirm, in terms which apparently extended those Lacan uses here, this link which profoundly unites psychoanalysis and Hegelian phenomenology in an interpretation whose central theme is the following:

> The notion of truth as unveiling is effected by the intercommunication of the consciousnesses of human beings, by mutual recognition, and by the language that is substituted for the very problem of God. While, for example, for the Cartesian, consciousness in its solitude addresses itself to God to guarantee its

truth, then returning armed with divine testimony about its fellow creatures, for Hegel it is only in the play of intercommunication between consciousnesses, in language, that the universal self-consciousness is elaborated and the truth is disclosed.[15]

From this determination by language results what Hyppolite calls the "unconscious function of consciousness." Because "consciousness sees and does not see itself, the consciousness in knowing misrecognizes [méconnait]. Perhaps here is the key to the problem of the unconscious: it is not a thing situated behind something, but fundamentally a kind of soul of consciousness, a certain inevitable means for the natural consciousness to be itself."[16] Let us note that this rereading of Hegel through Freud is based on two implicit presuppositions: one, which concerns Hegel, restores the Logos, in its constitutive role, to the play of consciousness as it is described in the *Phenomenology*; the other, which concerns Freud, reinscribes the unconscious within whose order it has become the instrument, by the intermediary through which it appears to itself, in the complex procedure that links it to truth. Is it not the primacy of the unconscious which is thus surreptitiously reintroduced to the great dismay of Freudian psychoanalysis, but perhaps also of Hegelian philosophy? It falls precisely to Lacan to instigate, at least partially, this interrogation.

Let us return to Lacan's first intervention in his seminar of February 1954. The result of all that precedes is that the crucial problem for analysis is the "dialectical" problem of the relation to the other, that is, of its place and its status in and for the subject's speech.

> It is precisely here that the question begins. Through what kind of otherness does the subject become interested in this existence? For it is from this otherness itself that the subject's ego participates.... In short, we expect the subject to respond by posing the typical question that most often liberates it from the silence that should signal to you the privileged moment of resistance: it is the moment at which the subject shows you *who* speaks and *to whom*, which constitutes one and the same question.[17]

For the question "Who am I?" must be interpreted as: "To whom do I address myself in the discourse I sustain and by which I speak for an other, this other which I also am, since I do not exist without it?" Therefore, this other which organizes my discourse, and in the absence of which it would not take place, is at once different from me, in that I am this individual bearer of a singular consciousness in which I identify myself. It is also in me in so far as I am this divided subject which brings into its own organization, its "structure," the necessity of this recourse to the other in and through dialogue: unconscious recourse, existing only because the nature and place of this other to which I refer remains, at least provisionally, unidentified.

All these themes are assembled in the fundamental formula introduced and justified in 1953 by the Rome discourse that Lacan recalls here to conclude his intervention: "The unconscious is the discourse of the other."[18] We reproduce this formula here in the typographical form in which it appeared in 1956, in the first issue of *La Psychanalyse*: but when he takes it up again ten years later in his *Ecrits*, Lacan revises and rectifies it, replacing the lower case with the upper case in his inscription of the other, marking it as: "the discourse of the Other."[19] But in 1956, and *a fortiori* in 1954, the distinction between the other and the Other, even if it is in formation, is not yet explicit. For in the earliest version, which is also the most confused on this point, this phrase is notable above all for the enigmatic perspective it opens retrospectively on the nature of this "other" it continues to maintain in such obscurity: is it a question of the "other" of the imaginary relation, or of the "Other" of the symbolic relation? This question, which could not be more precisely posed, must remain unresolved and in a way suspended, in the ambiguous discourse through which the subject interpellates itself, without even knowing that this discourse is addressed to it.

Because the truth of the unconscious, at the very moment that it is disclosed in the revealing aphorism, must also founder in the forgetting of itself: this is the very theme of Heidegger's text, *Logos*, which Lacan translated and published along with his interventions on Hyppolite's commentary on *Verneinung*.

> All this is to reveal the veiling that is present. The act of revealing requires concealment. *A-lethia* rests in *Lethe*, since it produces that which by its crossing is confined. The *Logos* is in itself at once a revelation and a secret. It is *A-lethia*. The unveiling needs *Lethe*, as a reserve from which revelation could in some way draw.[20]

Here again we encounter a tradition which begins with Kojève: it consists of reinterpreting, literally transcribing, Hegel's dialectic in terms of a hermeneutic of Heideggerian inspiration, to rethink the struggle unto death of consciousness that the *Phenomenology* delineates, to begin from the being-toward-death with which *Sein und Zeit* is concerned inasmuch as this is authentically the subject of truth, the only possible subject for a truth which reveals itself only by hiding. Let us yield the floor to Lacan:

> For the man who, in the act of speaking, breaks the bread of truth with his double, shares the illusion. But is this all there is to say here? And can the speech here not be extinguished before being-for-death when it will be approached at a level where only the joke is still viable, the appearances of seriousness in response to its gravity seeming nothing more than hypocrisy? Thus death brings us to the question of what denies discourse, but also the question of whether that is what introduces negation there. Because the negativity of discourse brings us back to the question of knowing what

nonexistence, which is manifested in the symbolic order, owes to the reality of death.[21]

There is no direct access to the truth for the divided subject that is constituted in the order of language, because it is communicated to the subject only by negative paths of subjection and annihilation, alienation and death.

If there is a dialectic of the subject, it is thus in so far as the subject is a subject for an other, or even, literally, subject of another which obscurely determines it more profoundly than itself—this other is a "lure," it is posed only as it is denied, through the imaginary or the symbolic, inhibited or repressed reality of the "not-me" (non-moi) with which it is confronted within the limits of its own discourse. Hence, the power of affirmation that links and restores it to itself—the Eros that is Verneinung, pure positivity—cannot be dissociated from this negativity which separates it in itself—and which proceeds, at least mythically, from the destructive drive through which the subject is also a being-toward-death. The theme is identical to that of Freud's article on Verneinung: and the moment has come for Lacan to yield the floor to Hyppolite, who must propose an explanation for it.

But before hearing Hyppolite, let us ask what place he occupies in the space of dialogue that will be established. He does not figure there under the title of an established specialist, coming from outside, since he speaks on the contrary from inside the seminar, of which he is regularly, this year and those following, an auditor and participant—the summaries testify to this. However, in the seminar he held a position which remained foreign, if not indifferent, to analysis, since—it is in these terms, so the stenographic record of the meeting tells us, that Lacan introduces the speaker—he represents "those philosophical disciplines which we could not do without in our present capacity."[22] This apparently means that Hyppolite is required here, according to his area of competence, Hegelian and philosophical, to comment on a work of Freud's whose signification exceeds the order of technique: however—and we can say in advance that this is the essential lesson that will be drawn from the meeting of 10 February 1954—the interpretation he will propose will not be left enclosed in the field of philosophical speculation, but will on the contrary burst its boundaries. Does this not mean that the relation established here between psychoanalysis and philosophy is the inverse of the presentation through which it first appears? Rather than the interrogation of psychoanalysis by philosophy, Freud in the light of Hegel, isn't philosophy put to the test of psychoanalysis, prey to its discourse, which is thus "the discourse of the other"?

Returning to this session in 1966 in his Ecrits, Lacan will specifically credit Hyppolite with a literal reading of Freud's article on Verneinung: a reading not only to the letter but also and above all a reading of the letter of Freud's text, which it avoids reducing to one meaning, philosophically, by means of one interpretation. This literal commentary is valuable as a privileged mode of access to the "truth," inasmuch as it is revealed only when it is hidden.

> That any text, whether it claims to be sacred or profane, sees its literality increase in relation to what it actually implies as an affront to the truth, it is this of which the Freudian discovery shows the structural reason. Precisely in what the truth that it brings, that of the unconscious, owes to the letter of the language, to what we call the signifier.... The truth-effect freed in the unconscious and the symptom demands from knowledge an inflexible discipline to follow its contour, for this contour runs contrary to intuitions which are too convenient for its security. This truth-effect culminates in an irreducible veil where the primacy of the signifier is marked.[23]

The reading of Freud proposed by Hyppolite will allow precisely such a residue to appear, resisting properly philosophical rumination, which will have every chance to be, if not the truth, at least a truth of the unconscious: pushed to this limit, his commentary will go on to demarcate or unmask that which in the article on *Verneinung*, beyond or rather short of its manifest clarity, testifies to the persistence, not of an assignable and comprehensible meaning, but of the unassimilable, indeed the unthinkable of his signification. Hence, from the moment when philosophy will be dismissed from power and the privilege of its concepts revoked, the unconscious, unrecuperated and unrecuperable, will triumph.

However, we are not yet there: for when Hyppolite begins to speak it is—and this should not surprise us—in order to distil from Freud's text a sort of dialectical atmosphere: a Hegelian halo. And for this he will exploit at bottom the determination of *Verneinung* as *Aufhebung* which he discovers in Freud's text. "*Verneinung* is an *Aufhebung* of repression"[24]: these are Freud's very words. Here, as in Hegelian discourse, the *Aufhebung* expresses an ambivalent relation, since it simultaneously signifies suppression and conservation: it lifts the repression while maintaining, through the intermediary of its mark, a negation, which persists through this "negation of the negation" which is also *Verneinung*. The "denegation"—following the translation which Hyppolite and Lacan propose of the term *Verneinung*—realizes the acceptance, access to the consciousness of a representation, even if it is repressed, provided that it bears the seal of the negation that is, says Freud, like a label, a certificate of the origin, the "Made in Germany" of repression. Hence, the analysand's words: "You ask me who is in my dream. It is not my mother," is interpreted by the analyst in the following way: "The person in the dream reminded me of my mother, but I do not want to accept this association." The place of negation in the discourse designates here, not an unequivocal signification, but a division by which this discourse functions at two levels at once as acceptance and refusal: to the extent that negation is also denegation, that is, a negation of the negation, it is the condition for a repressed content, without ceasing to be repressed, to attain consciousness, through ambivalent speech whose double meaning expresses and resolves, at least verbally, the conflict.

A dissociation of the intellectual—that which reaches representation— and the affective—the irreducible residue of repression that persists through denegation—also takes place. The affective, in so far as it is an *Aufhebung* which includes both acceptance and refusal, marks the point at which intellectual judgement or thought is separated, detached and even demarcated from the original drive (with respect to which it is posed as the direct opposite) through the intermediary of negation. Here we encounter a kind of dialectical process, in the course of which the intellectual is formed out of the affective, through the labour of the negative, in the shape of a genesis. This genesis, Hyppolite insists, is not a real genesis in the same sense that a psychologist would give to the word—that of an evolution proceeding through stages and identifiable through various traces—but is a mythic or symbolic genesis that allows the conditions of intellectual activity as such to be delineated: these conditions are given by negativity. This means that there is intellectual judgement or activity of thought from the moment that processes of primary affectivity are set off. This separation is effected by the intervention of the negative, by means of which what must remain hidden at the level of the functioning of the drives is recognized intellectually, that is, symbolized. Therefore, symbolizing activity in which the admission of the real thought is realized, has as its condition the intervention of the negative.

Although Hyppolite only alludes to them very discreetly, it is not difficult to rediscover the Hegelian terms that accompany and indeed sustain this analysis, even if those themes are inscribed in it *en pointillé*. In 1959 *La Psychanalyse* had published in its fifth issue a text by Xavier Audouard explaining this *rapprochement*.[25]

If the psychoanalyst is interested in Hegelian texts, it is not just because he finds them to be like a conceptual transposition of his own experience, but rather because analysis is in itself a technique for the suppression of every reflexive solidification in the same sense, with the same range, and thanks to the same means as the dialectic. Analytic technique is the implementation of the dialectic, in so far as reflection or, in other words, rationalization, comes to light in an individual's history. Conversely, the dialectic is the conceptual justification of what happens from the moment that an individuality agrees to be confronted with its desires under the non-reflexive, that "free" form of association.[26]

The dialectic, which reveals "the immense might," "the magical power" of the negative, discovers in negation the negation of the negation: this is what enables us to understand that beyond the explicit refusal that affects a representation—across the negative formulation, for example, that "this is not my mother"—there is an implicit affirmation of what is hidden behind this rejection and which manifests itself through it indirectly. This is why we can speak about the "identity of analytic experience and dialectical experience"[27]: this conclusion had already emerged from Hyppolite's presentation, at least at the beginning.

For Hyppolite's reading of Freud's text doesn't stop here: if it did, it would be content to find in that text a Hegelian terminology and problematic from the perspective of a philosophical interpretation. In the presentation he gave the following year for the *Société française de la psychanalyse*,[28] Hyppolite justified his undertaking a *rapprochement*, or parallel reading, of psychoanalysis and phenomenology: it isn't a question of reducing Freud to Hegel but, on the contrary, of rereading Hegel in the light of Freud: doesn't that presuppose that there is something more or less other in psychoanalysis than in the Hegelian dialectic, which allows the latter to be clarified by a kind of recursive procedure? In fact, the commentary on Freud's text on *Verneinung* attains its genuine goal at the moment that a new question is posed: from where does this negativity that we have just recognized as the condition of possibility for intellectual activity come? What is its origin? By means of this question we remain within the perspective already indicated: a mythic genesis of thought which can be deepened by pushing back its limits. It is not enough to notice that the negative is at work in this genesis; we must know from where it derives its miraculous power.

The solution to this problem that Hyppolite discovers in Freud's text is quite surprising: it consists in saying that negativity is already inscribed in the primary situation that precedes intellectual development, and is determined, therefore, at the level of affectivity:

> The primal form of relation known psychologically as the affective is itself situated within the distinctive field of the human situation, and if that engenders intelligence, it is because it already, from its beginnings, brings with it a fundamental historicity. There is no pure affective on the one hand, entirely engaged in the real, and pure intellectual on the other, which detaches itself from it in order to grasp it once again.[29]

There is not, on the one hand, first, a pure positivity and then, on the other hand, pure negativity. Rather, there is from the outset, inscribed in the origin—in which "before" and "after" already succeed one another in the form of a necessarily mythic "historicity"—the confrontation of positive and negative that takes the shape of a splitting at the level of the drive itself. It is here that the dissociation between the two fundamental drives—Eros, which tends toward *Verneinung*, and is therefore affirmative in its essential movement, and the instinct of destruction, *Destruktionstreib*, or death drive, which expresses in itself the opposite movement of expulsion and suppression—intervenes in Freud's text. Thus, the fundamental distinction of inside and outside, which makes possible the respective constitution of subject and object, is determined by "the <formal couple> of two primary forces: the force of attraction and the force of repulsion,"[30] which act in an absolutely primitive manner. That is, they are not reducible, from the perspective of a new genesis, to a still more original principle from which they themselves are emanations. What is absolutely primary is their conflict; one doesn't preexist its division into two: there is nothing but this very division.

The result is that symbolization, that is, the representation of the real in thought, is not something that comes after the real, in the form of a double which both substitutes itself for it and constitutes its negation, but is given from the outset as the condition of access to the real, which already implies a relation to the negative. Thus it is that the real is split into two levels or moments: it exists first in a primary, libidinal or prejudicative form in which negation is not yet posed, nor for a very good reason represented as such. It is only afterwards that it affects the explicit symbol of negation: it then becomes the conscious form of the negative, in so far as the latter constitutes the mark, the label that distinguishes intellectual activity from affectivity and assures its autonomy. This is why recognition, to the extent that it depends on this negation which is also a denegation, is always at the same time a misrecognition, because it is limited in its undertaking by the condition that makes it possible: the destructive drive from which it arises in the last instance inscribes a kind of blind spot in it, whose place can only be marked negatively, as a gap within the symbolic system of its representation. As we have said, to explain the genesis of thought, we can go as far back as—but not beyond—this negative tendency, within the framework of the antagonism that opposes it to affirmative Eros.

This seems to be what is essential to the commentary delivered in a much more improvised and disjointed way by Hyppolite. How should we characterize it? What lesson can we draw from it? We can content ourselves with a critical appreciation of it, of the kind presented by J.M. Rey in the margins of his own explanation of the text on *Verneinung*:

> Jean Hyppolite's commentary on *Verneinung* draws a parallel between Hegel and Freud which seems to us to be unsustainable, a parallel constructed on the basis of the presence of the term *Aufhebung* in the text on *Verneinung*. This term can be summarized as follows: the text on *Verneinung* has to do with establishing "the very origin of intelligence" (whereas Freud speaks about "judgement" and "thought" grasped from an economic perspective). Introducing, without real justification, the Hegelian notion of "negativity," Hyppolite

infers from it that *Verneinung* is in the last analysis nothing other than a "negation of the negation" and that as a result "there can be produced on the margins of thought an appearance of being in the form of not being, which is produced with denegation." Finally, everything that arises from the inside or the outside (in fact essential terms in this text) is only a "myth," as also is the opposition of life drives/death drives. It does not seem to us that the introduction of Hegelian notions as complex as those of "negativity" and "negation of the negation" can contribute in any way to a clarification of the text on *Verneinung;* especially in that their use ends up obscuring the specificity of the concept of "repression" as it is progressively formulated by Freud. . . .[31]

The term "obscuring" (*occultation*) is taken here in a radical and univocal sense: it characterizes a reductionist reading in which the dialectic effaces what is original in the Freudian concepts. But isn't obscuring also a form of unveiling? If Hyppolite had done nothing other than to set Freud alongside Hegel, it isn't clear what Lacan would himself have sought in Hegel, except a philosophical prudence that would allow him to pursue his own undertaking as theorist and practitioner of analysis under the guise of a similar dialectical recuperation. For the dialogue between philosophy and psychoanalysis that is consummated on this occasion, even if it has its difficulties and its misunderstandings, nevertheless constitutes, in our view, a complex exchange that perhaps cannot be reduced to an operation as elementary as exploitation or betrayal— whether it is Hegel who exploits and betrays Freud or vice versa.

In the same way, the essential problem posed by Hyppolite's commentary, constantly cited and reproduced by Lacan, who will include it in the appendix to his *Ecrits*, is that of his mode of operation, which does not directly follow from the commentary itself. This is why this commentary takes its value from the "response" that accompanies it and proposes its interpretation to us: not only a new commentary on Freud's text but a commentary on the commentary that has already been proposed and whose meaning itself needs to be determined. Which way is the interpretation that Lacan proposes of Hyppolite's text going to lean? Will it be towards an alignment of the Freudian dialectic and the Hegelian dialectic—which, perhaps, was one of Hyppolite's motives at the beginning, but doubtless does not explain his undertaking any longer? Or will it lean, on the contrary, towards a divergence, a demarcation which is going to allow Freud's position to be specified by putting at a distance the risk of Hegelian reduction? Such a question can be posed because Hyppolite's commentary offers a dual reading: at the first level, it constitutes a more or less successful attempt to rediscover, in Freud's texts, the concepts and problems of Hegelianism, a reading that seems to facilitate Freud's philosophical recuperation; but, more profoundly, it leads to the discovery of an irreducible residue which can itself be retranslated into the language of the Hegelian dialectic.

For Freud's text "resists" philosophical interpretation, even if this resistance is expressed from the perspective of other philosophical references which also belong to the field of philosophy but are inscribed elsewhere in the space of discourse. In fact, if the first level we have just noted undeniably, and thus especially, bears the mark of Hegelianism, the second contests it in terms that seem to have been borrowed from Kantian philosophy. For these primitive forces whose explicit antagonism explains the genesis of thought at the foundation of the unconscious whose ultimate determination they constitute are reminiscent of that very singular concept of the negative expressed in 1763 in the *Attempt to Introduce the Concept of Negative Magnitudes into Philosophy*[32] and which we find again in Kant at the foundation of his metaphysics of nature and history as the first principle of their rationality. It is here and not with Hegel that antecedents might be sought for the idea of a primitive negativity not yet affected by the symbol of negation and the logical marks that result from this symbolization. This negativity is the fundamental condition for the subject's relation to the real, such as it is first lived in the opposition of inside and outside, and afterwards translated into the distinction of subject and object.

What does this *rapprochement* with Kantian philosophy teach us? It reveals to us the presence in Freud's text of a concept of the negative which is not Hegel's but is no longer Kant's either. For we should recall that if Kant reserves the operation of this antagonistic mechanism for nature and history, it is to the extent that it maintains the exteriority of nature and history to reason, which itself situates its own ends beyond such a conflict.[33] Now it is clear that for Freud no consciousness of rationality will make us autonomous in relation to such a determination which unavoidably affects us, if not pathologically, in so far as we are not reasonable beings in general but human beings, who are born and develop in the gaps of nature and history. Psychoanalysis no more confuses its objects and interests with those of the philosophical speculation of Kant than of Hegel, even if it must cross their path. This is precisely the lesson Lacan himself is going to draw, by basing himself on new alliances which are also borrowed from the domain of philosophy by means of Hyppolite's commentary.

If this is so, the recourse to philosophy takes on a very different meaning from the one that might be attributed to it: if Hyppolite serves here as proof, it is not from the perspective of an alignment of philosophy and psychoanalysis through the intermediary of the Hegelian dialectic but, on the contrary, from the perspective of a differential characterization of their problematics. Now it is the "specialist," the "one who is supposed to know [*supposé savoir*]," in Hegelianism who himself brings to bear the arguments that allow such a specification to be established and the "dialectics" of Freud and Hegel to be distinguished.

So what happened during this session of the seminar on 10 February 1954? Now we can answer: it represents, in Lacan's progression, not a moment of philosophical recognition but, on the contrary, a moment when distance could be taken with respect to the Hegelian reference and, through it, with respect to every philosophical reference, and perhaps once and for all. On this day, then, accounts are settled: with Hegel in particular and, through his intervention, with all of philosophy. But let us note that this rupture occurs under enigmatic conditions which are characterized from start to finish by misrecognition and misunderstanding, after the manner of the dialectical exchange to which the cure amounts here. This session of the seminar was indeed a "session" in the sense proper to analytic practice, in which philosophy was put to the test of the transference, in order to expose its symptom and hand it over to the work of interpretation. In this dialogue *Verneinung* was present twice: as the object spoken about, but spoken about precisely in this ambivalent situation in which acceptance is superimposed on refusal, and in which truth is unveiled only by retaining that part of the shadow which constitutes the foundation from which it springs and to which it finally appears.

Now we can understand Lacan's response to Hyppolite: it is presented, we have said, as a commentary on a commentary, whose meaning we must now explain. Lacan returns to Freud's text, to which he applies—in order to make it "work"—a new philosophical reference borrowed from Heidegger. Does this mean that the philosophical import of psychoanalysis can be sought in the ontology of *Sein und Zeit* rather than of the Hegelian dialectic? But here it is perhaps instead a question of counterbalancing the effects of one philosophical interpretation by means of another, which serves in a way as an antidote to it, without substituting its revelation for the one it contests. The genuine object of the analysis of *Verneinung*, says Lacan, is "a relation of the subject to being and not of the subject to the world."[34] The world is "Being" (*être*) as "being" (*étant*), given in a way completely independent of the subject: it is the world presented to ordinary consciousness in the form of external reality. Being is reality as given to a subject in a relation which is not simply a relation of exteriority, because its possibility is inscribed within the subject, in so far as it is opened into itself onto this Being for which it "ek-sists," toward which it is "thrown" (*jeté*) and "projected" (*projeté*). Thus, in the *Letter on Humanism* that Heidegger wrote in 1946 can be found those formulations which very directly evoke those used by Lacan:

> [Man] stands out into the openness of Being. Being itself, which as the throw has projected the essence of man into "care," is as this openness. Thrown in such a fashion, man stands "in" the openness of Being. "World" is the clearing of Being into which man stands out on the basis of his thrown essence. "Being-in-the-world" designates the essence of ek-sistence with regard to the cleared

dimension out of which the "ek-" of ek-sistence essentially unfolds. Thought in terms of ek-sistence, "world" is in a certain sense precisely "the beyond" within existence and for it. Man is never first and foremost man on the hither side of the world, as a "subject," whether this is taken as "I" or "We." Nor is he ever a mere subject which always simultaneously is related to objects, so that his essence lies in the subject–object relation. Rather, before all this, man in his essence is ek-sistent into the openness of Being, into the open region that clears the "between" within which a "relation" of subject to object can "be."[35]

The opening of Being, such as it appears in the "ek-sistence" of the subject, is not the external and abstract relation between a subject and an object which are indifferent to one another, but is that movement which traverses both and ties them indivisibly, from the beginning, through their common division, the reciprocal "care" that connects them by dividing them and unveils them by hiding them.

This relation of the subject and Being is also the primordial symbolic relation, the order of language or the signifier, in so far as the latter is constitutive of the recognition of the real: the real is that which is imposed on the subject according to the order of the symbolic, into which system the subject itself must be integrated in order to attain consciousness of what is said and what it is. The fundamental lesson of Freud's text on *Verneinung* is precisely that it poses a "primordial symbolization"—determined by the antagonistic relation between the drives— which "preserves its effects as far as discursive structuration."[36] This symbolization constitutes the condition of access of representations to the level of conscious speech. Thus, the duality, the splitting, that is the form through which the subject attains consciousness of the real, is already inscribed in it, in the shape of this primitive division which forms the structure of the subject as such. "It is to mistake the meaning of the pleasure principle to fail to recognize that in theory it is never posed in isolation,"[37] but precisely in relation to the antagonistic, destructive drive with which it coexists. This confrontation imparts, at the deepest level of the subject—behind that which it represents as itself and the surrounding world—the distinction of inside and outside, the latter being the condition for the subject to attain consciousness of reality. For this subject to recognize the real as such is precisely to recognize it in a sense quite close to Platonic recollection or reminiscence, to which Lacan alludes several times: it is therefore to return to this first division which from the outset assigns to the real its place in the symbolic order, that is, in the system of the signifier itself that is the place *par excellence* where this splitting occurs.

In order to develop this idea, Lacan borrows from analytic literature some examples of which we shall take only one: that of the hallucination of the severed finger in the case of the "Wolf-man," which makes manifest in a converse way the conditions by which the real is recognized through the singular experience of false recognition. To begin, let us recall the subject's account of his adventure:

> When I was five years old I was playing in the garden near my nurse, and was carving with my pocketknife in the bark of one of the walnut trees that also come into my dream. Suddenly, to my unspeakable terror, I noticed that I had cut through the little finger of my (right or left?) hand so that it was only hanging by its skin. I felt no pain, but great fear. I did not venture to say anything to my nurse, who was only a few paces distant, but I sank down on the nearest seat and sat there incapable of casting another glance at my finger.. At last I grew calm, took a look at the finger, and saw that it was uninjured.[38]

What happened? The threat of castration has the object of a *Verwerfung*, of a "foreclosure" (*retranchement*), which Lacan following Freud distinguishes from *Verdrangung*, from "repression" (*refoulement*); that is, the threat of castration no longer has any place in the subject's discourse to be made the object of a positive or negative judgement: it is as if that threat had never existed. Lacan discovers in this "symbolic abolition"[39] the manifestation of that primary, prejudicative negativity which belongs to the original functioning of the drives: "it is exactly this which is expelled."[40] The representation is removed from the symbolic order through which it might be expressed, that is, verbalized. Does this mean that it completely disappears? No, for "that which hasn't come to light in the symbolic appears in the real,"[41] in the form of a hallucinatory symptom (the illusion of the severed finger).

The representation that has been foreclosed from the symbolic order reappears outside, that is, in the place that the symbolic order assigned to it, not within its system but external to it.

> There was first the primary expulsion, that is, the real as exterior to the subject. Then at the interior of the representation (*Vorstellung*), constituted by the (imaginary) reproduction of the first perception, the discrimination of reality as that which from the object of this first perception is not only posed as existing by means of the subject, but can be rediscovered (*wiederfungen*) in the place where it can grasp it. It is in that only that the operation, completely divided as it is by the pleasure principle, escapes its mastery. But in that reality which the subject must compose according to the well-required scale of its objects, the real, in so far as it is foreclosed from primordial symbolization, *is already there*. We could even say that it is the only cause. And the subject can see emerging from it the form of a thing which is far from being an object which could satisfy it, and which interests its present intentionality only in the most incongruous way: it is here a hallucination in so far as it is differentiated radically from an interpretative phenomenon.[42]

The feeling of reality at the basis of hallucination, in the absence of the real itself, is therefore the manifestation of a necessity whose principle is found in the ordinary interplay of drives and in the opposition of inside and outside that results from it. As we have said, a representation which has not been repressed at the level of verbal expression is expelled; but to where is it expelled? Into the real, where it is "rediscovered," where the representation waits for the real to receive it, in that outside which has been posed as an alternative to the inside by the original system of exclusion in which the reality principle coexists, without being confused, with the pleasure principle.

Between the real and the symbolic—which is here distinguished from the imaginary realm that is only a projection or a redoubling of the subject itself which, through this mirror-effect, fictively resolves the internal division by which it exists or "ek-sists"—there is, then, a close correspondence, even if the latter takes the form of an antagonistic reciprocity in which order arises from disorder, presence from absence, plenitude from void. This means that access to the real proceeds by means of the law of the symbolic, under conditions that the latter has determined and anticipated.

> It is only by the symbolic articulations that bind them to an entire world that perception assumes its character of reality. But the subject won't experience a less convincing feeling to clash with the symbol that it has from the beginning foreclosed from its *Bejahung*. For this symbol doesn't enter for all that into the imaginary. It constitutes, Freud tells us, what properly doesn't exist; and it is as such that it ek-sists, for nothing exists except in so far as it doesn't exist. This is what appears as well in our example. The content of the so massively symbolic hallucination owes its appearance in the real to that which doesn't exist for the subject.... In the symbolic order, voids signify as much as plenitudes; indeed, it seems that to understand Freud today, it is the gaping hole of a void that constitutes the first step of its dialectical movement.[43]

The confrontation of the subject with reality, which occurs across the relation of an inside to an outside, is not an arbitrary encounter between independent entities that preexists their being put into relation—this is how psychology presupposes the reality of an autonomous ego progressively adapting itself to a world external to it—but is inscribed within the constitution of the subject itself, by means of the mediation of symbolism, in so far as it is "ek-sistence," that is, both being and not being, admission and refusal, speech and silence.

In the text we just cited, the term "dialectic" was again employed to signify precisely this relation of exclusion which ties the real and the symbolic into a circle which, even if it is broken, does not fail to constitute an insurmountable limit. If there is a dialectic of the subject, it is a dialectic without resolution; it is therefore severed from any Hegelian reference. If Hegel's words always have their place—but let us note that with the exception of "dialectic" Lacan refrains from using them in his response—it is provided that they are deprived of their initial meaning. Strictly speaking, it could be said again that a hallucination is an

Aufhebung, a negation of the negation, but on the condition of specifying that it is not in this sense that the effect of reality aroused by it could simultaneously reconcile subject and object through a recognition of their common belonging to a third moment—Consciousness or Spirit—which would surpass their opposition: on the contrary, it affirms that their duality is irreducible to the extent that it is the condition for the subject itself to attain existence and form adequate or inadequate representations of itself and the surrounding world. Here Lacan distances himself in particular from Kojève's teaching by following a path on which Bataille, the "non-philosopher," had preceded him. The relation of the real and the symbolic is not reducible to that of the real and the rational as it has been established in the Hegelian Logos, because it is achieved only through a dialectical process of recognition in the course of which a divided subject would reestablish its lost unity by being absorbed into a system of absolute knowledge. From the standpoint of this final recognition, which gives meaning to the entire experience at the same time that it orders the course of the phenomenology, the Hegelian "subject" is not very different from the Cartesian "subject," whose imaginary reflection in some way constitutes it. If the Hegelian subject does not receive full consciousness from the origin in the form of a unique and unquestionable revelation, it finally attains full consciousness by following a progression in which the unconscious, or rather, to take up Hyppolite's expression again, "the function of the unconscious of consciousness,"[44] is only an intermediary, the instrument by means of which the contradiction that itself serves as the motor of this development is resolved. In this sense dialectical "genesis" is only a development of the *cogito* for the length of a history which abolishes itself at the moment it reaches its end: and the *cogito* consists, then, of an imaginary identification instead of the obscure revelation of the symbolic. In the context of such an interpretation, the unconscious, restored to a diachronic presentation, is deprived of its synchronic structure, whose form is anterior, and posterior, to every process, to every genesis, which constitutes only a partial realization of it.

The *rapprochement* of psychoanalysis and Hegelian philosophy on the basis of their common reference to a "dialectic" leads, then, to a positing of divergence. If Lacan enters into a dialogue with Hegel, with Hyppolite serving as interpreter, it is not in order to obtain and to validate the inscription of his theoretical undertaking—which was then formulated as a "return to Freud"—in the philosophical field but, on the contrary, in order to dissociate himself from it. Lacan is more concerned with leaving Hegel than with entering him. We find confirmation of this tendency in the remarkable dialogue that will conclude—ten years later, at the moment when Lacan's seminar resumed after the split with the *Société française de la psychanalyse*—the session devoted to "alienation."

J. A. Miller: *Do you not wish to show, all the same, that the alienation of a subject who has received the definition of being born in, constituted by, and ordered in a field that is exterior to him, is to be distinguished radically from the alienation of a consciousness-of-self? In short, are we to understand—Lacan against Hegel?*

Lacan: What you have just said is very good, it's exactly the opposite of what Green just said to me—he came up to me, shook my paw, at least morally, and said, *The death of structuralism, you are the son of Hegel.* I don't agree. I think that in saying Lacan *against* Hegel, you are much closer to the truth, though of course it is not at all a philosophical debate.

Dr Green: *The sons kill the fathers!*[45]

In fact, the session devoted to *Verneinung* seems indeed to have been the occasion of a totemic feast: and one cannot avoid thinking here of the "parricide" committed by Plato in the encounter with Parmenides, as he presents him and makes him speak in the presence of Socrates in the *Sophist*. For in philosophy, too, sons kill fathers, and that is what its entire history amounts to: didn't Hegel himself think that he had digested all the knowledge accumulated and transmitted by his predecessors? But if philosophers devour one another, it is in order to do philosophy. What happens when a "dialectician" like Lacan sits down at the great speculative table in order to flush philosophers out and manipulate their lures? What happens is that philosophy itself is consumed, or consummated, in the sense that it finds itself relieved of its place and its claims to tell the truth about everything, and in particular about that which concerns the analyst's competence, while remaining completely unconscious of the opposite movement that leads it back, a lured lure, to the hunter's fist, in order to make it the living instrument of a capture which surpasses it.

Notes

1. Thanks to Erika Thomas for her assistance in the translation of this article. (Trans.)
2. Lacan 1966, 829–50.
3. Ibid., 831.
4. Ibid., 837.
5. Translated by Hoesli (*Revue française de psychanalyse* VII, 2, 1934) with the title "Négation."
6. Lacan 1988. The account of the session on *Verneinung* is found on pp. 52–61.
7. *La Psychanalyse* (the publication of the *Société française de la psychanalyse*) 1–covering the years 1953–5 (P.U.F., 1956); the account of the session on *Verneinung* is given in pp. 17–58.
8. Lacan 1966, 363–99; Hyppolite's presentation is reprinted in the appendix, pp. 879–87.
9. Drafted in 1956, published in *La Psychanalyse* 2, 1957, 1–44, and reprinted as an introduction in the *Ecrits*, pp. 11–60.
10. In our explication we shall refer first to the version of the seminar on denegation published in 1956 in *La Psychanalyse* 1, reprinted in 1966 in the *Ecrits*.
11. *La Psychanalyse* 1, 17–28; Lacan 1966, 369–80.
12. Lacan 1966, 370.
13. Ibid., 373.
14. Ibid., 374.
15. Hyppolite 1957, 18.

16. Ibid., 19.
17. Lacan 1966, 374–5.
18. *La Psychanalyse* 1, 27.
19. Lacan 1966, 379.
20. *La Psychanalyse* 1, 73.
21. Lacan 1966, 379.
22. Lacan 1988, 55.
23. Lacan 1966, 364–5.
24. According to the translation of Freud's sentence proposed by Hyppolite; see the bottom of p. 269 of Hoesli's translation.
25. Audouard 1959.
26. Ibid., 247.
27. Ibid.
28. Hyppolite 1957, 17f.
29. Hyppolite 1988, 293. (Translation modified)
30. Ibid., 294.
31. Rey 1974, 129 note.
32. Kant 1992. Lacan himself refers to this *Attempt* in the second session of the 1964 seminar (Lacan 1978, 21).
33. As Lebrun 1970 shows.
34. Lacan 1966, 382.
35. Heidegger 1993, 252.
36. Lacan 1966, 383.
37. Ibid., 385.
38. Freud 1959, 563–4.
39. Lacan 1966, 386.
40. Ibid., 387.
41. Ibid., 388.
42. Ibid., 389.
43. Ibid., 392.
44. Hyppolite 1957, 19.
45. Lacan 1978, 215.

5

At the Sources of
Histoire de la folie:
A Rectification and its Limits

Histoire de la folie appeared in 1961: it was Foucault's first important theoretical work and the effective point of departure of all his later investigations. In 1962 the Presses Universitaires de France reprinted under a new title, *Mental Illness and Psychology*, and in a considerably restructured version, a short work which had been published by Foucault in 1954, in the collection "Initiation philosophique" directed by Jean Lacroix, *Mental Illness and Personality*.[1] If one would carry out the archaeology of Foucault's thought, it is to this latter book that one must return, in order to know the initial state of his reflections on mental illness and madness. The comparison between the two versions of this text, that of 1954 and that of 1962, is rich in lessons: it allows one to measure the path Foucault had to travel before engaging in the completely original approach he was to follow during the next twenty years, until the *History of Sexuality* of 1984; above all, through this theoretical rectification of a primitive text, carried out in the light of the discoveries also presented in *Histoire de la folie*, this comparison highlights the specific characteristics of the new problematic on the basis of which these discoveries were possible; finally, it allows us to see at the beginning of the 1960s the limits within which the interpretation proposed by Foucault of these practices and knowledges of man, which until the end of his *oeuvre* would constitute the object of his study, remained.

Let us consider first the general introduction to the book, although it is only very slightly corrected. It presents the general question to which all the later analyses refer: under what conditions has one come to speak about "mental illness" and to develop in relation to it discourses taking the form of knowledges? In the first version of his text, Foucault proposed to confront this representation with "a reflection on man himself" (1954: 2), a formula he rewrites in the following way: "a certain relation, historically situated, of man to the madman and to the true man" (1962: 2). Thus are announced two ideas to be found in all the rest of the book of 1962, and which also delimit the theoretical field of *Histoire de la folie*: first, there is no reflection except on historically situated human reality, and it is only in history that this reflection finds its actual foundations; on the other hand, madness, which is something essentially different from mental illness, enters into a fundamental relationship with truth. In what follows we shall have to ask ourselves if these two ideas are in agreement, and to what extent they prefigure Foucault's later philosophical positions. Let us point out again that at the beginning of *Mental Illness and Personality*, Foucault characterized the polemical orientation of his investigation as follows: "to show of what preconditions medicine must be conscious in order to find a new rigour" (1954: 2). For if mental pathology attains historically situated and diversified forms of rigour which constitute its "preconditions," it has become clear for Foucault in 1962 that the economy of his discourse does not arise from theoretical "postulates," whether the latter have a scientific value or not; nor will it ever be able to rid itself completely of these preconditions, in order to attain the objective status of a science, but only to become conscious of them, through a historical reflection on its own conditions of possibility.

The first chapter of the book, in its two versions, takes up these introductory themes again by developing them. It explains how from the concept of mental illness, previously defined from the perspective of a general or "metapathological" pathology common to organic medicine and mental medicine, under the guise of a proper psychological study of the phenomena of madness, a study emerged which reveals its specific characteristics, which are irreducible to the explanatory models used in the context of organic pathology. The text of *Mental Illness and Personality* reasserts, then, the necessity of freeing the notion of mental illness from the abusive postulates that prevent it from attaining scientific rigour: "Mental pathology must be free itself of all the abstract postulates of a metapathology: the unity assured by the latter among the diverse forms of illness is never anything but artificial; it is the real human being who supports their unity." (1954: 16) This latter formula, reminiscent of Politzer, by whom Foucault was doubtless inspired while writing his first book in 1954, is clearly ambiguous: to the abstract essence of illness, this formula opposes an actual and concrete truth of the human being, which is its mirror image. This is why the 1962 text substitutes this new version: "that is, it belongs to a historical fact that is already behind us" (1962: 13); for the "subject" of mental illness is not an authentic or objective nature, persisting behind the artificial interpretations that conceal it, but a historical being, about whom nothing says that he is himself ill, and the unity of this subject arises from conditions in perpetual transformation, which exclude any permanence. This is why to account for the specificity of mental life is not "to seek the concrete forms it can assume in the concrete life of an individual" (1954: 16), as the text of the first edition said, but, according to the corrected version, "to seek the concrete forms that psychology has managed to attribute to it" (1962: 13)—and this in the sense of a historical attribution which must be studied without reference to a real foundation, whether the latter is given in the singular existence of an individual or in an abstract human essence generally conceived. For this, it is no longer enough to "determine the conditions that have made possible these diverse aspects (of mental psychology) and restored the totality of the causal system that has founded them" (1954: 17); one must "determine the conditions that have made possible this strange status of madness, a mental illness that cannot be reduced to any illness" (1962: 13). To restore to the concept of mental illness its historical and social dimension is to remove its object from the mechanistic chain to which its insertion submits in a causal system, and on the contrary is to seek to think of this concept in relation to its presuppositions and conditions, that is, its "preconditions." Thus one understands why in the final lines of this introductory chapter, in contrast to the first version of his text where he proposed to reduce mental illness to its "real conditions" (1954: 17), in the corrected version Foucault is engaged on a different path, envisioning "psychopathology as a fact of civilization" (1962: 13). It is no longer a question of explaining illness itself but of relating the discourses and practices whose object it forms to the conditions that historically constitute the latter outside of every real determination arising from an objective or positive signification.

The rest of the book develops in two parts, of which the first presents—it is its title—the "psychological dimensions of illness"; it shows how the various psychological approaches to mental illness have gradually tried to detach mental illness from an essential or naturalist representation, by interpreting it either as a fact of evolution (according to the Jacksonian point of view, presented and criticized in the second chapter: "mental illness and evolution"), or as a moment in the history of the individual (according to the point of view of psychoanalysis, analysed in the third chapter: "mental illness and individual history"), or as a meaning offered to an existential understanding (according to the phenomenological point of view, presented in the fourth chapter: "illness and existence"). In the second version of the book, the text of this first part is reproduced with trivial changes. In 1962 Foucault continues to think that by proposing a description of mental illness not simply based on the negative representation of deficiencies—as is done on the contrary by organic pathology—and by putting forward the representation of conflicts (between the past and present existence of the individual, between his internal world and the external world, etc.), psychology has characterized the latter with what he has just called "a new rigour" (1962: 2). But the limit of these psychological interpretations appears from the moment that the latter present what only has a descriptive value as having explanatory value, revealing the meaning and origin of illness: they emphasize what is contradictory in the notion of mental illness, but they are not capable of resituating this contradiction within the structural system of its conditions, which are "historical" rather than "real"; in fact, they remain attached to the presuppositions of a given human existence, whose laws they claim to reveal. This is why, in the second part of the book, the question of the meaning and import of this notion of mental illness will be transported to a completely different terrain.

Here is how, in the final lines of the fourth chapter of his book, Foucault articulates this new investigation with the previous descriptions:

> But here we may have touched on one of the paradoxes of mental illness that demand new forms of analysis: if this subjectivity of the insane is both a call to and an abandonment of the world, is it not of the world itself that we should ask the secret of this enigmatic subjectivity [2nd edition: the secret of its enigmatic status]? After having explored the external[2] dimensions isn't one necessarily led to consider its external and objective conditions? [2nd edition: isn't there in illness a whole nucleus of significations that belong to the domain in which it appeared—and, to begin with, the simple fact that it is in that domain that it is circumscribed *as* an illness?] (1954: 69; 1962: 56)

This simple editing of the last three lines of the first part of the book shows that the apparent permanence of his text in fact conceals a shift in its meaning: for the characterization of psychology, in the words identically reproduced in the second book, lead to a new order of problems. The formulations used in *Mental Illness and Personality* could suggest the necessity of going further than the various psychologies do in the sense of the reconstitution of a human reality explained concretely on the basis of its "external and objective conditions," thus maintaining the illusion that the concept of mental illness refers to a real content of which it offers only a mystified interpretation. *Mental Illness and Psychology*, however, draws attention to a new question: the notion of illness refers to a meaning only to the extent that it is identified as such within a certain historical context, or inside a system of conditions which objectifies its content; hence, this objectification does not arise from a preestablished objectivity; it must not be questioned, then, about its real foundation but about its "historical constitution," and this is precisely what provides the subject of the second part of the book, in this new edition of 1962.

These considerations allow one to propose an explanation for changing the title of the whole work. By attempting to measure the relation of mental illness to personality, as he did in his 1954 text, Foucault engaged in an explanatory approach which sought the conditions of mental illness and its concept alongside the personal existence of the sick person, and of the general situation that determines this existence. The new titling of the book in 1962 indicates another orientation: it is no longer a question of studying the relationship that illness really enters into with the personality, but of examining its historical and discursive relationship with a "psychology" that delimits the epistemological field inside which its concept becomes thinkable and refers to a positive study, at least in appearance. From the perspective defined in this way, it is no longer possible to speak of mental illness, of personality, of psychology, as if these notions corresponded to objective contents whose contours could be defined and isolated without previously taking account of the historical system of conditions on the basis of which they correlatively take on meaning for one another.

This shift is confirmed by the new editing of the first lines of the second part of the book. Returning to the previous three chapters in order to specify their import, Foucault had first written: "The preceding analyses have determined the coordinates by which one can situate pathology inside of personality" (1954: 71); in 1962 he alters this formula as follows: "the preceding analyses have fixed the coordinates by which psychologies can situate the pathological fact." (1962: 60) This means that there is not, as the first text might lead one to think, any pathological fact in itself, hence no real relationship of determination between mental illness and personality; instead, the reality of the pathological fact, on the contrary, can itself only be thought on the basis of a psychology which inscribes it within this perspective. The essential question is indeed, then, to know what are the relations between mental illness and psychology, without passing through the intermediary reference to a "personality," whose intimate structure psychology would supposedly expound by giving a positive explanation of it.

The modifications made to the second part of the book are extremely important. The subject treated here stands out from its confrontation with the first part: until now the forms of the appearance of mental illness have only been exhibited from the point of view of the various psychologies that, under the pretext of presenting its explanation, have only described it; now it is a question of taking up the study of the conditions of the illness. At the end of chapter 5 Foucault writes that one must interrogate the "real origins" (1954: 89) of illness, instead of holding to the "mythical explanations" that immediately emerge from its simple observation, or out of what apparently is given as such. For these real origins of the illness are not found in the personality of the sick person or in the forms of existence imposed on him, the latter constituting the object of an investigation in which psychological analysis would still have its place, and even attain a scientific rigour; instead, they coincide with the historical conditions that simultaneously make possible the pathological fact and its interpretation, without it being possible to establish any relation of precedence or determination between the former and latter. In *Mental Illness and Personality* this inquiry is carried out under the title "the conditions of the illness" (1954: 71), which is an ambiguous expression, since it holds out the possibility of an objective explanation of the illness, in so far as the latter corresponds to a real datum capable of being related positively to its conditions. In order to bring this ambiguity to light, it would perhaps be enough to write this title a little differently: the conditions of the "illness," the quotation marks added to the word illness showing precisely that the conditions from which its object emerges determine at the same time and concurrently the fact and the representation of it that is given, without these two aspects being separable, and without it being possible to present one with respect to the other as the principle of its reality. In the second version of his book Foucault expressed this idea by entitling its second part "madness and culture."

Let us first consider the introduction of this new development. If psychologies, writes Foucault, "have shown the forms of appearance of the illness, they have been unable to show its conditions of appearance" (1954: 71; 1962: 60). And the text continues as follows: "It is in these conditions, no doubt, that the illness manifests itself, that its modalities, its forms of expression, its style, are revealed. But the roots of the pathological fact [2nd edition: the pathological deviation] are to be found elsewhere." (ibid.) In fact, from the point of view of this "elsewhere" in which are found the real origins of the illness, that is, from the point of view of this system inside which it is inseparable from its image, one no longer needs to speak of "pathological fact"—as if the latter existed in itself according to its own reality—but about "pathological deviation": this latter expression designates pathology as a deviation in relation to a norm that is simultaneously a norm of existence and a norm of evaluation, on the basis of which the illness coincides exactly with its image, such as it is constructed historically in conditions that are at once objective and subjective.

The rest of this introductory text has not been altered. Nevertheless, some attention should be paid to it, if only because, put back into a new context, the same analyses take on a different meaning and import. In these pages Foucault considers the "sociological" or "cultural" interpretations of mental illness, which precisely allow one to relativize the notion of mental illness, by plunging it back into the system of collective representations. Yet these interpretations, which actually present the psychological fact as a deviation in relation to a norm—"mental illness takes its place among the possibilities that serve as a margin of the cultural reality of a social group" (1954: 73; 1962: 62)—offer, according to Foucault (who in 1962 does not return to this critique), the drawback of providing only a negative characterization of it, the pathological thus being thought as a defect in relation to the norm. Yet "this, no doubt, is to ignore the positive, real elements in mental illness as it is presented in a society" (ibid.). In the 1954 text, pervaded by numerous reminiscences of a realist epistemology, this sentence is not surprising: it refers to the idea that there is a specific content of the pathological fact which escapes the global perspective of sociological explanation. But it is astonishing in the 1962 text, which seems otherwise purged of every positivistic reference. This is because, in the meantime, the formula has changed meaning: breaking with the "cultural illusion" (1962: 63) from which sociologism proceeds, it manifests now what connects the pathological fact to the system inside which it is represented in the form of a positive relation of determination.

> The analyses of our psychologists and sociologists, which turn the patient into a deviant and which seek the origin of the morbid in the abnormal, are, therefore, above all a projection of cultural themes. In fact, a society expresses itself positively in the mental illnesses manifested by its members . . . (ibid.)

In fact, positively: these words no longer signify, however, that there is an actual reality of the pathological, which is accessible to a positive explanation, but rather that the insertion of illness into a cultural and social context, far from implying a de-realization and denial of its concept, is precisely what constitutes its "positive" reality, in conditions which are obviously no longer those of a nature but of a history. The limit of sociologism and of culturalism is that they give illness a definition which is common to all forms of society and culture. The terms of such an analysis should be reversed: illness is not recognized as such because it is a deviation in relation to the norm; but it is a deviation in relation to a norm because it is identified as a pathological form, in conditions which remain to be elucidated, with respect to which collective norms should be thought of not as causes but as effects, not as realities in themselves—it is in this that on the contrary the culturalist illusion resides—but as phenomena.

Having set aside the perspective of a culturalist sociology, one must respond, then, to the following two questions: "How did our culture come to give mental illness the meaning of deviancy and the patient the status that excludes him? And how, despite that fact, does our society express itself in those morbid forms in which it refuses to recognize itself?" (ibid.) In fact, if illness is considered within a mechanism of exclusion, it is not within the context of culture or society considered in general but within the context of a certain type of culture and society, which thus assigns illness the form of its appearance. This is what Foucault means when he writes that a society "expresses itself positively" in the pathological forms it isolates, even if—and perhaps because—it refuses to recognize itself in them. But we are going to see that this idea of expression doesn't mean quite the same thing in *Mental Illness and Personality* and in *Mental Illness and Psychology*.

In fact, in the 1954 book chapter 5 is entitled "the historical sense of mental alienation," and in the 1962 book "the historical constitution of mental illness." To speak of the "historical sense" of alienation is to show how a society "expresses itself" through the morbid forms on which it imposes their modes of recognition: but this "sense" and this "expression" are then to be considered not according to the orientation of a hermeneutics of mentalities, this way being closed in any case, but from the materialist perspective of an explanation of the superstructure by means of the infrastructure, rather close to the Marx of *The German Ideology* who defined ideology as a "language of social life." This perspective, characteristic of *Mental Illness and Personality*, refers to the presupposition of a realist epistemology, explaining the psychological fact in relation to the real conditions that determine it as "alienation," within the framework of a society itself alienated; one will then say that this society projects its alienation into modes of behaviour which it imposes on certain of its members, thus moulding their personality. The truth of alienation thus resides in the social relations that human beings enter into among themselves in their existence, which in any case, whether ranked under the category of the normal or under the model of the pathological, is disrupted by the material conflicts that determine their forms. When in 1962 Foucault returned to the study of "the historical constitution of mental illness," he moved away from this conception of an alienation which was original because collective, which *a priori* accounted for all forms of social exclusion and would thereby provide even "the conditions of illness": for alienation must be thought not as a cause but as an effect, the latter arising from a "historical constitution," which does not amount to a real relation of determination, presupposing in the primitive materiality of its principle (the social structure) the content of what it seeks to explain. If there is alienation in a certain type of society, it is not by virtue of an alienated essence of that society, preexisting its appearances and having only to reproduce itself in them: but the materiality of the pathological fact only forms the object of a realization or an evaluation because it is constructed historically, in other words, because it is the product of a process which does not at all anticipate its reality at the beginning, but which brings about its conditions through a chain of unforeseeable events, whose succession remains to be reconstructed.

In the first paragraph of this fifth chapter, the 1954 text proposes a genesis of the modern forms of alienation from those original forms which are the *possessed* of the Greeks, the *captivated* of the Romans, and the *demoniac* of the Christians. "The primitive form of alienation is no doubt to be found in this possession in which, since Antiquity, one has seen, with the major sign of madness, the transformation of man into something other than he is." (1954: 76) By following the transformations of these primitive forms, it should be possible to show the historical sense of alienation, represented first as the irruption of the inhuman within human existence, then progressively integrated into the universe of men, until it finds its place in the contradictory system, combining exclusion and inclusion, characteristic of bourgeois society, which imposes itself on Europe in the final years of the eighteenth century. Yet the book published in 1962 rejects this conception of a continuous evolution leading from possession to mental illness by gradually specifying a concept of alienation whose sense takes shape only by developing progressively through this history, instead of actually being constituted in and through it. To adopt this latter point of view of a historical constitution is to reveal, in opposition to this continuous evolution, the succession of breaks which, by accumulating their effects, will end up producing the modern concept of mental illness within the specific conditions of a given culture. This is how in its new version chapter 5 begins: "It was at a relatively recent date that the West accorded madness the status of mental illness. It has been said, only too often, that, until the advent of a positivist medicine, the madman was regarded as someone 'possessed.'" (1962: 64) Yet this is precisely what Foucault had himself said in the first edition of his book, in which he presupposed a kind of permanence of alienation through history which exhibits it in its various forms. But history doesn't offer just one meaning, or meanings, to alienation; history governs the "constitution" of alienation, through a discontinuous approach which does not orient in advance the reference to a common form of alienation which from the outset establishes the general appearance of its trajectory. Let us note that logically, with this change of orientation, the allusion to a "West," which is itself mythical and refers to the same illusion of a permanence and a "sense," should also disappear.

To present the problem of the historical constitution of mental illness is thus to abandon the search behind the latter for the objective basis whose appearance it would be. Foucault writes, in *Mental Illness and Psychology*:

> And all histories up to the present day have set out to show that the madman of the Middle Ages and the Renaissance was simply an unrecognized mentally ill patient, trapped within a tight network of religious and magical significations. According to this view, it was only with the arrival of the calm, objective, scientific gaze of modern medicine that what had previously been regarded as supernatural perversion was seen as a deterioration of nature. (1962: 64)

The recursive reading of history projects even on to the primitive forms it presupposes this final truth which in fact only corresponds to the limited point of view from which it operates, as if it were the same madness that had first been ignored as possession so as next to be known, and recognized, as mental illness. In fact, a realist epistemology only maintains the substantial existence of the object to which it is applied in order to confer on this object the rightful permanence of a unique knowledge which traverses all of history, without its movement fundamentally altering it. But this representation of knowledge and its object is itself attached to a historical conjuncture—the one that in the nineteenth century will give rise to the discourse of positive medicine—and cannot escape its conditions. The continuity this representation presupposes has no real foundation but depends on the singularity of a point of view and a moment. The notion of mental illness—which was not only ignored until then but unthinkable within another context—appears to this point of view inside a system of practices and discourses which confers on this notion its exclusive value as truth.

Let us open a parenthesis here: immediately after having denounced this retrospective illusion of positive knowledge which annexes to the domain of mental illness all sorts of previous forms, assembled under the general notion of alienation, Foucault refers to the "confiscation" of the various experiences of madness within the very concept of illness (1962: 65). Yet this term confiscation simultaneously evokes two things: on the one hand, it indicates the process of abstraction that assimilates original historical features, incomparable by reason of the irreducibility of the conditions on which they depend, in a single representation, which amounts to privileging unduly one among them in order to make it the model by which the others should be uniformly measured; on the other hand, it also suggests the free proliferation of these singular experiences, arbitrarily retained within the limits of a mythical discourse which obscures its moving reality. One might think that a new realism is sketched here, a realism that would no longer be a realism of science but a realism of experience, in its turn promoted to the status of an original and true form, freely traversing history, which would only be the occasional place of its manifestation: it would be a question here of a realism of madness, as the object not of a knowledge but of an experience. Actually, all of *Histoire de la folie*, whose great shadow falls on the text of *Mental Illness and Psychology*, is haunted by this presupposition of a fundamental experience of madness, represented by the slightly mystical trinity of Nerval, Roussel and Artaud, an essential experience that would escape the limits of a historical constitution. This search for "secret ontological sources," to take up an expression of Dreyfus and Rabinow,[3] is entirely characteristic of the interpretive system adopted by Foucault at the beginning of the 1960s, at the moment that he is engaged in his great enterprise of a genealogy of the forms of human experience: it is precisely this presupposition that his later works will more or less clearly call into question.

We have just undertaken the analysis of a concept which is at the centre of all of Foucault's thought: the concept of experience, which appears at the end of the first paragraph of the fifth chapter in *Mental Illness and Psychology*. It intervenes then as an alternative to the representation of a positive fact which would be at the heart of the notion of mental illness. That which, in the recurrence of a knowledge which eternalizes its discourse by projecting it onto the past, appears in a continuous and permanent way as alienation, in fact corresponds to diversified and incomparable experiences. These experiences are not linked to one another on the basis of an undifferentiated essence of which they are the successive expressions, but they are articulated with one another, and in a way engaged, during this slow labour of historical constitution which is not predestined by the presupposition of a preestablished sense, but which always advances beyond its current forms, without depending on norms imposed by a preconceived rationalization, since on the contrary it engenders the criteria of its rationalization as and when needed.

From this point of view, the essential contribution of the 1962 text consists in the fact that, between the considerations on the ancient figures of possession and those which are devoted to the medicalization of the phenomenon of alienation, is inserted an analysis (pp. 67–9) bearing on the classical experience of madness, which takes up in a very summary form what is essential to the discoveries also detailed at length in *Histoire de la folie*. "About the middle of the seventeenth century, a sudden change took place: the world of madness was to become the world of exclusion." (1962: 67) The new "experience," issuing from this mutation, is ordered around an institution without precedents: the Hôpital Général. The structure of separation that is then put in place refers to a social pathology which mingles in the same category, by also enclosing them in the same place, the mad, the poor, the elderly, libertines, the rebellious, lumped together in this unique and monotonous figure of the deviant that society expels to its margins, so that society no longer has to recognize itself in the inverted image it reflects from itself onto this figure.

> These houses had no medical vocation; one was not admitted in order to receive treatment; one was taken in because one could no longer cope with life or because one was no longer fit to belong to society. The internment to which the madman, together with many others, was subjected in the classical period concerns the relations, not between madness and illness, but between society and itself, between society and what it recognized and did not recognize in the behaviour of individuals. (1962: 68)

It is at this moment that, alongside the other cases arising from the same sentence of internment, madness is perceived and lived as an absence of works, because it is reflected through an essential relation to idleness and laziness, which justifies the fact that it is cut off from the useful world of production. Thus it is that the system of internment precedes the constitution of madness as mental illness, providing a positive knowledge with its object. The medical experience of madness, which will come later, will occur on the basis of the precondition of this exclusion, whose structure it will transpose, from the hospital to the asylum without modifying its two fundamental characteristics: the imprisonment of silence and moral condemnation. The relation between mental illness and madness is therefore not the one that, by virtue of the recursive illusion that is its own, positive knowledge represents: the medical experience of madness as mental illness is not at all prefigured in the classical gesture of exclusion; but the latter, which precedes the former in the historical labour of its constitution, on the contrary imposes its own models of representation on it. Thus it is that at the moment when medicine will take over from the police, it will not be in order to become progressively closer to a natural truth of madness, but in order to pursue, in other conditions, the movement of elaboration that leads to its current forms.

From all this, it seems that one should conclude that there is no original experience of madness but only a discontinuous succession of experiences in the subject, concerning which there were no grounds for predicting, by virtue of a preestablished logic of facts, that it would be ordered in this or that sense. Foucault will thus show in these last works that there is no longer a nontemporal, immemorial experience of sexuality, whose alternations of licence and repression arise from or mask the essential foundation; instead, there are only conjunctural mechanisms of the desiring subject, which successively organize the experiences during a history which remains constantly open, because it is not subjected to the presupposition of any teleology, whether rational or not. However, it is not certain that *Histoire de la folie* is completely relieved of the weight of these origins: we are going to return to this matter.

On the basis of this analysis, and of the new fact it points out, the interpretation of the modern forms of internment in medical institutions which appear as the implementation of a knowledge of man, an interpretation sketched in the 1954 text, takes on a completely different significance in the 1962 text. In fact, what does Foucault show in his first book? That the liberation of the mad at the end of the eighteenth century, at the moment that humanist bourgeois ideology discredits the institution of the Hôpital Général, by reason of its too obviously carceral nature, and decides on its suppression, is a deceptive appearance, since this liberation coincides with the new practices of asylum medicine that, pushing madness a little more into its status of alienation, in fact return to deprive the individual of his humanity and personality. Undertaking in 1954 an inquiry regarding the "conditions of illness" (it was, let us recall, the title of the second part of *Mental Illness and Personality*), Foucault promised to respond to the following question: "How has our culture come to give illness the sense of deviation, and to the patient a status of the excluded?" (1954: 75) But this time the intermediary link presupposed by Foucault's explanation—the classical experience of internment—makes this explanation a complete failure and can only bring to the question thus posed an indicative response which relies on the interpretation of the general phenomenon of alienation. This interpretation rests on the analysis of the contradictions of bourgeois ideology that, at the same time, reintegrate madness into humanity and propose its positive study in the global context of the human sciences whose programme it then defines, and dispossesses the madman of his nature as a human being by forcing onto him a "prohibition" which removes from him the fundamental rights also attached to the human essence. "The mental patient in the nineteenth century is one who has lost the use of liberties that the bourgeois revolution conferred on him." (1954: 80) There is then a conflict between the ideal representation of an abstract humanity and the real practices of concrete society: this contradiction opens up within bourgeois society a space in which there is room for an alienation, and thereby constitutes this society itself as an alienated society.

> The destiny of the patient is established henceforth for more than a century: he is alienated. And this alienation marks all his social relations, all his experiences, all his conditions of existence; he can no longer recognize himself in his own will, since one presupposes that he doesn't know it; he only encounters strangers in others, since he is himself a stranger for them. Alienation is therefore for the patient much more than a juridical status: a real experience; it is necessarily inscribed within the pathological fact. (1954: 80)

There is an experience of alienation, then, which is not only the fact of the madman as an individual, but which belongs to the entire society inside which he is recognized as a patient. The knowledge of madness, as it develops through the discourse of medical pathology, thus does nothing other than express after the fact a structure of the social relations of which in a way it constitutes the reflection. Illness refers to the social, and not cultural, experience of dehumanization. This is why Foucault can conclude his analysis as follows: "One can presume that on the day when the patient no longer undergoes the fate of alienation, it will be possible to envisage the dialectics of illness in a personality which remains human." (1954: 83) To restore to the individual his personality— which can occur only in the context of a society itself disalienated ("on the day when")—is by the same token to suppress the form of alienation in order to substitute for it the "dialectics of illness."

In the 1962 text this theory of social alienation has been completely erased, and in its place is found an analysis of the means through which, at the end of the eighteenth century, internment was not suppressed but converted, transformed from a police practice into a medical practice: it was then that the asylums were set aside for mental patients, onto whom are transferred the former practices of imprisonment. This transformation takes place in the mythical form of a double advent: that of humanism and that of positive scientificity. But the human nature thus revealed is only a fictive essence: far from returning to the natural experience of the pathological fact rid of the prejudice of a social evaluation, the doctor in the asylum on the contrary applies to mental illness the collective verdict that condemns it; he is "the agent of moral synthesis" (1962: 71). The perception of madness as illness takes place, then, on the basis of a social space of exclusion, assimilating anomaly and error. It is in these conditions that for the first time the specificity of mental illness is recognized, through the mediation of the discourse of psychology which then parts with the discourse of organic physiology once and for all.

> In the new world of the asylum, in that world of a punishing morality, madness became a fact concerning essentially the human soul, its guilt, and its freedom; it was now inscribed within the dimension of interiority; and by that fact, for the first time in the world, madness was to receive psychological status, structure, and signification. But this psychologization was merely the superficial consequence of a more obscure, more deeply embedded operation—an operation by which madness was inserted into the system of moral values and repressions. (1962: 72–3)

This is because the constitution of this knowledge does not depend on the supposed nature of its object, but on the global system of evaluation inside which the latter is identified, and precisely recognized, as an object. This system, which is set up at the beginning of the nineteenth century, defines the conditions of a new experience of madness, whose style and general appearance are completely novel in relation to its previous experiences. So novel that, as has already been noted, the allusion to the "Western world," and to its seeming homogeneity or permanence, by the same token seems to lose its pertinence.

The last part of the chapter on "the historical constitution of mental illness" in the 1962 book is devoted to showing how psychology has been produced by the asylum structure inside which madness has become mental illness. In relation to the interpretation given to it at that time, the relation of mental illness to psychology must in fact be inverted, as we have just seen. "In other words, man became a 'psychologizable species' only when his relation to madness made a psychology possible, that is to say, when his relation to madness was defined by the external dimension of exclusion and punishment and by the internal dimension of moral assignation and guilt." (1962: 73) Foucault never says that this relation is contradictory but that it is "ambiguous," because it rests on the histori-cally established confusion between determinations which are foreign to one another from the start, and whose coincidence arises from neither a natural foundation nor a rational justification. "The whole epistemologi-cal structure of contemporary psychology is rooted in this event, which is contemporary with the French Revolution and which concerns man's relation with himself." (1962: 74) The discourse of psychology draws its legitimacy from an event which communicates its necessity to it, and of which only an artificially objectified representation has to be given, according to the model of *homo psychologicus* who is also inseparably the subject of internment.

Thus it is the experience of madness that allows the enterprise of psychology to be understood, instead of psychology itself allowing madness to be understood. However, one may wonder if there is not sketched here a new fiction, a new utopia, which is exactly symmetrical with the one in the 1954 text when it evokes the eventuality of a society which would be disalienated because it would be purged of all its contradictions once and for all ("on the day when"): the fiction of another knowledge of man, a naked knowledge, an authentic knowledge, a true knowledge, a de-psychologized because de-pathologized knowledge, as social upheavals reveal.

> Psychology can never tell the truth about madness because it is madness that holds the truth of psychology. . . . If carried back to its roots, the psychology of madness would appear to be not the mastery of mental illness and hence the possibility of its disappearance, but the destruction of psychology itself and the discovery of that essential, non-psychological because non-moralizable relation that is the relation between Reason and Unreason. (1962: 74)

This "essential relation" of man to himself puts into play another kind of truth, no longer arising from any kind of positive determination: this is why this truth constitutes an absolute norm of evaluation. This is the precise theme taken up in the sixth chapter of *Mental Illness and Psychology*, which is devoted to "madness: an overall structure." Here is its programme: "One day an attempt must be made to study madness as an overall structure—madness freed and disalienated, restored in some sense to its original language." (1962: 76) But doesn't this evocation, whose dazzling line also traverses many a page of *Histoire de la folie*, rest on a new myth, a myth so primordial that it cannot constitute the object of any examination, any evaluation, since it does not itself arise from any "condition"? This myth is the myth of essential madness, persisting in its original nature, this side of the institutional and discursive systems that alter its first truth, or "confiscate" it, according to an expression already commented on. Such a myth takes the place held, in the text published in 1954, by the myth of a disalienated human essence: as if the reference to Nietzsche and Heidegger, implicit throughout *Mental Illness and Psychology*, substituted for the reference to the young Marx, who for his part haunted the text of *Mental Illness and Personality*. This representation of a definitive relation of man to himself, which precedes all his historical experiences and relativizes them by measuring them by his own fundamental truth, in a way constitutes the theoretical unthought on the basis of which at the beginning of the 1960s Foucault wrote *Histoire de la folie*. One grasps then the limits that surround Foucault's correction in 1962 of his text of 1954: by displacing the idea of a psychological truth of mental illness toward the idea of an ontological truth of madness, this correction leaves intact the presupposition of a human nature, even if the latter arises from a poetic evocation instead of from a positive knowledge.

One then understands that in his 1962 book Foucault had been able to retain the pages that served as a conclusion to the fifth chapter of the 1954 book (pp. 73–5), by deferring them until the end of this sixth chapter, which is devoted to "madness: an overall structure." Why this postponement? Because by rejecting in conclusion considerations on the historical and social conditions of internment—considerations that by the fact of their insertion into a new context also take on a considerably different significance—Foucault was able to eliminate that which, under the title of "the psychology of conflict," gave its content to the sixth chapter of *Mental Illness and Personality*. The pure and simple suppression of this chapter is certainly the main reason for the overhaul of the work at the time of its reedition: for it is clear that nothing—either in its content, or in the detail of its formulations—corresponded any longer to the conception of the relations between mental illness and psychology that Foucault put forward after his works on the history of madness. In fact, this sixth chapter of the book published in 1954, relying on data and concepts borrowed from Pavlovian psychophysiology, restores a place, alongside an analysis of social conditioning ranked under the general rubric of "alienation," for a properly psychological study of recognized behaviours, under the effect of this conditioning, as pathological. It is then a question of showing how the collective forms of alienation held on to individual behaviours, in order to imprint on some of them a characteristic of normality, reserving for the rest the catastrophic appearance of deviant behaviours, sanctioned as such by a medical diagnosis. This implies that mental illness arises from two kinds of conditions: from general conditions, common to healthy behaviours and to those which are identified as pathological; and from conditions which are specific to the individual's personality, at the level of which operates the *caesura* of the normal and abnormal.

Such an analysis arises from two presuppositions. On the one hand, by situating the research of psychology—or rather what a little later in his

1954 book Foucault called "true psychology" (1954: 110), that is, a psychology finally liberated from the prejudices imposed on it by the alienation of society—in the margins of historico-social explanation, in order to show how the general contradiction of society can be internalized by these individual consciousnesses according to a model of conflict, this analysis is maintained from the perspective of a psychological realism: it implants in consciousness the phenomena of mental illness, and it attaches them to it even more as it brings this consciousness back to a totality of processes, jointly psychic and organic, whose mechanism, governed by objective determinisms, thus attains a kind of material necessity.

On the other hand, by revealing that all behaviours are subjected to the same laws on the basis of the fundamental relation of excitation and inhibition, the examination of these processes makes them depend on a general psychology which by the same token is also a pathology. Arising from the same explanatory principles as normal behaviours, illness then appears as a phenomenon of adaptation, that is, as the more or less coordinated system of responses to stimulations having come from an external environment, in which in the last instance are found the causes of the conflicts of which illness is only the manifestation.

> There is illness when conflict, instead of leading to a differentiation in the response, provokes a diffuse reaction of defence; in other words, when at the level of his reactions the individual cannot master the contradictions of his surroundings, when the psychological dialectic of the individual cannot be found in the dialectic of his conditions of existence. (1954: 102)

Alienation is an appearance at the level of the individual, because it is a reality at the level of the conditions of collective existence: and a materialist and dialectical psychology was absolutely required to confirm and specify this objectification of pathological phenomena, whose actual nature is thus displaced from the individual to his surroundings, in which is found their real foundation. "Alienation, with this new content, is no longer a psychological aberration; it is defined by an historical moment: it is in that alone that it is made possible." (ibid.)

But Foucault can no longer, it is obvious, reason in this way after having written *Histoire de la folie*. First, because such an objective explanation restores to a psychology the function of accounting for mental illness, whereas in the meantime it has become clear that it only legitimates *a priori* the practices on which its discourse depends. Next, and above all, because, at the same time that this explanation connects pathological phenomena with the historical moment that makes them possible, it derives from them the characteristics that, within a well-defined historical context, make them recognized as pathological even before identifying them as "facts." In 1962 it has become essential for

Foucault to show that the alienated individual is not only maladjusted, that is, a reject from the mechanisms of adaptation about which it is no longer very clear whether they arise from a psychological or sociological study. For the alienated individual is in fact something completely different: he is the product of an institutional regime inside which there is room for the patient precisely to the extent that there is no room for the madman. In his first text Foucault concluded that abnormality was an effect of alienation, the latter being the objective principle on the basis of which illness can be explained: "Thus one is not alienated because one is ill, but one is ill to the extent that one is alienated." (1954: 103) And again he wrote: "To seek to define illness on the basis of a distinction between the normal and the abnormal is to reverse the terms of the problem; it is to make a condition out of a consequence, in the undoubtedly implicit goal of masking alienation as the true condition of illness." (1954: 105) In his 1962 book Foucault shows on the contrary that the concept of mental illness has no meaning except on the basis of this procedure of exclusion, whose origins or reasons are not to be sought in any form of positive knowledge, a procedure that, even before recognizing and describing it as alienation, establishes an impassable frontier between illness and other forms of human existence, this separation alone conferring on pathological phenomena their reality as objects offered to knowledge. It is true that at the same time Foucault transfers from alienation to madness this characteristic of objective fact, for which mental illness is, instead of the symptom or manifestation, the substitute, since, in the conditions of a historical experience, it manages almost completely to obscure its primordial nature. But then too it is no longer a question, at any level whatever, of presupposing a psychological explanation of illness: for it is obvious that no psychology will ever manage to account for the phenomenon whose conditions of appearance it must precisely render forgotten.

Between the two successive versions of the same work, of *Mental Illness and Personality* and *Mental Illness and Psychology*, there is thus a genuine reversal of perspective. It is this reversal that allows us to specify the conditions within which, by breaking with his previous orientations, Foucault engaged in his first great theoretical construction, *Histoire de la folie*. However, a reversal is a movement that in a certain way preserves, since it also presupposes a permanence. By carrying out a decisive rectification of his previous analyses of mental illness, Foucault has made possible a labour of historical investigation liberated from the *a priori* conditions that imposed on it a preestablished explanatory dogma, and especially from the teleological presupposition of a meaning of history: one understands that afterwards, having experienced it himself, Foucault distrusted like the plague everything that came from "dialectical materialism." But does this mean that he managed, in this unique gesture of rupture, to establish once and for all the new theoretical pedestal on which rests a study of history returned to its exact conditions and authentic origins? Nothing could be less certain. And in order to be convinced that this rectification itself only has the limited, and not a definitively foundational or fundamental, value of a discursive act which is itself inserted into the general movement of a mechanism of knowledge of which *Histoire de la folie* is only the first milestone, it suffices to read the conclusion of *Mental Illness and Psychology*: for in these pages appear in a striking way the heuristic nature and also the limits of the new problematic that Foucault defined at the start of the 1960s, and which were to serve as a point of departure, but only a point of departure, for his later investigations. Here is sketched an interpretation of history as a process of obscuring the truth, whose inspiration is indisputably Heideggerian: if there is no psychological truth of madness—*homo psychologicus* being only a late invention of our culture—it is because madness itself, in its essential and timeless truth, rends history with its lightning flashes which, although intermittent (Hölderlin, Nietzsche, Artaud . . .), are no less the indisputable signs of its unalterable permanence. The history of madness is thus not madness as history, or madness in so far as it arises from a historical constitution which produces it in the form of its various experiences; instead, it is the history that has happened to madness, because one has done it to madness, a history regarding which arises a suspicion, that of its inauthenticity, and also a hope, the hope that since history has been made, it could be unmade, in such a way that at last this first truth of which history demonstrates only the absence would return. "There is a very good reason why psychology can never master madness; it is because psychology became possible in our world only when madness had already been mastered and excluded from the drama." (1962: 87) Mastered or confiscated madness is fundamentally madness which is denatured at the same time as it is socialized. The question posed by reading Foucault's great later works, from the archaeology of knowledge that is *The Order of Things* to the *History of Sexuality*, is to know if these works maintain the same division between history and truth, which finally relates back to an abstract distinction between the orders of nature and culture, or else if in their turn these works bring about new rectifications of this problematic.

Notes

1. I have made my own translation of the passages Macherey cites from Foucault's 1954 text that do not appear in Foucault's 1962 text, which has already appeared in translation as Foucault 1987. (Trans.)
2. Here there is plainly a mistake in the text: "external" is printed for "internal."
3. Foucault 1983, 12.

6

Foucault: Ethics and Subjectivity

In the conclusion to the *Use of Pleasure* Michel Foucault clearly laid out the orientations and stakes of an ethical investigation:

> If one wanted to assign an origin to those few great themes that shaped our sexual morals (the idea that pleasure belongs to the dangerous domain of evil, the obligation to practice monogamous fidelity, the exclusion of partners of the same sex), not only would it be a mistake to attribute them to that fiction called "Judaeo-Christian" morals, it would be a bigger mistake to look behind them for the timeless operation of prohibition, or the permanent form of law. The sexual austerity that was prematurely recommended by Greek philosophy is not rooted in the timelessness of a law that would take the historically diverse forms of repression, one after the other. It belongs to a history that is more decisive for comprehending the transformation of moral experience than the history of codes: a history of "ethics," understood as the elaboration of a form of relation to self that enables an individual to fashion himself into a subject of ethical conduct.[1]

The same argument as the one that in the *History of Sexuality* had sustained a critical reflection on the great themes of psychoanalysis, here leads to a denunciation of the effort to interpret the ethical experience of the subject on the basis of the primitive fact of the law, a mythical origin embodied this time in the ahistorical fiction of "Judaeo-Christian morality." Instead, one must understand how the law, to the extent that it assumes the juridical form of prohibition, is itself only a particular and derived effect, whose production occurs in a more fundamental process which is not strictly speaking one of morality, in relation to certain systems of obligation and codes, but of ethics.

How does ethics differ from what we usually designate by the term "morality"? The form of the relation to self considered by ethics is not defined with reference to a law, and therefore to a universal. Whereas the moral subject must conform to a preexisting law, in the double sense that it is obligated to do so and also that it is supposed to have to do so, the ethical subject is not constituted through its relation to the law under which the justification of it falls, but on the basis of "the elaboration of a form of relation to self that permits an individual to be constituted as a subject of moral conduct." Ethics studies how, without a law intervening or before a law intervenes, the individual is transformed into a subject for moral conduct. The subject is thus not given as such at the origin, already completely constituted; it is the outcome of a procedure of transformation which constitutes it. Ethics is interested precisely in this production of the subject.

This also means that the subject is not given apart from its own history, that is, the forms of its constitution. Ethics does not reveal a figure of the subject in itself, prior to the historical conditions of its realization, but the history of the subject: it shows how, under certain conditions, individuals become subjects.

Yet to think the subject in its history is not only to present the latter as constituting its context or environment: rather, it is to show how, in the subject itself, history thoroughly constitutes, it determines and defines, the conditions of its existence as a subject. For such a conception, one must abandon considering the subject as substantial, defined by its essence as a subject and thus constituted prior to the cycle of its production and its transformations. In other words, the subject must no longer be considered on the basis of universality—as it is, for example, in the Cartesian experience of the *cogito*—but, on the contrary, in relation to a singularity. Or again: the subject that, for an ethics in the strict sense of the word, has no substantial reality no longer has anything but a form. It is defined as a subject-form, which is never fixed once and for all but is historically determined, and thus carried along into an incessant movement of transformations.

One understands, then, why according to Foucault the notion of a "practice of the self" specifies the field of an ethics. This notion is, in fact, precisely the opposite of the presentation of an autonomous ego which, due to the fact that it is defined by its first essence, communicates from the start with a universal and, already really itself, precedes its own history. "Self," in the sense of ethics, is precisely the opposite of this essential ego. In fact, it is the result of a practice, that is, of a labour. The object of ethics is this labour of subjectification, which restores to the notion of the subject its processive character and its historicity. From the standpoint of an ethical history of the subject, it is a question of understanding how, at every moment of this history, it "subjectifies," it "makes the subject," it "subjects." And this, without seeking to bring back this labour of subjectification to the ideal presupposition of a substance-subject, which would be the "subject" of this labour of transformation of individuals into subjects, whereas the subject is itself only the result, the product of this labour.

But an objection arises here, which one cannot avoid taking into account: to turn the subject into a historical product in this way, that is, to consider the subject as the result of a process of which it is not initially the principle—isn't this to "objectify" the subject and thus also to deprive it of its quality as a subject? Completely "subjected" to the singular conditions of its effectuation, thus deprived of all its pretensions to the universal, isn't the subject, at the same time as it is reinserted into the history that constitutes it, deprived of that margin of autonomy, initiative and responsibility that ensures its properly ethical function as a subject? Isn't a subjectified subject, in the sense of practices of subjectification, also a desubjectified subject, a shadow of itself, finding and capturing its position only by giving up its freedom?

What is a Subject?

So the question must be posed again: what does it mean to think about the subject as such? Where should one situate the margin of initiative and interest that constitutes it specifically as a subject? For it is not enough to say that the subject is in its history, from which it cannot be extricated; it remains necessary to specify where it is situated in this history. It is necessary to identify the place where the subject is produced and which defines the proper domain of ethics. We have just spoken of a margin of initiative and interest that should be maintained for the subject not to lose itself in its own shadow. Yet the question posed in this way already points toward its solution: the place of the subject is a margin; the place occupied by the subject in its history is its margins. To say this, Deleuze uses an extremely striking formula in the book he has devoted to Foucault. He has written: "The inside as an operation of the outside: Foucault seems haunted by this theme of an inside which is merely the fold of the outside, as if the ship were a folding of the sea";[2] and again: "the boat as interior of the exterior."[3] It is as though the subject were the same of the other—the law being, on the contrary, dialectically, the other of the same—that is, this "identity" without substance, which has no other thickness, no other materiality, than that of a difference or a limit. In this sense, the "place" of the subject is indeed the margin, a limit: a place that strictly speaking no longer occupies a space but which, at the extremities of a space, defines its own singularity.

To situate the subject at the limit, to identify it by its difference, is in a certain way to think about its singularity, to think about it as "self." What does this mean? In order to understand, perhaps it would be useful to recall the paradoxes of individualism. Individualism is that attitude which tries to establish the reality of the individual apart from that which constitutes its "outside" and which considers it, then, as an autonomous entity, which is self-sufficient, closed onto itself and onto the world of its interests, which all refer to the primordial interest that the individual carries in itself. In a way, it is to treat the individual as something completely singular, by detaching it from every relation to an external universal represented by the existence of everything it is not and all the others it is not. But it is clear that to reflect in this way the singular outside of the universal, as constituting an independent and preexisting order, amounts—surreptitiously and no doubt unconsciously—to returning to the illusion of the universal, to reproducing it in the opposite sense: for the other of the universal is still a universal. Such is the very operation of the classical subject that reinjects the universal into the singular: thus the Cartesian *cogito* makes it seem that the subject, in its singular experience, is a bearer of universal values of truth whose knowledge constitutes its essence, since to think and to be are the same thing (*cogito ergo sum*: I am only to think, I am only what I think). To think about the universal outside of the universal is still to think about it as universal, since it is to present it as an abstract entity.

The only remaining way to think about the singular as such is not to detach it from the universal or to oppose it to the universal, but on the contrary to include it in the universal, by showing that there is something singular in the universal, and thus that there is a singular of the universal. In this sense, the subject is neither pure interiority nor pure exteriority but remains precisely at the limit of the interior and the exterior, in a relation which is simultaneously one of inclusion and exclusion, at the place that the practices of the self must allow it to be found or invented. It is precisely at this point that the field of a properly ethical problematic opens up.

Here a remark is in order: formulated in these very general terms, this approach not only characterizes Foucault's final works, but concerns the totality of his investigations, since the first form given to it by *Histoire de la folie*. The latter might be read in relation to this fundamental preoccupation: to make elements of singularity appear in all the universal figures that cross our existence—knowledge, power, and the subject itself. In fact, to adopt the standpoint of history in order to treat these problems—by substituting a history of the forms of knowledge for a reflection on knowledge, a history of the forms of power for a reflection on power, a history of the forms of subjectification for a reflection on the subject—is precisely to bring out this very particular relation of inclusion and exclusion which in the constitution of all these practices connects the universal and the singular.

Now this enterprise is precisely subjective: having lost the faculty of contesting from outside the historical system that conditions it (as if it constituted itself a counter-system), the subject that has understood that the project of liberating itself was illusory, maintains the possibility of contesting it from inside by demonstrating that which reveals its singularity against the grain of its claims to universality. In this way the games of knowledge and power, contrary to what they would have us believe, don't proceed from the self, because the evidence they reveal is of a historical kind, and can therefore only abusively aspire to an absolute and definitive character.

The actual freedom of the subject begins with this propensity to singularize the system to which it belongs, at the moment when, inside the framework established by this belonging, appears the possibility of establishing a certain detachment in relation to it, and hence to a certain extent of detaching itself from it. In the fact of revealing what there is that is historically singular in the orders of knowledge and power, for this reason there is something subjective, in the full sense of the manifestation of a possible freedom. But, as one can see, the singularity affirmed here is quite the contrary of a given singularity: it corresponds instead to the act of singularizing, to the fact of disclosing singularities.

The Aesthetics of Existence

In an interview published in the 30 May 1981 issue of *Libération* under the title of "Est-il donc important de penser?", Foucault said:

> Each time that I've tried to do theoretical work it has grown out of elements of my own experience: always in relation to processes which I saw unfolding around me. It's precisely because I thought I recognized cracks, muffled shocks, dysfunctionings, in the things I was seeing, in the institutions I was dealing with, in my relations with others, ... that I went to work—some autobiographical fragments.[4]

So to "think," in the true sense of the word, is always to think about systems or norms, not for the purpose of legitimizing or justifying them, but in some way to make apparent what isn't going well, or at least what, in them, isn't going well with the self: from this point of view, every authentic thought is "autobiographical." But that doesn't mean that, by thinking about "objects," which by definition are external to it, the subject would do nothing in reality, through their mediation, but think by itself, think itself, and therefore project onto them its own preoccupations as a subject, its subjectivity: this is precisely the conception of the subject–object relation that the idea of subjectification developed by Foucault deprives of any significance. It means instead that, by discovering the faults of the system in which it is inscribed and is produced as subject, the subject opens up for itself a domain of intervention, inside not outside the system, by taking the position from which a certain claim to freedom becomes meaningful.

It is indeed in this sense that the subject, and incidentally the thinking subject, is defined by the manifestation of a limit. It is not a question of the limit that falls between two independent orders, for example, between a world of exteriority, where there is the other, and a world of interiority, where there is only the same. But it is a question of that limit which, in every order, in every normed system, reveals a margin (a certain possibility of refolding) in it and not outside it, and—at the inside of the outside, as Deleuze says so well—detaches from this margin a domain of identity and relative initiative. In other words, in every social and cultural system, there must be a point or line of subjectification, a point or line without substance and without weight, from which individuals are reproduced as subjects, by engaging in that very particular kind of practice which is a practice of the self.

One understands, then, that by privileging the problems of ethics in his final works, Foucault had not at all sought to close the subject back into itself, according to the tradition that in general would be that of individualism; from the point of view of such an individualism, it is first and foremost a question of understanding or revealing how the subject, whose determination is then anthropological and not ethical, would be radically separate from the historical order inside which it appears, and that it must reject in order to capture its own essence.

It must be said, to the contrary, that this practice of singularity, which defines the subject as such, is possible and thinkable only within the historical conditions of a culture. These conditions are themselves singular because the figures of knowledge they strive to promote, as much on the side of knowledge as on the side of power, are never fixed once and for all, but are carried into an incessant movement of transformation. Also, with his study of the Greek world and its modes of thought, Foucault developed the theme of what he called an "aesthetics of existence," the development of this theme meaning for him not the pursuit of the dream of a life outside-of-power and in some way outside-of-society, which, by establishing its own rules for itself, by the same token would be "liberated" from every relation to an external system: Foucault is just the opposite of an ideologue of liberation. His opposition to this concept runs through all his books without exception. The aesthetics of existence consists only in discovering those points and lines of subjectification giving room to practices of the self through which individuals become subjects: that is, in the very order which includes and constrains them, they are constituted as being beyond-the-law—but not beyond power or beyond the system of the norm—to the extent that power and norm are not defined by the law but define the law as one of their particular effects.

In an interview published in the book that Dreyfus and Rabinow have devoted to him, Foucault declares:

the political, ethical, social, philosophical problem of our days is not to try to liberate the individual from the state, and from the state's institutions, but to liberate us both from the state and from the type of individualization which is linked to the state. We have to promote new forms of subjectivity through the refusal of this kind of individuality which has been imposed on us for several centuries.[5]

Thus, it is not at all a question of returning the individual to itself, as if it were waiting, subsisting somewhere in its immutable and unaltered essence, to be delivered from the weight of the historical constraints that alienate it. Rather, new forms of subjectivity must be promoted, to see whether, inside the cultural system to which we belong, certain "folds" (Deleuze) are not in the process of formation, folds which it is possible to open up and enlarge in order to bring about in that system forms of singularity constitutive of the existence of subjects.

In this sense, there is no room to think subjectification outside of or against the belonging to this system; it must be thought as one of its products, by way of an eventuality which always remains open to it in a certain way, but never in the same way, nor identically for all. Also, to identify forms of subjectification belonging to a historically determined social system does not amount to defining subjectivity by the fact of its complete integration into this system, which would be represented ideally through it by manipulating it, by "possessing" it. One must understand how, in a system, there must always be room—"there must" not in the sense of obligation but of *aléa* and event—for phenomena of disintegration or detotalization, through which individuals become subjects, in relation to the practices of the self that make possible these effects of rupture or refolding with respect to the historico-social totality. This equally presupposes that a historical and social system is never full and homogeneous, as a structure definitively closed onto itself would be, but "must" leave room somewhere within itself for practices of the self to develop at its limit, in its margins or folds. Thus the "structure" itself brings about the conditions of a possible freedom, since the subject is what seeps into the faults of every system, and in a way emanates from its decentring.

A Philosophy of the Event

With all his might, Foucault rejected the method of a philosophy of history. For two reasons: on the one hand, it is impossible to assemble all the moments and aspects of historical development in a global and homogeneous process, like a universal history; on the other hand, for each of the moments of this development grasped in its specificity—in the sense in which Foucault speaks, for example, of the "classical age"— there is no longer any spirit of unified time, from whose viewpoint the absolute convergence of all the elements that constitute it could be demonstrated. Also, for Foucault history is first of all the place in which singularities are produced, these singularities not having a status apart from this place and the conditions fixed to their production. This method restores all its meaning to the notion of event, as, for example, in the concept of a "discursive event." This is why Foucault never tried to reduce the distinctive nature of the event by reintegrating it into the order of a structure, but always strove, on the contrary, to think the production of the event from the perspective of a history in which there is everywhere and always the event and in which one must seek, at all levels, what constitutes an event.

From this privilege granted to the event and to the forms of its recognition, it follows that the ethical problematic remains, or "must" remain permanently open. Since it is ruled out that any system can form a bloc and concentrate on itself, to the point of suppressing the possibility of the event, as if it were not itself an event; it always remains possible to situate "oneself" in relation to the system to which one belongs, so as to evince in it this inevitability of the event. The subject's practice of the self is precisely nothing else.

These themes appear, for example, in a 1982 interview devoted to Pierre Boulez in *Le Nouvel Observateur*:

> He precisely expected thought to allow him at any moment to do something other than what he did. He asked thought to open up a new free space in the game—so regulated, so thoughtful—that he played. One heard some accuse him of technical liberties, others of an excess of theory. But what was essential for him was the following: to think practice as closely as possible to its internal necessities, without submitting to any of them as if they were sovereign demands. What, then, is the role of thought in what one does, if it must be neither know-how nor pure theory? Boulez would show it: to give the strength to break rules in the very act of putting them into play.[6]

A certain number of propositions of general import are stated here, propositions characterizing the subject's position in its relation to the practice of thought: to "think" is always, as one has seen, a fragment of autobiography. "To think practice as closely as possible to its internal necessities, without submitting to any of them as if they were sovereign demands"; "to give the strength to break rules in the very act of putting them into play": these formulas apply precisely to Foucault's work, they reveal its essentially "subjective" nature.

In this sense, to think, which is also an ethical operation, is to think limits. This refers to the great orientations of the Kantian critique: but the latter are then completely reoriented. For Foucault, it is not a question of thinking about limits so as to constitute from them the legality or the regularity of a system, within the order of experience for knowledge, outside of experience for action. It is instead a question of an effort to think at the limit, by carrying oneself to the limits of these systems, in order to grasp them where they are formed (which is also the point at which they are undone), and thus to open up a certain margin of freedom by "problematizing" them. In the article published in the United States, "What is Enlightenment?," Foucault explains

> what may be a philosophical ethos consisting in a critique of what we are saying, thinking, and doing, through a historical ontology of ourselves.... This philosophical ethos may be characterized as a *limit-attitude*. We are not talking about a gesture of rejection. We have to move beyond the outside–inside alternative; we have to be at the frontiers. Criticism indeed consists of analyzing and reflecting upon limits. But if the Kantian question was that of knowing what limits knowledge has to renounce transgressing, it seems to me that the critical question today has to be turned back into a positive one: in what is given to us as universal, necessary, obligatory, what place is occupied by whatever is singular, contingent, and the product of arbitrary constraints? The point, in brief, is to transform the critique conducted in the form of necessary limitation into a practical critique that takes the form of a possible transgression.
>
> This entails an obvious consequence: that criticism is no longer going to be practiced in the search for formal structures with universal value, but rather as a historical investigation into the events that have led us to constitute ourselves and to recognize ourselves as subjects of what we are doing, thinking, saying. In that sense, this criticism is not transcendental, and its goal is not that of making metaphysics possible: it is genealogical in its design and archeological in its method.[7]

In fact, Foucault's approach is exactly the opposite of Kant's. First, in that for Foucault ethical concern does not have as its correlate the delimitation of a domain of intervention reserved specifically for action: it is not outside the system open to knowledge but within this system, or more precisely at its limit, on its margins, that the position of the subject is played, through its ethical relation to itself. This is indeed why, in Foucault's *œuvre*, ethics did not constitute a late preoccupation which, like a second critique written after the first, was added on to the investigations devoted to the games of knowledge and power so as to add a new domain of questioning: rather, from the outset ethics had its place in the critical examination of discourses and institutions which try to legitimize forms of knowledge and powers, thus conferring on this examination its "autobiographical" nature. On the other hand, instead of bringing out universal conditions of legitimacy in response to the questions What can I know? What ought I to do?, this critical examination leads to a delegitimation of the systems of knowledge and power, on the basis of emphasizing what the latter contain that is arbitrary and contingent, that is, singular.

The Specific Intellectual

Thus it appears that, contrary to an entire tradition, to think is not to think the universal, but to think the singular in its irreducible singularity. This is what Foucault meant by speaking of the "specific intellectual," which he opposed to the "universal intellectual." The universal intellectual is someone who denounces an alienation and proclaims the necessity of an emancipation in the name of a common right, hence of a universally recognizable principle of legitimacy: it has fallen to someone like Habermas to constitute the theory of this position today. The specific intellectual is one who, instead of seeking to universalize his position, on the contrary declares its autobiographical nature, not in the sense of the defence of individual rights supposedly distinct from those of the community, but in the sense of the disclosure, necessarily situated, of what there is that is essentially singular in the fact of right, that is, in the fact of living under norms. The specific intellectual speaks in his own name: and not in the name of Man, the (present or future) State, or the Proletariat, for these entities, precisely from the fact of his intervention, are themselves relieved of their promotion to the universal. And for the specific intellectual there is no longer any question of proposing models of life and thought, nor of envisioning the conditions necessary for their actual realization, from a "constructive" perspective, oriented by the spirit of utopia. The specific intellectual proposes only to think about the present in its singularity, without seeking to include it within the process of a universal history endowed with a coherent and univocal meaning— and this in view of a freedom not for tomorrow, which all ideologies of liberation are concerned about, but for today.

Finally, this means that to think is not limited to the fact of developing a thought by giving it the form of a system: it is, according to Kant's magnificent formula, to orient oneself in thought, that is, to situate oneself in thought, not with a view to occupying a central position in it, but by seeking on the contrary to win its frontiers, so as to grasp it, not face-to-face, but from an angle. This clarifies in particular the way in which Foucault reads other philosophers, such as Plato in the *Use of Pleasure*, Descartes in *Histoire de la folie*, or Kant in the *Order of Things*. For Foucault does not at all seek to enter into their systems in order to reconstitute their global logic—as if Plato, for example, had only made it possible to think Plato's thought—but treats them in an incidental way, by taking a sample in their discourses of some singular elements that he isolates, in a seemingly arbitrary way in relation to the totality inside which they are formed, in order to emphasize their nature as events. As opposed to the architectonic effort of integration to which the classical philosophers are devoted, it is a question of revealing what remains in itself irreducible to such a procedure of totalization, and can be detached from it. Thus, Descartes's "but whoever are mad" which, even outside the argumentative progression of the first *Meditation*, produces an unsuspected effect of meaning. This strictly scandalous way of doing the history of philosophy retains from the great systems of thought only their downfalls, without even seeking to carry out afterwards a rereading of everything they said in the light of these particularities considered as symptoms within the framework of a hermeneutical enterprise which would finally recover their overall meaning.

It goes without saying that Foucault also had to apply to himself this operation of disintegration and detotalization, and renounce proposing a thought which was first measured by criteria of coherence and enclosed on its own problems and concepts, thus remaking the world according to its own idea. Engaged in a singular practice of thought, he had to disperse it into a multiplicity of punctual interventions, of which the next was ordered on the basis of no preestablished principle from which it would have drawn the illusion of an absolute beginning. This clarifies the inaugural parody with which the *Discourse on Language* opens:

> I would really like to have slipped imperceptibly into this lecture, as into all the others I shall be delivering, perhaps over the years ahead. I would have preferred to be enveloped in words, borne way beyond all possible beginnings. At the moment of speaking, I would like to have perceived a nameless voice, long preceding me, leaving me merely to enmesh myself in it, taking up its cadence, and to lodge myself, when no one was looking, in its interstices as if it had paused an instant, in suspense, to beckon to me. There would have been no beginnings: instead, speech would proceed from me, while I stood in its path—a slender gap—the point of its possible disappearance.[8]

For to affirm the autobiographical nature of thought is also to recognize the anonymity of every discourse, the formula "I am an author" having just as much sense—that is, just as little—as the formula that gives its title to Magritte's famous painting, *This is not a pipe*. This is how Foucault, for example, considered Raymond Roussel, at the moment that the latter is involved in the literary act he explains and that explains him:

> Apropos of the "I" which speaks in *How I Wrote Certain of My Books*, it is true that a disproportionate detachment at the heart of the sentences he pronounces makes him as remote as the third-person "he." They become confused in the distance, where self-effacement brings out this third person who has been speaking at all times and who always remains the same.[9]

It is no more possible to begin a discourse absolutely than it is to close a discourse once and for all, since a discourse has always already begun. Since there is always discourse, the only possibility that remains open to the subject is to say the discourse, by folding it back onto itself, that is, to "give the strength to break rules in the very act of putting them into play." For in a world in which there is only already organized and normed discourse, it always remains possible to ask oneself: "What is so perilous, then, in the fact that people speak and that their speech proliferates?"[10] Yet this defines a properly ethical questioning, in the sense not of the search for a new conformism, prophesying what we should do, but in the sense of the effort to free oneself from every conformism at the very interior of the operation that determines norms of conformity.

Notes

1. Foucault 1985, 251.
2. Deleuze 1988a, 97.
3. Ibid., 123
4. Foucault 1992, 35.
5. Foucault 1983, 216. (Foucault's remarks actually come from a lecture, not an interview. Trans.)
6. Foucault 1982.
7. Foucault 1984, 45–6.
8. Foucault 1972, 215.
9. Foucault 1986, 155–6.
10. Foucault 1972, 216.

From Canguilhem to
Canguilhem by Way of Foucault

Aside from the personal and particular considerations that lead us to relate the theoretical approaches of Georges Canguilhem and Michel Foucault, such a connection is justified above all for one basic reason: these two bodies of thought have developed around a reflection devoted to the problem of norms; reflection in the strong, philosophical, sense of the expression, even if in these two authors it has been directly associated with the use of materials borrowed from the history of the biological and human sciences and from social and political history. Whence this common questioning which, in very general terms, could be formulated as follows: Why is human existence confronted with norms? From where do norms derive their power? And in what direction do norms orient this power?

For Canguilhem these questions take shape around the concept of "negative values," taken from Bachelard and reworked. This point is clarified in an exemplary way by the conclusion to the article "Vie" in the *Encyclopaedia Universalis*, which, on the basis of a reference to the death drive, states this thesis: life becomes known, and recognized, only through the errors of life that, in every living thing, reveal its constitutive incompleteness. And this is why the power of norms becomes apparent at the moment that it trips over, and eventually falls at, the limits it cannot pass and toward which it is thus indefinitely returned. In this sense, before quoting Borges at length, Canguilhem presents the question: "Is not the value of life, along with the acknowledgement of life as a value, rooted in knowledge of its essential precariousnes?"[1]

The problems that are thus at stake will be here placed in a narrowly delimited framework, on the basis of a parallel reading of the two works of Canguilhem and Foucault that address precisely this question: the intrinsic relationship of life to death, or of the living to the mortal, such as it is experienced on the basis of the clinical experience of illness. To begin, let us briefly recall in what chronological space this confrontation is deployed: in 1943 Canguilhem published his medical thesis, *Essai sur quelques problèmes concernant le normal et la pathologique*; in 1963, "twenty years later," in the "Galien" collection, devoted to the history and philosophy of biology and medicine, which he directed at the Presses Universitaires de France, Canguilhem published Foucault's second great work after *Histoire de la folie: Naissance de la clinique*; the same year, at the Sorbonne he offered a course on norms, preparing the reedition, in 1966, of the *Essai* of 1943, combined with *Nouvelles réflexions concernant le normal et le pathologique*. Let us rehearse the successive stages of this journey.

The 1943 *Essai* opposes the objectifying perspective of a positivistic biology—at that time represented in an exemplary way in the works of Claude Bernard—to the actual reality of illness: the latter having essentially the value of a problem presented to the individual and by the individual, on the occasion of the failures of his own existence, a problem taken charge of by a medicine which is not first a science, but an art of life, illuminated by the concrete consciousness of this problem considered as such, apart from attempts at solutions which try to suppress it.

This entire analysis revolves around a central concept: that of the "living," the subject of an "experience"—this notion is found throughout the *Essai*—through which it is exposed, in an intermittent and permanent way, to the possibility of suffering, and more generally, of living badly. From this perspective, the living simultaneously represents two things: it is first the individual or the living being, grasped in its existential singularity, as it is revealed in a privileged way by the conscious lived experience of illness; but it is also what one could call the living of the living, that polarized movement of life which, in every living thing, pushes it to develop to the maximum what there is in it that is or exists. In this latter aspect, no doubt one can find a Bergsonian inspiration; but one could equally see in it, although Canguilhem does not himself mention the possibility of such a connection, the shadow cast by the Spinozist concept of *conatus*.

This living (thing) is defined by the fact that it is the bearer of an "experience," which itself appears simultaneously under two forms: a conscious and an unconscious form. The first part of the *Essai*, in opposition to the procedures of the biologist who tries to turn him into a laboratory object, insists above all on the fact that the sick person is a conscious subject, by striving to express what makes him feel his experience by declaring his disease through the lived lesson that links him to the doctor; in this sense, Canguilhem writes, referring to Leriche's conceptions: "We think *that there is nothing in science that has not first appeared in the consciousness,* and that ... it is particularly the sick man's point of view which forms the basis of truth."[2] But the second part of the *Essai* takes up the same analysis by deepening it, which leads to the rooting of the experience of the living in a region situated short of or at the limits of consciousness, where is affirmed, in a confrontation with the obstacles opposed to its complete disappearance, what we have just called the living of the living, and which Canguilhem also designates as being a "spontaneous effort, peculiar to life,"[3] an effort that is spontaneous and thus prior—and perhaps external—to its conscious reflection: ". . . we ask ourselves how the normativity essential to human consciousness would be explained if it did not in some way exist in embryo in life."[4]

Emphasizing this "experience," with its two dimensions—conscious and unconscious—leads, in opposition to the objectivism characteristic of a positivistic biology willfully ignorant of the values of life, to the following conclusion: "It seems to us that physiology rather than searching for an objective definition of the normal, ought better to recognize the original normativity of life."[5] Which means that since norms are not objective data, and as such directly observable, the phenomena to which they give rise are not the static phenomena of a "normality," but the dynamic phenomena of a "normativity." One sees that the term "experience" here again finds a new meaning: that of an impetus which tends toward a result without any guarantee of attaining or maintaining it; it is the erratic being of the living, subject to an infinity of experiences, that is in the case of the human living thing the positive source of all its activities.

Thus the traditional perspective concerning the relationship of life and norms is reversed: it is not life that is subjected to norms, the latter acting on it from outside; but it is norms that are produced by life's very movement in a completely immanent way. Such is the central thesis of the *Essai*: there is an essential normativity of the living, the creator of norms which are the expression of its constitutive polarity. These norms account for the fact that the living is not reducible to a material datum but is a possibility, in the sense of a power, that is, a reality which is given from the beginning as incomplete because it is confronted intermittently with the risks of illness, and the risk of death permanently.

To read *Naissance de la clinique*, the book published in 1963 by Michel Foucault under the authority of Georges Canguilhem, is to note shared views without excluding the difference, indeed the opposition, of points of view. These two works criticize on all sides biological positivism's claim of objectivity. We have just seen that Canguilhem had carried out this critique by committing himself to the side of the concrete experience of the living, and thus had been led to open up a perspective on the play of norms which could be called phenomenological, grasped at the point that it issues from the essential normativity of life.

But for the consideration of this essential origin, Foucault substitutes that of a historical "birth," situated precisely within the development of

a social and political process: he is thus led to carry out an "archaeology"—the opposite of a phenomenology—of medical norms, seen from
the side of and even from behind the doctor, from the side of medical
institutions much more than from the side of the sick person, who thus
appears as the great absence in *Naissance de la clinique*. In this way
Foucault explains the deployment of a medical space in which illness is
subjected to a simultaneously normed and norming "gaze," which
determines the conditions of normality by being subjected to those of a
common normativity:

> Medicine must no longer be confined to a body of techniques for curing ills
> and of the knowledge that they require; it will also embrace a knowledge of
> *healthy man*, that is, a study of *non-sick man* and a definition of the *model man*.
> In the ordering of human existence it assumes a normative posture, which
> authorizes it not only to distribute advice as to healthy life, but also to dictate
> the standards for physical and moral relations of the individual and of the
> society in which he lives.[6]

It might be said that the living has ceased to be the subject of
normativity in order to become no more than the point of application, if
Foucault did not practically erase from his analyses every reference to
the notion of the living, which is as rare in *Naissance de la clinique* as it is
frequent in the 1943 *Essai*. It is at this cost that a genesis of normality—in
the dual sense of an epistemological model, governing knowledges, and
of a political model, governing behaviours—can be presented.

The concept of "experience" recurs as often in Foucault's analyses as
in Canguilhem's; but, in relation to the requirement formulated by
Foucault of "taking things in their structural severity,"[7] this concept is
given an entirely different meaning. It is no longer a question of an
experience of the living, in all the meanings this expression can have, but
of a historical experience, simultaneously anonymous and collective,
from which the completely deindividualized figure of the clinic is freed.
Thus, what Foucault calls "clinical experience" proceeds at several levels
at once: it is what allows the doctor to perfect his experience, by putting
him in contact with experience through the mediation of observation (the
"medical gaze"), and this within the institutional framework that determines a socially recognized and controlled experience. In the preceding
sentence, the term "experience" intervenes in three positions and with
different meanings: the correlation of these positions and these meanings
precisely defines the structure of clinical experience.

This is the triangle of experience: at one vertex, the sick person occupies
the place of the object gazed upon; at another vertex, one finds the
doctor, a member of a "body," the medical body, recognized as compe-
tent in order to become the subject of the medical gaze; finally, the third
position is that of the institution that makes official and socially legitim-

izes the relation of the object gazed upon to the gazing subject. Thus one sees that the play of the "said" and the "seen" through which such an "experience" is established passes over the sick person and the doctor himself, in order to realize this *a priori* historical form which anticipates the concrete lived experience of the illness by imposing its own models of recognition on it.

This analysis profoundly differs, and perhaps even diverges, from the analysis presented by Canguilhem in his *Essai* of 1943. And yet, in an unexpected way, it leads to some rather similar conclusions. For clinical experience as it has just been characterized, at the same time that it offers the sick person a perspective of survival by restoring him to a normal state whose criteria it itself defines, the latter being validated only after the fact by the constructions of objective knowledge—this experience confronts the sick person with the risk and the necessity of a death which then appears as the secret or the truth of life, if not as its principle. This is Bichat's lesson, laid out in chapter 8 of the *Naissance de la clinique*, which Canguilhem has often cited.

It is thus the historical structuring of clinical experience that establishes the great equation of the living and the mortal: it inserts morbid processes into an organic space whose representation is precisely informed by the conditions that promote this experience; and these conditions, by virtue of their historicity itself, are not reducible to a biological nature which is immediately given in itself, as an object permanently offered to a knowledge whose truth values would be by this fact unconditioned.

> This is why the concern to describe the vicissitudes of the doctor/patient duo in terms of encounter, distance, or "understanding" should be left to phenomenologies . . . At the original level takes shape the complex figure that a psychology—even depth psychology—is hardly able to master; since pathological anatomy, the doctor and patient are no longer two correlative and external elements, like subject and object, observer and observed, eye and surface; their contact is only possible on the basis of a structure in which the medical and pathological belong to the interior in the fullness of the organism . . . . The open and externalized corpse is the internal truth of disease; it is the displayed depth of the doctor/patient relation.[8]

In the conditions that make the clinical experience possible, death—and with it life, too—ceases to be an ontological or existential absolute, and simultaneously acquires an epistemological dimension: as paradoxical as this might seem, death "clarifies" life.

> It is from the height of death that one can see and analyse organic dependences and pathological sequences. Instead of being what it had so long been, the night in which life disappeared, in which even the disease becomes blurred, it is now endowed with that great power of elucidation that dominates and reveals both the space of the organism and the time of the disease.[9]

Let us note that it is here regarding Bichat that, with a view to relativizing the content, *Naissance de la clinique* makes one of its very rare references to the notion of the "living":

The irreducibility of the living to the mechanical or chemical is secondary only in relation to the fundamental link between life and death. Vitalism appears against the background of this "mortalism."[10]

For this reason, to decompose this clinical experience by revealing the structure that supports it is also to expose the rules of a kind of art of living, in relation to everything included under the notions of health and normality, the latter no longer having anything to do with the representation of what Canguilhem would himself call a "biological innocence." And one could see here the outline of what, in his final writings, Foucault will call an "aesthetics of existence," so as to explain how one defies norms by playing with them, that is, by making them function, and at the same time by opening up the margin of initiative that frees their "play." This art of living presupposes, on the part of one who exercises it, that he knows himself to be mortal and that he learns how to die: Foucault also developed this idea during the same year 1963 in his work on Raymond Roussel, in which the experience of language to some extent has taken the place of clinical experience.

In 1963, at the same time he read Foucault's book, Canguilhem reread himself and prepared his *Nouvelles réflexions*, which would be published three years later. In this later text Canguilhem does not cease to insist on the fact that he sees no reason to return to the theses he had sustained in 1943 in order to inflect or depart from them. But if this is really so, how can one explain the necessity of presenting these reflections, in which it was indeed necessary that something "new" come to light?

Yet their novelty first of all has to do with the fact that these reflections again present the question of norms by shifting it to another ground, which considerably enlarges the field of functioning of norms. To put it briefly, this enlargement proceeds from the vital toward the social. Whence this question which is in fact found at the centre of the *Nouvelles réflexions*: can the effort to think the norm on the basis of normativity instead of on the basis of normality—which had characterized the 1943 *Essai*—perhaps be extended from the vital to the social, in particular when all the phenomena of normalization concerning human labour and the products of this labour have been taken into account?

On the whole, the response to this question would be negative, owing to the impossibility demonstrated by Canguilhem of inferring from the vital to the social, that is, of aligning the functioning of a society in general, in so far as it carries out a project of normalization, with that of an organism. In this argument, one can see a resurgence of the traditional debate between internal finality and external finality. Does this mean that it would be necessary to distinguish radically between two types of norms, by refusing to favour either the vital or the social?

Yet to this last question, the response will also be in the negative—essentially for two reasons. First, the *Nouvelles réflexions* emphasize the fact that vital norms, in the world of man at least—and isn't man the being who tends to make all things enter into his own world?—are not the expression of a natural "vitality," abstract because strictly confined within its order, whereas these norms express an effort to surpass this order, an effort having meaning only because it is socially conditioned. On the other hand, the *Nouvelles réflexions* also present the idea of a social normativity, proceeding by means of the "invention of organs,"[11] in the technical sense of the term invention. This suggests the necessity of overturning the relationship of the vital to the social: it is not the vital that imposes its unsurpassable model on the social, as the metaphors of organicism would have us believe; but it is rather, in the human world, the social that draws the vital before itself, if only because one of the "organs" that pertains to its "invention" is the knowledge of the vital itself, a knowledge that is social in its principle.

To think norms and their action is thus to reflect a relation of the vital and the social which is not reducible to a unilateral causal determinism. This evokes the very particular status of the concept of the "knowledge of life" in Canguilhem, who used it, of course, as the title of one of his books.[12] This concept corresponds simultaneously to the knowledge one may have of the subject of life considered as an object, and to the knowledge produced by life which, as subject, promotes the act of knowledge and confers its values on it. That is, life is neither completely object nor completely subject, nor is it entirely intentional consciousness, nor is it matter to be worked on, unconscious of the impulses at work on it. But life is power, that is, as we said at the beginning, incompleteness: and this is why it is experienced only by being confronted with "negative values."

The following can be read at the end of the *Nouvelles réflexions*: "It is in the rage of guilt as in the clamor of suffering that innocence and health arise as the terms of a regression as impossible as it is sought after."[13] Michel Foucault could perhaps have written this sentence to illustrate the inevitable myths of normality: those myths which, through their idealized expression, speak of nothing but suffering and death, that is, of the threat that reminds every living thing of itself, both of its individuality of living and of its living of living.

Notes

1. Canguilhem 1994, 90.
2. Canguilhem 1989, 92–3.
3. Ibid., 126.
4. Ibid., 127.
5. Ibid., 178. (Translation modified.)
6. Foucault 1973, 34. (In this essay Macherey quotes from the first edition of *Naissance de la clinique*, published in 1963. Unfortunately, the English translation, which appeared in 1973 as *Birth of the Clinic*, was based on the revised second edition of *Naissance*, published in 1972. When possible, then, I have used the English translation; otherwise, I have translated directly from the original French. Trans.)
7. Foucault 1963, 138. (This phrase appears only in the first edition of *Naissance*. Trans.)
8. Ibid. (These sentences appear only in the first edition of *Naissance*. Trans.)
9. Ibid., 144.
10. Ibid., 145.
11. Canguilhem 1989, 253.
12. I.e., *La connaissance de la vie* (1952). (Trans.)
13. Canguilhem 1989, 243.

IV
Spinoza

Deleuze in Spinoza

An important part of Deleuze's *oeuvre* is devoted to the reading of philosophers: the Stoics, Leibniz, Hume, Kant, Nietzsche, Bergson, etc. But a rather singular position in this list would be assigned to Spinoza, owing to the philosophical interest that corresponds to him:

> It was on Spinoza that I worked the most seriously according to the norms of the history of philosophy—but he more than any other gave me the feeling of a gust of air from behind each time you read him, of a witch's broom which he makes you mount. We have not yet begun to understand Spinoza, and I myself no more than others.[1]

One cannot say that Deleuze is a historian of philosophy, given that his method keeps such a distance from disciplinary divisions and by this fact ignores such artificial dilemmas as those of explanation and understanding, and commentary and interpretation. For Deleuze, when he presents Spinoza's thought, the fact of analysing with the greatest precision the text in which it is advanced, by showing how this text is composed and manages to state what it has to say, does not at all exclude an evaluation of its speculative content, from the point of view of a theoretical investigation concerning not only an historical past, in relation with something that has been thought, and could no longer be thought except in the past. Rather, it also coincides with the effort of a thought in the present, recreating the act through which this thought is realized in the very person who reads it.

Rather than rethinking him, in a way Deleuze sets out to think Spinoza, or to think "in" Spinoza, by establishing himself in the midst of the speculative surroundings, of the living element in which the totality of this *oeuvre* develops, the latter not being reducible to a doctrinal combination, to a "system." Instead of taking a philosophy, Spinoza's, as it is, or as it is supposed to be, and giving it a description which is in principle objective and exhaustive of its discourse from a static point of view, it is rather a question of dynamically producing, rather than reproducing, the intellectual movement through which this philosophy has become what it is. Instead of "following" Spinoza, taking great care to repeat everything he has already said, it is as if Deleuze preceded him, intervening in the history of a thought at the same time that he makes it known, and making it known only inasmuch as he intervenes in it, or with it: for Deleuze in Spinoza is also Spinoza in Deleuze.

Perhaps more than in the reading of his books, it is in his teaching that Deleuze has astounded his audience through this faculty of penetration which has allowed him to assimilate and communicate a philosophical thought from the inside, and in its depth, far beyond a formal or abstract study of its articulations. Here his method is apparently opposed to Foucault's, who on the contrary read classical philosophers obliquely, and one can also say diagonally, in a systematically partial way, by neglecting the overall organization of their thought and considering only certain of their particular statements completely isolated from their context. In Deleuze philosophies find a centre and a foundation, he would himself perhaps say a sense, from the point of view of which they are illuminated in full. One could be tempted to see here the symptom of a dynamic and synthetic reading, which a 1912 text on "Philosophical Intuition"[2] had precisely illustrated with the example of Spinoza. But the Bergson expressing himself here, himself revitalized by reading Nietzsche, speaks the language of a dynamics of forces, for which the power of meaning is simultaneously pouring out of the depths and spreading out on the surface, according to a dual principle of manifestation and composition, such that he extricates himself from a structuralism which would have completely assimilated the lessons of a genealogy.

In fact, although he carries it out quite differently, Deleuze is less opposed than one might first think to Foucault's reading of philosophers. A formula Deleuze has used several times well expresses how he finds himself "in" Spinoza: "to take him by the middle,"[3] "to try to perceive and to understand Spinoza by way of the middle."[4] The "middle" of a philosopher, or of a philosophy, if one reflects on it, can be two things. First, as we have just seen, it is the element in communication with which that philosopher's thought is produced, something that would somewhat resemble what Foucault had called an "*épistémé*," that is, a field of problems or a new way of posing philosophical questions, the fact of posing these questions having a value in itself, apart from the solutions that can also be brought to it. From this point of view, the question of Spinoza, the question we ourselves must pose not "to" but rather "in" Spinoza, is the new problem he has introduced into philosophy, and which must be identified by reading him. According to Deleuze—we will return to this—the problem is that of *expression*, according to the term used as a title of the work he has wholly devoted to Spinoza's *oeuvre*.[5]

But the "middle" of a philosopher is also that which "in" his thought constitutes neither his final objective nor his first principle, but precisely connects the two, by interposing itself between them. To take Spinoza by the middle is to abandon an attempt to accompany his reasoning step by step, from the moment his discourse begins until the moment it is finished, for no philosophical discourse truly begins or ends. Rather, to take Spinoza by the middle is, anticipating it, to grasp his reasoning directly at this central point from which its problems arise. Deleuze has subtitled a little book in which he has gathered together several texts devoted to Spinoza: "practical philosophy."[6] Spinoza's *Ethics*, as its very name indicates, is not just a theoretical work, which should be read in order to know the way in which he resolves certain questions, but it is above all a certain way of posing these questions, an attitude of thought and of life, or even a kind of "ethos," in the very sense of ethology. In an incredible passage, in which Deleuze connects Spinoza with the theorist of the *Umwelt*, Uexküll, is found the following reflection:

> there is a strange privilege that Spinoza enjoys, something that seems to have been accomplished by him and no one else. He is a philosopher who commands an extraordinary conceptual apparatus, one that is highly developed, systematic, and scholarly; and yet he is the quintessential object of an immediate, unprepared encounter, such that a nonphilosopher, or even someone without any formal education, can receive a sudden illumination from him, a "flash." Then it is as if one discovers that one is a Spinozist; one arrives in the middle of Spinoza, one is sucked up, drawn into the system or the composition.[7]

This is Spinoza's singularity, through which speculation becomes practical.

To read a philosopher like Spinoza, or to "practise" him, is precisely to decipher the indices of his singularity, that is, to discover that which, in his thought, causes a problem. Yet what causes problems in philosophy? It is neither theories nor doctrinal systematizations, that is, everything that can be reduced to an analytic order of reasons: but rather it is the concepts that work it. "A philosophy's power is measured by the concepts it creates, or whose meaning it alters, concepts that impose a new set of divisions on things and actions."[8] Yet the concept that permits one to enter into Spinoza, or to grasp him by his middle, in the two senses of this formula, is, according to Deleuze, that of expression.

By choosing to present the totality of Spinoza's *oeuvre* by confronting it with this single problem, that of expression, whose Leibnizian connotations would have seemed more obvious, Deleuze from the beginning deviates from traditional forms of the history of philosophy and the concern proclaimed by the latter for a narrow orientation to the very letter of texts. In fact, the singularity of Deleuze's reading of Spinoza, a singularity also allowing Deleuze to find himself "in" Spinoza because it is also Spinoza's singularity, is that the concept Deleuze has singled out is nowhere to be found explicitly formulated or thematized in Spinoza. Deleuze comments on it precisely at the beginning and end of his book: "The idea of expression is neither defined nor deduced by Spinoza, nor could it be."[9] Thus, the "central" idea of this philosophy is strictly speaking also absent from it. That which produces meaning in Spinoza is not the determinate plenitude of a theoretical object, capable of being connected to a given segment of his discourse; but is instead that which, without being attached once and for all to only one of its points in a definitive way, justifies the possibility of everything stated in that discourse, and thus spreads out on or radiates at the surface of Spinoza's entire text, which it organizes without really belonging to it. As middle, centre and element, expression is not "a" concept, that is, a single concept, representative of a determinate content. Rather, expression is the dynamic movement of conceptualization, which must be found everywhere in its explicit concepts: it is what Spinoza thinks, what causes Spinoza to think, and also what allows us ourselves to think in Spinoza.

All this means that the demonstrative order of Spinoza's philosophy, arranged "according to the order of geometers," only apparently constitutes a rigid structure: grasped from the central point of view of expression, Spinoza's philosophy is animated by an intense life, which in practice transmits what was first presented in the form of a purely theoretical discourse, or what historians of philosophy are wont to call a "doctrine." The idea of expression does not figure as such in Spinoza's text, in the sense that the substantive term which could designate it, that of "expression," is never used, let alone reflected, in it. Spinoza's philosophy does not develop a theory of expression but is a practical philosophy of expression: one might say Spinoza's philosophy "expresses."

This is why the idea of expression is found marked in Spinoza's text all the same, for in no case can one say that this idea is behind the text: rather, it is found in a form which, without being that of an objectified concept, refers to the very fact of conceptualizing. This form of the verb *exprimere*, for which Emilia Giancotti's *Lexicon spinozanum*[10]—the best existing study of Spinoza's terminology—lists thirty occurrences in the *Ethics*, the first of which (E IDef6) sets the tone for all the others: "By God I understand a being absolutely infinite, that is, a substance consisting of an infinity of attributes, of which each one expresses an eternal and infinite essence." Commenting on this definition, Deleuze brings out the principle of what he calls the "triad" of expression. In the fact of expressing, as the verb *exprimere* used by Spinoza suggests, three aspects are thus associated: an expresser (here substance), an expressed (here the essence), and a third element (here the attribute), which is not strictly speaking a term, to the extent that it is stated by a verb and not by a name; this last element is what allows the expresser to be expressed in the expressed. The true point of departure is therefore not what Spinoza seems at first to state: Martial Guéroult had also explained that the *Ethics* does not begin with substance. It is rather this third element, the act of expressing or of being expressed, which simultaneously constitutes every reality and renders it thinkable. And this same active element also allows nature to be simultaneously "naturing" and "natured": a formula according to which reality is again presented and stated with the help of a verb (*naturare*: in a way "to nature").

The problem of expression in Spinoza, that is, the idea problematizing his entire thought, is inseparable from the fact that he does not reflect on expression through a substantive term, a name, the latter (*expressio*) really remaining unpronounced, but in a verb. The order of expression does not correspond to a system of things, frozen in the inert reality that their names designate, but is nature in so far as it is effected in action, and at the same time is included in the action that brings it about. Seen from the middle of this expression, Spinoza's philosophy appears as an actual philosophy of actuality: one understands why, in all domains, it denies a rational significance to the notion of virtuality; it is also understood that it is a philosophy of pure expression, of an expression that does not require the mediation of signs in order to take place: and this is indeed what distinguishes the status of expression in Leibniz and in Spinoza, for one would search in vain in Spinoza for traces of a universal characteristic.

Expression in action is exactly the opposite of a representation: Spinoza refuted the representative conception of the idea at the heart of Cartesian thought. By substituting the triad of expression for what in *The Order of Things* Foucault called the "reduplication of representation," which presupposes a purely reflexive relationship of representer to represented, Spinoza would therefore have understood and explained expression in terms of constitution and production, that is, dynamically. For Spinoza knowledge is not "representation" of the thing to the mind through the mediation of a mental image itself capable of being relayed through a system of signs; rather, knowledge is expression, that is, production and constitution of the thing itself in the mind. "It is now the object that expresses itself, the thing itself that explicates itself."[11] This is how Spinoza escaped the representative "platitude" of classical rationalism in order to rediscover a certain expressive "depth" of the world,[12] with a view to "founding a postCartesian philosophy."[13]

The expressionist reading Deleuze makes of Spinoza, which greatly resembles the way he looks at Bacon's paintings, reveals this philosopher's absolute singularity and, as Deleuze also says, links Spinoza to "a rather hidden, and a rather forbidden, history of philosophy."[14] This reading causes a dangerous force of subversion to stand out from Spinoza's text, which confers on it in its time a paradoxical position, that of a limit-point which is neither entirely inside nor entirely outside: Deleuze would perhaps speak today of a fold. If within the framework of classical rationalism Spinoza constitutes a "savage anomaly," it is because in fact he is found elsewhere: this is also what Negri explains in a work in every way extraordinary and for which Deleuze wrote a preface to the French translation.[15] The presentation of the classical *épistémé*, defined as an order of representation, given by Foucault in *The Order of Things*, left no place for Spinoza: but this was precisely because Spinoza in no way has his place in this order, from which, with all his argumentative power, he extricated himself by rendering its global configuration problematic. It has been said before that Foucault and Deleuze do not read philosophers in the same way, because they do not handle them in the same way: but their approaches complement rather than exclude one another. By restoring to Spinoza's text its force and its demonstrative intensity, Deleuze enables us to understand, without recourse to the dialectical hypothesis of a labour of the negative, how the *épistémé* of classical rationalism could be destabilized from the inside, on its margins. This is what is still living "in" Spinoza's thought.

Notes

1. Deleuze and Parnet 1987, 15.
2. Henri Bergson 1946, 133–4.
3. Deleuze and Parnet 1987, 59.
4. Deleuze 1988b, 122.
5. Dekleuze 1990a.
6. Deleuze 1988b.
7. Ibid., 129.
8. Deleuze 1990a, 321.
9. Ibid., 19; also see 327.
10. Giancotti 1970.
11. Deleuze 1990a, 22.
12. Ibid., 324.
13. Ibid., 335.
14. Ibid., 322. (Translation modified.)
15. Negri 1982. (Deleuze's preface was not included in the English translation of this work; see Negri 1991. Trans.)

Spinoza's Philosophical Actuality

(Heidegger, Adorno, Foucault)

What allows one to say of a body of philosophical thought that it is actual, whereas historically it belongs to the past? In order to detect or measure this actuality, one might have recourse to very different criteria.

First of all, one might consider a philosophy "actual" to the extent that it is actually read and worked on, that is, studied for itself, because there exist the material and intellectual means indispensable to such an activity (editions, translations, commentaries, criticism . . .). Let us note that if, from this point of view, Spinoza is indisputably actual, it is because he has become so relatively recently, and in conditions that remain to be elucidated: for we know that if Spinoza played an important role for philosophical reflection in the eighteenth and nineteenth centuries, it was not always on the basis of such a study; whence the rather unusual situation reserved for him of being simultaneously present, perhaps even central, and relatively ignored.

At the same time, a philosophy can be considered actual from the moment that, independently of the objective conditions authorizing an authentic and actual reading of its *oeuvre*, it constitutes an important source of inspiration for other forms of philosophical thought, which are nourished by this reference: yet this approach, which leaves open the greatest margin of interpretation, does not necessarily coincide with the previous approach. In this way one could reconstruct a coherent history of Spinozist philosophy, whose peculiarity is somehow to have been reinvented in each century: for the "materialist" version predominant in the seventeenth century is substituted the "pantheist" version current during the greatest part of the nineteenth century, then the "political" version revealed in the twentieth. This history would show clearly that Spinoza's thought has never ceased to be "actual" in this sense, owing to its ability to resonate with the singular preoccupations of each time, which has allowed it to revive historically, by serving somehow as witness to all the figures of living thought.

Finally, alongside these two forms of actuality which are directly visible or legible, objectively as well as subjectively, perhaps it remains possible to detect a third form, which is less obvious, less immediately perceptible because it remains by definition implicit and latent. In fact, one can consider a philosophy to be living or present not only because it constitutes a source of reference or an object of study and reflection but because its problems and some of its concepts, independently of every explicit citation, nonetheless in the absence of their author continue to accompany other forms of thought which, elaborated in new times, are not content to go back to rediscover or reinvent what a philosopher like Spinoza would already have been able to theorize, but propose to bring new developments to philosophical reflection.

We shall especially concern ourselves with this third aspect of philosophical actuality, by asking how certain specific theoretical preoccupations of Spinozist speculation still have a certain value today, or at least offer some reference points around which philosophical thought seems to be knotted, and also seems to come undone. For this we must show—without a concerted intention necessarily being required for this effect—that some questions and themes treated by Spinoza are at work even today in philosophical reflection, even if it is in a language and according to perspectives which can no longer be Spinoza's. In order to bring out this latent actuality, we shall rely on three examples, borrowed from some contemporary authors who all apparently dismiss Spinoza, who are not obviously interested in him in a particular way, indeed are even uninterested in him, or who have condemned him, for specific reasons, but who, in a certain way, have nonetheless encountered him: at issue are Heidegger, Adorno, and Foucault.

1. Regarding Heidegger, let us begin by noting the rarity and paucity of explicit references to Spinoza.[1] So it is that in *The Principle of Reason* Spinoza is named in passing, within the framework of a very general evocation of the history of being: "After the preparation of Descartes, Spinoza, and Leibniz, Kant's philosophy carries out the decisive step in the fleshing out of being as objectness and will."[2] According to this simple indication, one understands that, according to Heidegger, Spinoza's philosophy does not constitute a significant stage in the history of Western thought. In *Identity and Difference*, within the framework of a paragraph devoted to the Hegelian conception of the history of philosophy, there is a brief allusion to the critique of Spinoza developed by Hegel, which amounts to characterizing him from the point of view of "substance . . . not yet developed into the subject."[3] The most sustained reference is found in the 1936 course on Schelling.[4] Here Spinoza is evoked as a characteristic representative of modern systematic thought, tied to the development of the natural sciences and to the model of

rationality extracted from it through which metaphysics is presented as
the double of a science itself elaborated in reference to a technical ideal.
Let us quote two significant passages extracted from this text:

> The fact that this metaphysics; that is, science of beings as a whole, is called
> "Ethics" is indicative that man's actions and behavior are of decisive import-
> ance for the kind of procedure in knowledge and the foundation of knowledge.

> The interpretations of Spinoza's system, which are very diverse in their
> orientation, usually contributed to thinking generally of a "system" of philos-
> ophy as something like this very definite and one-sided system.[5]

Here is sketched an apparently very restrictive reading of Spinoza's
philosophy, completely reintegrating the latter into the Western tradition
of metaphysics, of which it does not even constitute an especially
important moment. It appears, then, as if Spinoza had brought nothing
essential to the history of being, that is, to the history of the forgetting of
being, from which he cannot be isolated.

This makes it quite clear that any attempt to reinterpret Spinoza's
philosophy in Heideggerian terms, as well to reinterpret Heidegger's
philosophy in Spinozist terms, would be laughable: if Heidegger glosses
over Spinoza, it is not by chance, but by virtue of an explicit and
deliberate choice. But does this mean that these two forms of thought are
radically foreign to one another and that they do not intersect at any
point? In order to provide the beginning of a response to this question,
we shall rely on two particular occurrences, in which can be perceived
the germ of a movement, starting with Spinoza or Heidegger, and which
seems to proceed in the direction that the other has opened or followed.
Wouldn't this be the point of departure for a discussion whose very
possibility presumes the presence, on both sides, of some common
terms?

Let us first see how this discussion could be initiated with Heidegger.
In order to do so, we shall start with a well-known passage of *Being and
Time*, namely, the beginning of paragraph 9: "We are ourselves the
entities to be analysed. The Being of any such entity is *in each case mine*
[*das Sein dieses Seienden ist je meines*]."[6] At first glance, this last formula
seems to introduce a kind of philosophical anthropology, such as it can
be elaborated once the traps of the objectivist rationalism of which
Spinoza precisely offers an exemplary version have been dismantled. Is
this how the interpretation that Heidegger has himself given of his own
thought in his *Introduction to Metaphysics* proceeds?

> The qualification "in every case mine" means that being-there is allotted to
> me in order that my self should be being-there. But being-there signifies:
> care of the ecstatically manifested being of the essent as such, not only of
> human being. Being-there is "in every case mine"; this means neither "posited

through me" nor "apportioned to an individual ego." Being-there is *itself* by
virtue of its essential relation to being in general. That is the meaning of the
sentence that occurs frequently in *Sein und Zeit*: Being-there implies awareness
of being.[7]

In this passage one finds a commentary on Heidegger by himself which
has the value simultaneously of rectification and of warning: it is not—
or is no longer—a question of opposing the subjectivist approach of an
anthropology to the objectivist approach of a metaphysics; for one is
finally only the obverse of the other. Anthropology is a substitute for
metaphysics, whose effort it continues in order to embody being in the
positivity of a given "essent." This is the idea generally developed in the
Letter on Humanism. Here we see that, in a way which might recall
Spinoza, Heidegger rejects the temptation to consider the human being
"as a power in a power" (*tanquam imperium in imperio*), as if there were a
human essence entering into a privileged relationship with being in
general, since on the contrary "Being-there is *itself* by virtue of its
essential relation to being in general," in a sense close to that in which
Spinoza says of substance that it "is prior in nature to its affections"
(*prior est natura suis affectionibus*) (E IP1). Now this latter thesis is
extremely important for Spinoza, since it clarifies the essential notion
indicated by the formula "part of nature" (*pars naturae*), in which the part
is determined synthetically by the whole to which it "belongs," according
to a relation which must not be confused with a transitive causal relation
of the analytic type.

Now we turn to Spinoza, starting with the statement that has just been
cited: "Substance is prior in nature to its affections." This statement
expresses the relation of causal determination that connects modal reality
with substantial reality, in so far as these precisely do not constitute two
autonomous orders of reality, connected by a transitive network of
relations, this network restoring a relation of transcendence, on the
model of creationist doctrines, between them: it must instead be understood in reference to a completely different type of causal relation, the
one expressed by the idea of immanent causality, having nothing to do
with the mechanistic model in which Heidegger finds the exemplary
form of classical rationalism. Thus the formula "to have priority naturally" (*prior est natura*) does not mean an anteriority but precisely a
priority which can no longer be thought only on the basis of the relation
between a before and an after, that is, in the manner of a chronological
succession, as is the case for the transitive conception of causality, in
which the cause precedes—in the sense of preexisting—the effect. It is
instead a question of a priority whose meaning is simultaneously logical
and ontological. This meaning could be clarified by the Heideggerian
distinction between being and essent. In fact, this distinction has nothing

to do with a simple division, as if there were on the one hand the order of being and on the other the order of the essent: since for Heidegger being does not lie behind the essent in the sense of a relation of transcendence, as all metaphysics reflects, as if being were another essent posited beyond the essent; but it must instead be said that being is that which in the essent itself lies behind the essent, and thus is being of the essent, being that therefore cannot be apprehended anywhere else than through the "essential" relation that connects it with the essent. Now this is perfectly in accord with the definition of substance in Spinoza: the latter is not one being alongside others, as a kind of great mode would be; but even more than being in general, it must be said that substance is "being," in a sense in which the verbal form prevails over the substantive form (the latter still being marked by the presence of the definite article: "the" being). In other words, substance is the fact of being thought absolutely, hence from a perspective in which essence completely coincides with existence. Regarding this latter coincidence, one can say that there would be a Heideggerian resonance to the paradoxes of the exposition of the *Short Treatise*, which, in an apparently provocative manner, begins by proving "that God is" (KV I,1) even before explaining "what God is" (KV I, 2).

However, this connection makes sense only if one identifies the very narrow limits within which it has some chance of functioning. What does it mean for Spinoza to think being? It means something defined by the operation of an understanding (*intellectio*), for which there is no room to make the distinction between the fact of knowing and the fact of understanding. "Knowledge of God is the mind's greatest good; its greatest virtue is to know God." (E IVP28) Yet to "know" God, there is no room to resort, as on the contrary an interpretation of the Heideggerian type would suggest, to a privileged experience, for example, the experience the work of art generates by revealing "ecstatically" that which, in the essent, withdraws, as being of the essent, being whose "reality" has more to do with that of a nothingness than with that of any being-essent. In Spinoza knowledge of the third kind, which maintains all the characteristics of the "understanding," has nothing to do with such aesthetic ecstasy. We see as well that behind the confrontation opposing Heidegger and Spinoza is pursued a debate, whose stake is perhaps given less in the dilemma between an intellectualism or rationalism and an intuitionism—this would rigorously be the Heideggerian version of this discussion—than in the dilemma opposing in general a positivism and a negativism. By "positivism" must be understood here the possibility of understanding, in the sense of *intellectio*, being as such without mediation, that is, without the intervention of a negative relation to self of being. Yet this point is, one knows, at the heart of the refutation of Spinoza developed by Hegel. Whence this final suggestion we shall make to conclude: between Spinoza and Heidegger would be none other than Hegel.

2. In Adorno, as in Heidegger, references to Spinoza are rare and don't seem very significant. For example, Horkheimer and Adorno's *Dialectic of Enlightenment*, in its first text devoted to the "concept of Enlightenment," refers to a passage of the *Ethics*, the corollary of proposition 22 in part IV: "The striving to preserve oneself is the first and only foundation of virtue," presented as "the true maxim of all Western civilization, in which the religious and philosophical differences of the middle class are reconciled."[8] So it is that the formula of the *conatus* constitutes the characteristic expression of the so-called theses of possessive individualism, through which reason is itself subjected to an objective of domination and thus submits to an abstract and calculating model of rationality. This interpretation would rigorously apply to Hobbes; but an even slightly attentive reader of Spinoza knows that this is the exact opposite of what Spinoza maintains for his own account. In fact, for Spinoza, to preserve oneself—that is, according to the very definition of the *conatus*, "to persevere in its being"—is for everything, and not just for a human individual, to make an effort with a view to developing to the maximum the power of existing and acting that is in it. Yet this tendency, far from folding the individual onto himself, and onto the egoistic figure of his identity, as if the latter could constitute an autonomous reality, *tanquam imperium in imperio*—for this formula applied to human beings in general is *a fortiori* applicable to every human being in particular—on the contrary projects him towards other forms of existence which constitute the reason of his organic and intellectual development, literally associates him with these forms, and through them links him to all of nature, of which he is himself only a singular expression.

One sees that, in Adorno as in Heidegger, Spinoza's thought is integrated into a totality—Western metaphysics or bourgeois reason—with which it is so closely at one that it loses its originality from the fact of this assimilation. But here again one might wonder if this absorption means the radical erasure of every theme of Spinozist orientation or origin in the development of Adorno's critical reflection. In order to indicate the possibility of such a resurgence, we shall limit ourselves to a very specific reference: the introduction written by Adorno for the publication of the 1961 Colloquium on the social sciences held at Tübingen, an encounter dominated by the confrontation between Adorno and Popper, and also marked by Habermas's first public interventions.[9]

The argument presented by Adorno systematizes the totality of his criticisms against positivism, and leads him to specify his conception of the dialectic, which he opposes to positivism. First, contrary to what positivism in general maintains, which Adorno identifies with an empiricism, it is not possible to grasp facts for themselves, as pure phenomena, without relating them to the totality that essentially sustains and determines them, for this totality is properly what constitutes their essence: "positivism, following Schlick's maxim, will only allow appearance to be valid, whilst dialectics will not allow itself to be robbed of the distinction between essence and appearance.... One must adhere to Hegel's statement that essence must appear, [for it is in this way that essence enters into contradiction with appearance]."[10] The dialectic apprehends this contradiction: in a way the dialectic posits the phenomenon on the basis of essence, which does not mean that it reduces it to being simply the manifestation of an abstract essentiality, since on the contrary it distinguishes its singularity by opposing it to this essentiality from which it detaches it, or at the very least to which it opposes it. Precisely at this point a second thesis develops: for this totalizing essence whose phenomenon is only a particular determination to appear is to be opposed to facts, that is, to shirk any grasping at facts. "The interpretation of facts is directed towards totality, without the interpretation itself being a fact.... To this extent, totality is what is most real. Since it is the sum of individuals' social relations which screen themselves off from individuals, it is also illusion—ideology."[11] The essence or the whole only appears by disappearing, that is, by being concealed, since, being given only under particular perspectives, it is distorted or decomposed by being communicated. This idea also expresses a paradoxical formula, which is found in paragraph 29 of the first part of *Minima Moralia*: "The whole is the non-true."

Now this reasoning is not unrelated to what is at stake in propositions 20 to 22 of part IV of the *Ethics*, which have just been mentioned. What Adorno seeks to make understood is that since the essence to which every phenomenon is dialectically related is not a totality objectively given in the form of a positive existence, it is thereby irreducible to any immediate apprehension: it is therefore ruled out that essence finds its source in the individual consciousness, on the basis of which it is expressed, or to which it is addressed as a legislative reason; but, in relation to the lessons of this consciousness, essence must be held perpetually behind and in default; and this is why essence can itself only be aimed at according to a critical perspective which tries to destabilize every factual form of existence, regarding which essence appears as "non-true," and which, reciprocally, appears with respect to essence as unworthy of being maintained and preserved.

If one reflects a little carefully on it, one notices that Spinoza, while using a completely different language, is not so far removed from a conception of this kind. In fact, the *conatus* that, according to Spinoza, "speaks" in every individual does so independently of a conscious apprehension, and in any case precedes such an apprehension: at least this is how the concept of *conatus* is introduced in the sixth proposition of the third part of the *Ethics*. Thus, the *conatus* does not appear in so far as it would be rooted in the very individual it traverses, the latter for its part constituting an isolated and autonomous entity. On the contrary, the movement of the *conatus* incorporates the individual within the totality of nature which causes it to be and act, and by the same token disqualifies the individual's claim to be completely self-sufficient. And if the individual "understands" this situation, which is for it the only way to liberate itself from the constraints the situation imposes on it, it finds here precisely an argument, not to isolate or enclose itself mechanically within itself, but to link itself organically with all other beings which constitute nature with it, to the extent that they are not incompatible with the essence that singularly defines it; that is, the individual must seek to unite itself physically and intellectually with other figures of individuality, because this union is the true condition of its own perpetuation.

We see that the totality Adorno is talking about is not entirely unrelated to substance as Spinoza defines it, substance that conditions all modal determinations to the extent that substance itself cannot be apprehended modally. However, and thereby we return to the conclusion that the connection with Heidegger had already suggested, Spinoza rules out the idea of a dialectical type of relation between mode and substance, in the sense that the dialectic cannot be thought without reference to a negativity. But shouldn't one say, then, that Spinoza had invented a completely original form of dialectic: that of a dialectic of the positive? And the very fact that such a question could be posed confirms what had already been indicated: if one wants to speak of a philosophical actuality of Spinoza, it must pass through Hegel, which obviously does not mean that one must take up again as such the interpretation of Spinoza's philosophy that Hegel had proposed.

3. Foucault probably quoted Spinoza only once, but in a way that attracts attention. It is in *Histoire de la folie*, when he brings out the ethical problematic that, according to him, persists in the background of all classical thought:

> Classical reason does not encounter ethics at the end of its truth and in the form of moral laws; ethics as a choice against unreason is present from the origin of all concerted thought. . . . In the classical age reason is born in the space of ethics.[12]

In support of this analysis, Foucault quotes the paragraph of the *Treatise on the Emendation of the Intellect* that defines the ethical position of the subject by "the union that the mind has with the whole of Nature."[13] Nor is this formula, which we have also already found in Russell, unrelated to the formula that had occupied the attention of Horkheimer and Adorno. In fact, this ethical position simultaneously presents two characteristics: on the one hand, it makes it quite clear that the ethical subject's singularity is not an egoistic singularity, that of an isolated being determining itself solely through its relation to itself; and from this point of view we note that Foucault is far from comparing classical thought to a "bourgeois" reason, as Horkheimer and Adorno did quite simply. On the other hand, this constitution of the subject is ethical in the strict sense of the word, to the extent that it forms the economy of the relation that would submit the subject to the edicts of an autonomous, or intrinsically rational, moral law, that is, to the principle of an abstract universal. This is precisely what is stated in the passage quoted from the *Treatise on the Emendation of the Intellect*: the ethical subject is determined as such through the relation it enters with the whole of nature, a relation that, if it is intellectually carried out, which moreover is also the condition for it to be completely practised, by the same token ceases to be lived in the form of subordination or of constraint but becomes the figure *par excellence* of freedom.

One knows the importance assumed in Foucault's final works by reflection on the problems of ethics, in so far as the latter is not left enclosed within the framework and categories of a moral speculation, itself developed in terms of subjection to a law, whether the latter acts from inside or outside the individual it directs. Thus, this reflection develops in the direction of an ethics of freedom, completely separate from the preoccupations of a morality of liberation. In this regard one might quote an especially revealing text, which is extracted from a course given on 5 January 1983 at the Collège de France on the theme "What is Enlightenment?"[14] This text brings out the new philosophical question that, according to Foucault, emerges at the moment that Kant set about responding to the question "What is Enlightenment?" that still defines our modernity, a question Foucault himself reformulates in the following terms: "Who am I now?" "What is this present to which I belong?"

> It is a question of showing how he who speaks as a thinker, as a scientist, as a philosopher, is himself part of this process and (more than that) how he has a certain role to play in this process, in which he is to find himself, therefore, both element and actor. . . . And in doing so we see that when the philosopher asks how he belongs to this present it is a quite different question from that of how one belongs to a particular doctrine or tradition; it is no longer simply the question of how one belongs to a human community in general, but rather that of how one belongs to a certain "us," to an us that concerns a cultural totality characteristic of one's own time . . .
> All this—philosophy as the problematization of a present, and as the questioning by the philosopher of this present to which he belongs and in

relation to which he has to situate himself—might well be said to characterize philosophy as the discourse of modernity on modernity.[15]

What strikes the reader of this text is the haunting repetition of the term "belong," which Foucault uses to characterize what he also calls an "ontology of the present": to think today is first of all to think about a belonging, which constitutes thought itself, by grounding it in the historical conditions making it possible; it is to understand that thought is legitimated neither as a discourse of God, nor as a discourse of Man, but is brought about as a historical relation.

Yet what is suggested by this notion of belonging, which refuses to recognize in reason the illusory nature of an autonomous activity, decreeing for itself its own laws by resting on a divine or human sovereignty, and which on the contrary asserts that all thought is conditioned, and maintained within limits that, even before being consciously reflected, make possible its actual process? It refers to an idea which Spinoza developed: the idea according to which the individual has in itself no other reality than that communicated through its relation to the totality to which one can also say that it "belongs," a relation that governs its ethical destination. Perhaps in order to distinguish Foucault from a properly Spinozist tradition, one will say that the concept of belonging to which Foucault refers is just the opposite of a naturalism, since he refers to the idea of an historical belonging, hence irreducible to the universal laws of a nature considered in general. But this argument, in itself incontestable, can also lead us to reread Spinoza, by asking ourselves about the conception that lingers almost everywhere about his "naturalism." Perhaps then we shall take note that the eternity of substance is not, as Spinoza himself reflected, directly assimilable to the permanence of a nature already given in itself, in an abstract and static manner, according to the idea of "substance which has not yet become subject" developed by Hegel regarding Spinoza; but, to the extent that this substance is inseparable from its productivity, that it manifests itself nowhere else than in the totality of its modal realizations, in which it is absolutely immanent, it is a nature that is itself produced in a history, and under conditions that the latter necessarily attaches to it. Thus for the soul to attain the understanding of its union with the whole of nature is also to recognize historically what confers on it its own identity, and it is in a certain way, then, to respond to the question "Who am I now?"

We see that neither Heidegger, nor Adorno, nor Foucault is a Spinozist or Spinozan. But that does not mean that the preoccupations at the centre of Spinoza's thought are completely absent from their own reflection. Obviously, we should not conclude that one would have to read

Heidegger in the light of Spinoza, or Spinoza in the light of Heidegger, etc., so as formally to align with one another types of speculation developed on different theoretical terrains and historical conditions. But all this means that perhaps it would be possible to locate some intersections of these speculations—which is just the opposite of an alignment. On the basis of the points where these speculations cross, we would simultaneously see how they meet and also separate, since they certainly come from elsewhere, oriented as they are in different directions. And by the same token we could define more precisely what there is specific in their own problematics, by making them react on one another. From this point of view, if Spinoza is philosophically actual, it is probably because he still constitutes, regarding the great contemporary figures of philosophical thought, an irreplaceable reactor and developer. To read Spinoza today is also to seek to understand how the problems he took up, and the way in which he treated them, contribute objectively, if not subjectively, to enrich the thought of philosophers.

Notes

1. The references indicated in this paragraph have been communicated to me by Françoise Dastur.
2. Heidegger 1991, 65.
3. Heidegger 1969, 47.
4. Heidegger 1985, 33–4; 89–90.
5. Ibid., 33–4.
6. Heidegger 1962, 67. (Trans.)
7. Heidegger 1987, 28–9.
8. Horkheimer and Adorno 1989, 29. The rest of the development devoted to the concept of Enlightenment again presents a certain number of references to Spinoza, which are all used in the same sense. In the same edition, see p. 86 (in which the passage from the preface to part III of the *Ethics* on the necessity of reducing affective behaviours to geometrical figures in order to explain them is interpreted as a symptom of the bourgeois ascetic ideal and of his effort with a view to subjecting vital phenomena to a rational totalization), p. 95 (in which E IVP54 is supposed to reveal the inhuman obverse of the project of a complete self-mastery), p. 101 (in which the reference to E IVP50 and its scholium, as well as to chapter 16 of the Appendix of this same part, demonstrates, by the demystification that these texts propose, the "sadistic" content of bourgeois virtue).
9. Adorno et al. 1976.
10. Ibid., 11–12. (The second half of the last sentence does not appear in the English translation of this passage. Trans.)
11. Ibid., 12.
12. Foucault 1972, 157.
13. TdIE 13.
14. An extract from this course was published under the title "Q'est-ce que les lumières?" in *Magazine littéraire* 207 (May 1984), 35–9. A more developed account of the same ideas has been given by Foucault in an article published in the United States. See Foucault 1984.
15. Foucault 1988, 87–8.

Spinoza, the End of History, and the Ruse of Reason

As the title of this study suggests, our concern, from a singular—and perhaps unsuspected—angle, is Spinoza's relation to Hegel. To begin, let us say quickly what one can expect from such a *rapprochement*: we shall not seek, reading Hegel in Spinoza, or Spinoza in Hegel, to pursue the chimera of a Spinozist Hegel or a Hegelian Spinoza. We shall only be concerned to read Spinoza and Hegel together, that is, one with the other, but also one against the other, so as to draw out the eventual elements of divergence as they can appear through their very convergence. In an extremely summary fashion, the nature of this relation could be expressed in the following way: no doubt Spinoza and Hegel talk about the same thing—and this is why there exists a real community of thought between them—but they speak about it differently, and perhaps even in an opposite way—and this is why, if it is not permissible purely and simply to equate their philosophical positions, neither can they be completely separated. This is indeed why this *rapprochement*, which is in fact a confrontation, constitutes an irreplaceable intellectual stimulus which reveals, or at least throws into relief, aspects of each of these theoretical positions which would otherwise risk going unnoticed. And it does so all the more as the themes adopted here so as to realize such a *rapprochement*—themes borrowed from the domains of the philosophy of history and of political philosophy—are precisely those themes regarding which Hegel, while upholding positions which quite closely evoke Spinoza's, even as they simultaneously deviate from them, gave no explanation about the reasons and limits of this encounter, although he was able to do so about other, properly metaphysical or epistemological subjects.

Here we shall stage an encounter between two extremely well-known texts, whose significance is certainly crucial for their authors, who presented them in the form of veritable theoretical manifestos: the beginning of the *Political Treatise* and the preface to the *Elements of the*

Philosophy of Right. By carrying out parallel readings of these two texts, seen in a perspective which is no doubt rather cavalier, we find three essential, interdependent themes regarding which we can ask if Spinoza and Hegel really treat them in a comparable way: they are the appeal to political realism, the postulate of the end of history, and the doctrine of the ruse of reason.

First, political realism. Initiating a philosophical reflection on the fundamental problems of right, Spinoza and Hegel subordinate the rationality of their approach to a critical presupposition which could be formulated as follows: every speculation concerning what should be, that is, the possible, must be removed from this speculation, and the essence of right must be brought back to its actual reality. The whole question is then to know if, through this affirmation of the primacy and exhaustibility of the real, Spinoza and Hegel aspire to the same concept of reality: to take the State as it is, or States as they are, in order to discover its specific reason—is this to adopt the precepts of a positivism before the fact, or else is it to admit the presupposition of an immanent rationality which maintains the ideality of its object? In other words, is knowledge of the reality of politics a reduction of this reality to its phenomena, or else is it a highlighting of the finality that is in it and which allows this reality to be understood as it is in itself?

This appeal to realism leads to the affirmation of an end of history, which in fact constitutes its presupposition. In Hegel this theme is stated, proclaimed in a way that seems striking: one only philosophizes about what is, that is, about what has been realized, or even about that which is completed; and this is why actual rationality is a rationality that, being asked only to paint its grey on grey, is itself situated at the end of the real processes it recovers in thought by retrospectively bringing out their internal logic. It is surprising to find this suggestion—in an attenuated form, it is true—in Spinoza's text, when Spinoza declares himself "convinced that every form of commonwealth which can be devised to secure human concord, and all the means required to guide the multitude, or to keep it within definite bounds, has already been taught by experience" (TP I/3). The hypothesis adopted by Spinoza is that for experience, which can here be equated with the real history of human beings, having revealed everything that can be expected from it, all that remains is to take into account its results in order to draw out its main lessons by bringing about their synthesis. The problem is then the following: are the concepts of history at work in Spinoza and Hegel comparable? The difference is obvious between the representation of history as an oriented process, leading to the final revelation of a rationality it carries in itself from the beginning, and the reduction of history to a succession of experiences in which apparently only occasion and chance intervene. Let us note that the question just formulated ties in with the previous question: is or is not reality subjected to ends which condition its understanding? In what sense must one speak of an "end" of history?

Finally, Spinoza bases his requirement to measure right by fact, according to the lessons of experience, on the necessity of considering human beings "as they are" (*ut sunt*), instead of fictitiously substituting "a human nature which exists nowhere" (*humana natura quae nullibi est*) for "the one that exists in reality" (*ea quae revera est*)" (TP I/1). Here political realism is seemingly coupled with an anthropological realism: societies are as experience presents them to us, and it is futile to seek to imagine them otherwise, because the individuals they assemble are guided in their conduct not by an ideal "rational precept" (*dictamen rationis*), which resolves all problems of political power by evacuating the necessity of this very power, according to the logic of utopia, but by the power of their affects, in so far as this power spontaneously, hence before every reflection, coincides with their *conatus*, that is, with their innate tendency to persevere in their being. In this sense, political rationality—if it exists—must proceed through the mechanism of instinctive natural inclinations, which defines the proper content of its reflection, and marks out the ground of its interventions. Now this theme recovers an idea which, if it is not explicitly formulated in the preface to the *Elements of the Philosophy of Right*, underlies all of Hegel's political thought: the idea of the ruse of reason, according to which reason manifests itself in history only through the mediation of human passions which, even in their most unreasonable expressions, are the instruments of reason's operation. Thus, what in the preface to the *Phenomenology* Hegel calls "the monstrous labour of world history" (*das ungeheure Arbeit der Weltgeschichte*) is nothing other than the controlled exploitation of this material, animated by the dialectic of the recognition that plays primitively at the level of the experiences of consciousness.

The whole difficulty of Hegelian theory is attached to the metaphor of the "ruse" (*die List der Vernunft*), which seems to superimpose the schema of external finality, reason adjusting itself to the spontaneous elements that it diverts to its profit, on that of internal finality, according to which human affects are not only the instruments which reason uses, but the actual form of its realization. One might then wonder which of these two models of reference—the first model maintaining a *de facto* discontinuity between human reason and the passions, which it manipulates from outside, and the second model on the contrary presupposing an essential identity, at least at the level of their content, between what is immediately given to consciousnesses and the immanent order that orients their entire movement—is most related to the kind of *emendatio* that Spinoza applies to juridical reason: to follow the logic of this *emendatio*, to what point can reason perhaps be embodied in society and identify its own ends in society?

But is it possible, according to Spinoza, to speak of the ends of reason? Doesn't submission to the correctness of an adequate thought—achieving a complete understanding of its object prior to a rational theodicy that provides a foundation for a philosophy of history—amount to reintroducing into knowledge a teleological presupposition that contradicts its strictly genetic and causal demonstrative rigour? Yet what is here in question is indeed the relation between philosophy and politics in so far as it depends on the status of true knowledge: if to understand the social existence of human beings is to bring back the latter to necessary conditions, doesn't this mean that reflection about right is possible only on the condition of being enclosed within narrow limits, outside which, if not against which, the project of liberation characteristic of philosophy must be maintained? Now doesn't Hegel himself assert the necessity for pure thought, once it has traversed all the stages of its realization, of withdrawing "into the figure of an intellectual kingdom" (*in Gestalt eines intellektuellen Reichs*)?

Now one sees that the relation that passes between Spinoza's thought and Hegel's is complex in a different way from that of an abstract identity or irreducible difference: it can be grasped only as an exchange, through which the positions defended by one and the other correspond and respond without, however, ever being confused. This is why the confrontation of their discourses can be fruitful.

We must now return more precisely to each of the three themes that have just been stated superficially, so as to grasp the content of this exchange, that is, to measure its philosophical stakes.

Political Realism

On this point, we shall start with Hegel, in order next, in the light of his reflection on what is "actually real" (*wirklich*), to be able to reread Spinoza's text. According to Hegel, "reality" (*Wirklichkeit*) is intrinsically rational to the extent that it is the work (*Werk*) of reason, that is, the product of its labour: perhaps reason can be said to realize itself in the world through forms which are also extremely diverse, proceeding from the empirical *Erscheinung* to the ideal *Offenbarung*, that is, from realization in the strict sense to incarnation. To what extent can history be regarded as such a rational work? To the extent that, considered in its totality, as universal history, and stripped of the factual envelope arising from the pure contingency of the event that defines *Realität* in the strict sense, that is, the detail of what has happened, history reveals its mystical kernel, the eternally present substantial content (*das Ewige, das gegenwärtig ist*) which constitutes its immanent law. In this sense, for Hegel the refusal to transgress the limits of the world as it is, this transgression which is only capable of being realized in the name of an illusory because necessarily subjective transcendence, coincides with the recognition of the fact that reason is actually present in "this world-here" (*disseits* and not *jenseits*, an alternative which will be transmitted into German philosophical thought, by way of Feuerbach, up to the young Marx), because the world is the result of the labour that Spirit carries out, in so far as it is "Worldspirit" (*Weltgeist*), in order to realize itself necessarily.

This is why for Hegel the State, which is the most accomplished historical form, also represents "objective Spirit" (*der objektive Geist*), Spirit as it is itself objectified in the world in its most perfect figure, such that nothing else is rationally thinkable which could ideally—in the sense in which the ideal would be opposed to the real instead of being realized in it—be substituted for it. This is the reason for which it makes its peace with reality, it is nothing other than reconciling itself with the present, "to recognize reason as the rose in the cross of the present," "*reconciliation* . . . which philosophy grants to those who have received the inner call *to comprehend*, to preserve their subjective freedom in the realm of the substantial, and at the same time to stand with their subjective freedom not in a particular and contingent situation, but in what has being in and for itself."[1] In other words—Hegel uses this expression in the preface to his *Lectures on the Philosophy of History*—reason is "the Hermes who actually guides peoples" along this procession which leads them in turn to assume, each according to their rank and time, their spiritual destination; and this spiritual destination is to represent adequately, within the limits assigned to their respective situations, one and the same reality that confers its spiritual substance on their existence. The whole question, then, is to know if history, brought back to its rational norm, is *Vorstellung* or *Darstellung*, either a representation of the present through intermediaries which to a certain extent maintain it as separate, or an actual presentation which absolutely integrates reason within the limits of universal history, to the point of identifying completely the ends of reason with the ends of history.

The political realism noted by Spinoza is inscribed within an apparently quite different theoretical context, since from the beginning it appears as a realism of experience, which seeks its first references in practice. From this perspective thus opened, it is futile to seek outside experience a political model regarding which one would then have to ask how to put it into practice: whatever its form, right has always been elaborated in usage, in a completely empirical way, through the intervention of "politicians" (*politici*); it is the latter who have adjusted the procedures best adapted to human affects, procedures whose efficacy precisely permits the degree of this adaptation to be measured. This is why if, strictly speaking, politicians don't know how to talk about the nature of the State, in the sense of a theoretical knowledge, it is they who in fact know it best by right, since "experience has been their guide, they have taught nothing which was far from use" (*quoniam experientiam magistram habuerunt, nihil docuerunt quod ab usu remotum esset*) (TP I/2).

Now there is no other path in politics except the path thus shown in the facts and which, in order to understand the reality of right, leads one to take into account the experience that has been given of it: all of experience, but nothing but experience. To what extent is one entitled here to speak of empiricism? Spinoza invalidates the procedure that would consist of evaluating experience in the name of external principles, for such principles would disqualify phenomena by bringing them back to the status of simple appearances: the principles of an adequate knowledge must on the contrary be inherent in experience, in the sense that they are given in it or agree with it. But this does not mean that these principles, which are given in experience, are given by experience; for if, within its limits, experience generates all the effects of which the political nature of human beings is capable, it does not directly show the causes of these effects; and one might even argue that experience is in fact organized so as to conceal its causes, or to postpone their manifestation. To know within the limits imposed by experience is thus to reason about the objects of experience, so as to understand its true nature. Now this explanation arises from the same demonstrative requirement as every other form of rational knowledge, whether or not the object of the latter is immediately given in experience. Even if, in the *Political Treatise*, the arguments are not formally ranked according to the strict deductive model carried out in the *Ethics*, Spinoza's objective remains that of a necessary and reasoned Politics.

What constitutes the point of departure for such a demonstration? It is the real human being, that is, the actual practice of human relations: these expressions can appear anachronistic in that they anticipate a terminology which will only be in use much later and in a different context, and yet the idea they carry is certainly included in the concept of human nature as formulated by Spinoza. On the basis of a consideration of the affects and their spontaneous free play, independently of the awareness and rational judgement whose object they can ultimately form, it is a question, then, of drawing out the logic of human actions, in so far as the latter derive from a "nature" which is the real source of every right. A necessary connection is thus posed between anthropology and politics: it is simultaneously a question of concluding on the basis of experiences of life in society the common laws that emerge from them, and of demonstrating the validity of these experiences on the basis of the necessary laws that direct them. Thus, human beings, who all continually do politics without knowing it, by this very fact do right, in the sense that they make right, and, by their actions, confer on right the only kind of legitimacy of which it is capable.

But because the main principle of Spinoza's political naturalism is that nature establishes right, this does not mean that right follows from nature as if from a base that preexists it in an independent way. On the contrary, what Spinoza means is that nature is full of right, that nature is already right itself according to its essential constitution which, while maintaining the specific characteristics of social right, anchors social right to the greatest depths of the right of nature and circumscribes its field of action. No more than human beings themselves is society "as if a power within a power" (*tanquam imperium in imperio*); instead, society is thus subjected, in so far as it is a "part of nature" (*pars naturae*), to the common laws that govern all reality. Rather than say that right derives from nature, one must say, then, that right is entirely immersed in nature, and this is also why right constitutes its own "figures" (*species*) within the limits imposed on it by experience.

Spinoza's position, then, does not amount to a simple pragmatism. Nor can his position be identified with a kind of positivism before the fact. Yet this last connection stands out as if by itself on the reading of the first pages of the *Political Treatise*; and if the concept of science to which Spinozist politics is tied will be explicitly at the heart of philosophical thought during the first half of the nineteenth century, rather than in Hegel, with his attempt at a completely rational deduction of right as mediated realization of Spirit, it is in Comte, in so far as Comte makes the adequation of right to fact the condition of an authentic theoretical rigour, that the indices of such an intellectual community must be sought. For example, in the first text in which he defined the fundamental concepts of a positive politics, Comte writes:

> Admiration and reprobation of phenomena ought to be banished with equal severity from every positive science, because all preoccupations of this sort directly and unavoidably tend to hinder or mislead examination. Astronomers, physicists, chemists and physiologists neither admire nor blame their respective phenomena. They observe them, although these phenomena may afford ample subject for reflections of each sort, of which numerous examples may be cited. Savants, with reason, leave such considerations to artists, within whose sphere they really fall.[2]

At first glance, one would believe that this text was directly inspired by reading Spinoza. Yet it is obvious that Comte, if he had had knowledge of the Spinozist reference, would have energetically rejected it, in the name of his condemnation of the metaphysical approach. It is precisely then that the confrontation of Comte and Spinoza takes on meaning, at the moment that it reveals the intractable difference between them.

For Comte politics is a science like the others to the extent that, having previously circumscribed the level of studies in which it is situated, that of properly human phenomena, politics manages to formulate the necessary laws that these phenomena specifically obey, the natural laws of history, subject to a principle of rational progression whose necessary development seems to depend more on an "outline of nature," in Kant's sense, than a "ruse of reason," in Hegel's. Now, according to Comte, such a study presupposes that one has completely abandoned seeking the causes of these chains, in order to keep to the necessary relations that are established at the level of their effects alone.

On the other hand, Spinoza insistently asserts that, like every adequate knowledge, true political science rests on a complete understanding of its phenomena, which makes them known as they are in themselves, that is, as they are really produced by their causes. This is why this knowledge takes the form of a "deduction": "I have only applied myself to demonstrating in a certain and necessary way [certa et indubitata ratione demonstrare] those things which accord best with practice, or to deduce them from the condition itself of human nature [ex ipsa humanae naturae conditione deducere]." (TP I/4) One finds here the idea of an anthropological foundation of right: if societies are what they are, that is, ruled by laws which decide the just and unjust, it is because something happens in them that first belongs to the nature of human beings; this thing is "power" (potentia). Power is what determines all things of nature to exist and act: society, which is a natural thing, has no power except inasmuch as power has been imparted by the individuals comprising it, in which society has its source. This does not mean that, according to a mechanistic perspective, Spinoza seeks to compose complex social reality on the basis of an abstract construction assembling the simple elements that are human beings into the organized totality that is the political order. In fact, just like the beings they assemble, societies are individuals; and, on the other hand, social agents—or, if one prefers, political subjects—are individuals only inasmuch as they are themselves organized as complex systems, assembling still other elements into kinds of corporeal and mental communities, which one can visualize in their turn already as species of societies.

All this follows from the very particular notion of individuality developed by Spinoza's philosophy: this notion is never comparable to that of elementary entities, physical or psychic atoms, which would give an absolute end to an analysis of reality. It is at this point that this philosophy is clearly opposed to the materialism of the ancients. Spinoza always thinks of the individual synthetically, as the result of a movement of totalization which has begun well before it and is still pursued beyond its own limits. This is precisely what the definition of the individual as a "part of nature" (pars naturae) means, a definition that, let us note, is applied both to the singular human being and to the social body conceived in its specificity: "part," not in the sense of an element non-decomposable in itself, following the logic of a strictly analytic approach, but in the sense of a determination which itself finds its principle in the existence of everything to which it belongs interdependently, and from which it can only be provisionally and relatively detached. This is why the form *par excellence* of the realization of individual power is the *conatus*, an effort to persevere in its being which, far from isolating finite things or individual realities from one another, *tanquam imperia in imperio* one could say, on the contrary attaches them, through the mediation of their mutual relations, to all of nature, of which these things are precisely only "parts." For what defines the reality of individuals is that they are not existences independent in themselves; and this is why the *conatus* that delimits their power does not find its principle in their essence alone, since it is not concluded by their definition: "It follows that the power by which things in nature exist, and by which, in consequence, they operate, can be none other than the eternal power of God." (TP II/2) It is the power of nature considered in its totality that is continued in individual things, and "acts" in them by spreading to everything they do, to all their "operations"; and this is the reason why they can thus transmit this power to other configurations into which they themselves enter as constituent elements, which persist in asserting their own power in the dynamic of their fusion.

From this perspective, one can say that Spinoza's realism is first of all a naturalism, provided that one purges this term of every pragmatist or empiricist reference. Obviously, naturalism must be understood here in the sense of nature considered absolutely, that is, of the divine substance, which, because it produces all its effects in itself, also constitutes the principle of every existence and power. If there are societies, and if in the order that they define, human beings can realize the part of eternity that falls to them, that is, manage to live free, it is because these societies incorporate or inform, that is, there is no better word to say it, individualize, in their way, the global power that belongs to all of nature: for it is this power which truly constitutes their cause, on the basis of which they can be adequately interpreted.

When one has reached this point, one can wonder if the divide between Spinoza and Hegel isn't slightly reduced. Whether societies and the human beings they cause to live together are the product of an absolutely first nature, or the realizations of a Spirit which is in search of itself through the succession of its manifestations, the fact remains that right is answerable to a logic whose development coincides exactly with that of an ontology, and, from this point of view, Spinoza's and Hegel's "realisms"—whether a realism of experience or a realism of effectivity—can seem quite close to one another. No doubt the fact that Spinoza thinks of nature as substance, whereas Hegel on the contrary defines Spirit as subject, maintains an irreducible difference between them, a difference that separates a necessary order of causes from an absolute order of ends. The study of another theme, that of the end of history, should allow us to shed light on the presuppositions that this last alternative puts into play.

The End of History

This time, let us try to begin by characterizing Spinoza's position. In what way is the theme of the end of history inscribed in his text? Prior to the pure deduction of right, Spinoza asserts that all forms of right are from the outset realized in practice: "And so it is hardly credible that we can conceive anything for the benefit of an ordinary community which has not been suggested already by opportunity or chance, and which men intent on public business, and careful of their own safety, have not discovered for themselves." (TP I/3) One can consider, then, that experience has already shown—indeed, at the beginning of the same paragraph Spinoza writes *ostendisse* and not *ostendere*—everything that can possibly be attained by right in matters of social organization. All that remains is to recapitulate the acquisition of this experience, which has presented them in a dispersed form, as if they arose on occasion or by chance: that is, all that remains is to totalize them by bringing about their rational synthesis. This last approach, which consists in subtracting the object it considers from the contingent conditions of duration in order to take account only of the immutable, and hence untransformable, order that constitutes its truth, can seem quite traditional. Similarly, in the chapter of the *Theological-Political Treatise* devoted to miracles, by relying on the Bible's text itself, Spinoza confirms this position by virtue of which the order of things cannot be modified, because this order cannot be put into contradiction with itself:

> In certain passages Scripture asserts of nature in general that she observes a fixed and immutable order, as in Psalm 138 verse 6 and Jeremiah chapter 31, verses 35, 36. Furthermore, in Ecclesiastes chapter 1 verse 9 the Sage tells us quite clearly that nothing new happens in nature, and in verses 9, 10 to illustrate this same point he says that although occasionally something may happen that seems new, it is not new, but has happened in ages past beyond recall. For, as he says, there is today no remembrance of things past, nor will there be remembrance of things today among those to come. Again, in chapter 3 verse 11 he says that God has ordered all things well for their time, and in verse 14 he says that he knows that whatever God does will endure forever, neither can anything be added to it nor taken away from it. All these passages clearly convey the teaching that nature observes a fixed and immutable order, that God has been the same throughout all ages that are known or unknown to us, that the laws of nature are so perfect and fruitful that nothing can be added or taken away from them, and that miracles seem something strange only because of man's ignorance. (TTP end of chapter 6)

In an analogous way, doesn't the supposition that the political order could be radically changed entail engaging one's belief in impossible miracles, everything, in this as in other domains, having already happened?

If Spinoza sets himself up from the point of view of a history which is finished—let us also note that, if we hold to what has just been said, history would have been finished from the start, and in fact has never taken place, perfect order being by definition without history—it is thus for motives seemingly opposed to those that inspire Hegel. Spinoza's reasoning does not at all take into account a dialectic of innovation resting on the labour of the negative, but on the contrary develops all the consequences of what has just been called his political realism. Nothing new under the sun: if social forms have really been invented it was so long ago that memory of them has dissipated; and this is why all that remains is to accept these forms as they appear today, without claiming to add or take away any of them, by acting as if they held good for eternity.

However, it immediately appears that these formulations must no longer be taken literally, for political theory can no more be reduced to a simple recording of the facts: experience delivers genuine lessons only if it is considered "under the aspect of eternity" (*sub specie aeternitatis*), hence completely released from the accidental circumstances that confer its singular temporal situation on it. In addition, for Spinoza it is a question, by analysing the different forms of social structures, that is, political regimes, of resituating these structures or regimes within the framework of a general deduction which makes them derive from a common nature. Yet this approach is itself only possible by considering the optimal forms in which political power brings about its own organization: "So now that I have dealt with the right of commonwealths in general, it is time for me to discuss their best condition." (TP V/1) Presented in this way, as a kind of ideal type, or original form, this political order in fact corresponds to something perfectly novel regarding the current existence of society, as Spinoza himself points out a little later: "Finally, although there is no state, as far as I know, which incorporates all the constitutional provisions described above, we can confirm from actual experience that this form of monarchy is the best by surveying every civilized state and examining the causes of its preservation and downfall." (TP VII/30) It suffices, it seems, that the theoretical approach does not contradict experience in order to find itself by the same token in perfect agreement with it: but this also means that, in order to understand the substantial reason of phenomena, in the political domain as in all others, one must depart from their strictly factual reality by applying to them a consideration of norms which, without contradicting them, nonetheless remains unnoticed at their level.

One can say, then, that Spinoza does not passively resign himself to the facts, if only because the actuality in which the facts are embodied is by definition precarious and condemned sooner or later to come undone: the grave events that shook Dutch society in 1672 also come to offer a striking testimony to the moment in which Spinoza wrote the lines just quoted. No doubt it was these events that gave an initial impetus, indeed a theoretical object, to the reflection of the *Political Treatise*. There is no question, then, of denying that history is the place of constant changes, and that it is haunted by a dynamic that tends in a quasi-permanent way to destabilize its apparent figures. The objective of a rational knowledge, backed by demonstrations, is in a way to take this movement in an opposite direction, by bringing back society, every society, to its principle, which is not to be confused with a historical origin. But it would be utterly inconsistent to suppose that this deduction, which is carried out in a certain *a priori* way, could abandon seeing its objects realized in practice and be satisfied with giving them a purely scientific presentation, for the simple pleasure of understanding (although Spinoza also refers to this last argument, see TP I/4).

From the beginning of his *Treatise*, Spinoza is busy establishing the necessary unity of theory and practice, and it would be very difficult to conceive that this unity had only a theoretical significance: the fact that theory and practice don't contradict one another is the sign but not the foundation of their agreement. No doubt it is not permissible to read the *Political Treatise* as if it were a discourse addressed to a Prince, or a militant's manual, or even a treatise on civic instruction for the use of good citizens: for it basically is nothing other than a philosophical reflection on the best, or the least bad, use that the sage can make of the social state from which in any case he cannot free himself without abandoning his concrete project of liberation. But however theoretical and philosophical this reflection may be, it obviously could not cut itself off from every perspective of practical realization, it being understood that in the last instance this realization does not depend on the decisions and good intentions of anyone: to admit that the optimal form concerning each type of political regime could only exist as an idea would be illogically to confine theoretical thought to the consideration of a pure possibility completely separated from the conditions of its realization. On the contrary, to envision as realizable, inasmuch as the external circumstances allow it, the social structure that, in each case, would guarantee civil peace as much as possible, and by the same token would assure the best conditions for the freedom to think, is to draw out from this structure the irrational nature of an ideal possibility, reserved for the subjective reveries that specifically constitute the fictive universe of fables (TP I/5).

Nothing new under the sun: this consideration only holds good for the causes that command the right of societies, but not at all for the effects deriving from its causes, whose variety is indeterminate and transformation incessant. No doubt human beings are always the same, in the sense that, in all places and times, they are necessarily led by their affects, which necessarily derive from their nature: but these affects link human beings to always-new forms of association, whose configurations are never exactly identical. And this is why, if it is undoubtedly not possible in history, which remains subject to the general laws of nature, which rules out the possibility that something contradictory be produced in it—as Spinoza says, one will never make tables eat grass—the fact remains that everything that can be concluded from fundamental principles, that is, from the real causes of right, must happen one day or another: at least this eventuality can never be definitively excluded, which in particular means that the worst is not in all cases necessarily the most probable.

It must be said, then, that in a sense history is never finished, but that history always pursues, beyond its current forms, a movement of production which, if it alters none of its essential conditions, indefinitely varies the forms in which the latter are realized. Spinoza's "realism" leads him to consider an open history, for which any present moment never has anything but the relative nature of an occasional manifestation, and not that of an absolute expression. History is endless, and without ends, because it necessarily depends on causes which always act in it, whatever the conjunctures that establish the context of their interventions. This is also why, as has just been suggested, in the worst moments of this history, those moments in which civil power degenerates into an arbitrary constraint which seems to deny right itself, it nonetheless remains possible, provided that one considers things under the aspect of eternity, that is, returning to the real causes of right, to think of being free, to think freedom, in a mode that is not just that of an ideal without content. The eternal optimism of the sage.

To think of right is not, then, to think of history as such, nor is it to think without it or against it: but it is necessarily to think in history, in the horizon in which its successive experiences are pursued *ad infinitum*. However, if history is not absent from Spinoza's theoretical reflection, that is so to the extent that history is envisioned in conjunction with the unlimited power of nature, in the absence, then, of every teleological presupposition. Here again, between Spinoza's thought and Hegel's there emerges a motif of seemingly radical divergence. From Spinoza's point of view, the rational deduction of right can in no way coincide with the revelation of a rational progression, which would dispose the concrete forms of its realization throughout a continuous line, oriented by its own internal dynamic in a unique sense, uniformly ascendant. Of course it is possible to classify the forms of the State and its power, but in the

Political Treatise this order takes the form of a typology, a list of structures, inside which at each moment only the one best adapted to its specific requirements has to be chosen, it being understood that in the last instance this choice does not arise from individual takings of position which on the contrary always presuppose it. To the extent that Spinoza is engaged in a reflection on the logic of history, one can say that this reflection is limited to the observation that the monarchical drift threatening all forms of social organization, and little by little restraining the seats of their power, renders more and more precarious the conditions of their perpetuation (see TP VIII/12). If it is possible to reflect on universal history, it is thus rather from the perspective of a cycle indefinitely returning onto itself and not from the perspective of a progressive tendency heading toward the ideal of a society of intrinsically rational right, which it would embody at the end of its evolution.

Here again, one can see an occurrence of Spinoza's political realism: philosophy leads all kinds of societies back to common principles, which are those of nature, but it abandons privileging in any absolute way a certain structure of power and constituting this structure into a universal paradigm, which would be the unique form towards which every State would tend, whatever the conjuncture presiding at their formation. If there is an essence of the social, whose complete explanation in fact arises from the adequate knowledge of universal determinism, there is no essence of society preexisting the totality of its manifestations and being embodied in it, in a way, by traversing all history, to reach its complete realization. True wisdom is not to allow oneself ever to be surprised by the changes to which the social state is permanently exposed and, at every moment, to manage to identify the specific type of regime of power one is dealing with, so as to understand how it agrees, in its fashion, with the natural foundations of right, and to deduce as a result everything one can expect from it in practice, to envision the eventual improvements that could be made so as to assure it a maximum of stability, and thus to guarantee civil peace as much as can be done.

This comparative evaluation proceeds, then, from what could be called a historical scepticism: it narrowly limits the hopes—but by the same token also the fears—that can be attached to a given situation: if they are all valuable, it is because despite their heterogeneity, they express in an always different way this same common foundation on which they depend, and which is not even right, in so far as, from an actual or formalist perspective, its specificity would be irreducible, but consists in nature and its universal laws. For the ultimate horizon of right for Spinoza is not history envisioned as such, but nature. This point obviously opposes him to Hegel, who on the contrary traces the organization of all societies back to an essentially spiritual principle which, if it is realized in historically diverse figures, nevertheless obeys an internal logic of development. This logic in turn engenders the different figures of right as the successive moments of a unique series which finds its true beginning in its end: the rational State.

Here again, though, to recognize the radical opposition that arises between Spinoza's and Hegel's standpoints cannot be only to refuse to come out in favour of either of them, by simply noting their disagreement: for their disagreement makes sense only on the basis of an implicit understanding; their disagreement allows one to identify in their respective discourses the existence of certain common issues, indeed of certain common objects. If one reconsiders the Hegelian philosophy of history in the light of Spinoza's argument, as its major lines have just been reconstructed in a cavalier fashion, one perceives that its lessons are less simple, and especially less simplistic, than those which are ordinarily attributed to it. If Hegel had really formed the idea that the rationality of history can only be freed provided that history has actually attained its absolute end, history in fact coincides with the moment in which Hegel's very reflection is situated, and being established in the supposedly unsurpassable form of the Prussian State, it is clear that his entire doctrine would depend on a presupposition which is in itself unjustifiable, whether by reasons of fact or reasons of right—all this contradicting the rigour of its internal organization and, at the limit, putting the system into contradiction with itself. In addition, Hegel never said this, at least literally. But it is futile to scour all of Hegel's *oeuvre*, with the exception of some metaphorical formulas arising more from religious symbolism than from the scientific rigour of the concept, for a speculation about the terminal moment of history.

This is perfectly clear if one reflects carefully on what the notion of "present" means for Hegel. Hegel relates this notion to the eternity (*das Ewige das gegenwärtig ist*) of the concept and to the self-identity of Spirit that remains always beside itself, and not to the empirical actuality of a given temporal moment (*die Gegenwart als jetzt*), which is only its external finite form. If history is the place of an *Aufhebung* which directs it towards a maximum of rationality, it is because the infinite truth that continually haunts history does not proceed in it but persists through all its transformations. This is why philosophy never considers anything but the present: it is the present that gives a meaning to the past, and makes the past the object of an *Erinnerung* which, literally, integrates it in the actual reality of spirit as it is now, from the point of view of which the perspective of a possible future arises from an irrational "need to be" (*sollen*).

Returning, in his *Lectures on the History of Religion*, to the necessary reconciliation of spirit and reality, by resuming on this occasion the famous formula of the preface to the *Elements of the Philosophy of Right*, "to recognize reason as the rose in the cross of the present," Hegel refutes

the mythical conceptions of right by resituating its ideal in a lost origin
or in an anticipated Paradise, future, past or future but in any case
absent, whereas authentic thought applies only to what is present:

> This theory determines its ideal as past or future. It is necessary that it is posed
> and thus expresses the true in and for itself, but the mistake is precisely this
> determination of past or future. It makes of it something that is not present
> and thus immediately gives it a finite determination. That which is in and for
> itself is the infinite: however, once reflected, it finds itself for us in a state of
> finitude. Reflection rightly separates these two things; yet it has the drawback
> of being attached to abstraction and requires, however, that what is in and for
> itself must also appear in the world of external contingency. Reason assigns its
> sphere to chance, to free will, but knowing that in this world which is
> extremely confused in appearance truth is yet found. The ideal State is a sacred
> thing, but this State is not realized. If one represents the ideal State by its
> realization, the complications of right and politics, the circumstances as well
> as the multiplication of human needs that appear must all conform to the Idea.
> Here is found a ground which could not be adequate to the ideal but which
> must yet exist and in which the substantial Idea is nonetheless real and
> present. This present existence is only one side, and does not include the
> totality that belongs to the present. What determines the ideal can exist, but
> one has not yet recognized that the Idea is really present, because one only
> observes it with a finite consciousness. It is difficult to recognize reality
> through the husk of the substantial, and because one with difficulty finds the
> idea in reality, one places it in the past or in the future. It is a possible labour
> to recognize through this husk the kernel of reality—in order to pluck the rose
> in the cross of the present, it is necessary to take care of the cross.[3]

If there is a philosophy of history, it is because, according to Hegel,
reason is found "present" everywhere in history, and not only in any one
of its finite moments, improperly privileged in relation to all other
moments, and arbitrarily identified with its absolute culmination. In this
sense, for philosophy it is always the end of history, to the extent that in
all its moments without exception history must be reflected in a recursive
manner on the basis of its current state, so as to reveal the rational
conditions that render the latter necessary. And if Hegel pictures the
State as the completed form of objective Spirit, one must really understand that this form thereby never entirely coincides with the realization
of absolute Spirit, which arises from completely different conditions. The
State is eternal, precisely because the idea in it is never completely
identified with its circumstantial realizations but is irresistibly led to
"surpass" its realizations, the truth that inhabits it pushing it to seek
without ceasing, beyond the limits of a historical actuality, the conditions
of its fulfilment. Thus for both Hegel and Spinoza, if reason encounters
history, it is to the extent that reason is not exactly of the same order as
history and remains, in relation to its singular manifestations, in a
constant reserve. This is what allows one to say metaphorically that

reason "ruses" with history, for history is for reason only a chance instrument.

The Ruse of Reason

The study of this last theme will bring us back to the relationship between nature and reason as established by right. One might say that the method followed by Hegel is dialectical to the extent that it manages to reconcile these two terms by maintaining their contradiction to the end: reason is realized in right against nature, but at the same time it exploits the elements provided to it by nature in order to divert them from their own ends. "The passions realize themselves according to their natural determination, but they produce the edifice of human society, in which they have conferred on right and order power against themselves."[4] Does Spinoza mean anything else when he takes up in his turn the definition of the human being as a "social animal" (TP II/15)? Undeniably, this last formula means for Spinoza that right, founded in nature, is, if not of the same order, at least in continuity with nature: society after all being only the continuation of nature by other means. Yet for Hegel, if right rests on nature, it is to the extent that right is also at odds with nature, and this is indeed what the metaphor of the ruse means, which implicitly refers to a negativity, reference to which one would search for in vain in Spinoza's text.

For Hegel the genesis of right rests on the development of a contradiction which in the last instance amounts to the contradiction of the singular and the universal. In their empirical behaviour, human beings are led by the search for what satisfies their particular interest, and at the same time their actions must be inscribed within the framework defined by law, which on the contrary poses the preeminence of the common general good. In order for reason to be realized objectively in the world of right, it must take up this contradiction again on its own account and develop this contradiction to its end: that is, it must be integrated into the relation spontaneously established among human beings, through the free play of what they believe to be their interests, so as to control this relation and direct it; everything happens then as if reason manipulated human passions as a material so as to bend them to its own ends.

Now this reversal is only possible because reason introduces, or reveals, mediations between the extreme terms it reconciles. Within the context of universal history, these mediations are peoples, who simultaneously participate in the singular, through the specific characteristics that differentiate them among themselves, and in the universal, through the common spirit they elaborate, and which authorizes them, when the moment has come for each of them, to claim the function of representing the universal Spirit in the theatre of history. In fact, for Hegel history is like a stage on which reason is embodied in its cast, its peoples, who enter and exit this stage according to the requirements of their roles. If peoples are the true "actors" of history, it is precisely by reason of the intermediate situation they occupy between nature and reason, whose synthesis they bring about: the life of a people being precisely nothing other than the development of this contradiction, a fruitful development, since it carries in itself the promise of a supersession, in anticipation of the moment when another people will take over in the fulfilment of the same mission, which is to realize the state of right and to rationalize of human relations.

This means that for Hegel the matter of history is given in the existence of peoples and not of individuals; or rather, the existence of individuals is only involved to the extent that it is already informed by the collective cultural configuration inside which it is inscribed and which necessarily preexists it. This is why Hegel does not give right an anthropological foundation any more than he develops a humanist vision of history. In fact, he thinks that, considered in its objective movement, history does not enter into a direct relationship with the existence of individuals, and thus cannot be explained on the basis of individuals. If history is possible, it is because it labours, not on human beings themselves, considered in their singular individualities, but on already constituted human relations, which it progressively transforms, by playing on their internal conflicts, so as to confer on them the rational structure of the State. This point is essential, for it allows one to understand why Hegel is radically opposed to the tradition arising from Rousseau. Hegel attributes to Rousseau exactly the opposite conception to his own, one that attempts to deduce the spirit of right, defined, wrongly in Hegel's view, as "general will," on the basis of arbitrary decisions of individuals, whereas these decisions considered as such are only capable of a formal unification. Hegel's fundamental reproach to social contract theories is that they substitute an irrational psychological foundation for the rational juridical foundation of the State.

One can legitimately ask where Spinoza himself stands in this last discussion, when he attempts to deduce the forms of social organization on the basis of human nature: does he try to reduce the juridical to the anthropological, or else does he rely on a conception of nature whose presuppositions on the contrary invalidate, in its principle, such a reduction? We have already begun to respond to this question in attempting to disengage the original characteristics of the concept of individuality as it is used by Spinoza. To the extent that the individual is "part of nature" (*pars naturae*), there is no individual existence in itself whose limits are established and defined once and for all, but only individualized totalities which are formed and attenuated inside larger totalities by which they are in fact determined.

Now this reasoning, which applies first to singular human beings, also applies to peoples: the Spinozist conception of history seems not to recognize a privileged status in the existence of peoples—with the exception perhaps of the Hebrews: but aren't the latter instead, through their dream of election, a kind of anti-people?—and in any case it cannot recognize in peoples a necessary function of mediation between the singular and the universal. To the contrary, it claims to explain directly the relative forms of organization established by right on the basis of human nature as it is embodied immediately in individual affects. If one can speak of a ruse of reason in Spinoza, one must refer precisely to this method, which consists in finding, behind all collective motivations and behaviours, the necessary, because strictly causal, determination of the passions, the latter expressing the power of nature in the human being, in all human beings, whatever their historical situation, since these passions themselves do not appear to have a history. But neither is the nature that acts in a human being his nature, in the sense of its belonging exclusively to him and artificially detaching him from all other beings, human or not, to which he is on the contrary objectively connected by the fact that he belongs to the same nature as they.

When Spinoza speaks of human beings as social animals, he is not at all trying to assert a primacy of the anthropological over the political, because he is relying on a concept of human nature that prohibits thinking of such a primacy. What is "natural" in human beings? Spinoza tirelessly repeats that it is their affects, in so far as the affects are spontaneously at play and lead human beings without their even being conscious of it. These affects are the same, and are submitted to the same laws, whether they are related to individuals, according to the *jus naturae*, or to the collective relations they bind together inside social organization, acording to the *jus civile*: it is precisely the identity of these affects that grounds the necessity of right, according to an objective natural order which is not reducible to any artificial convention. But what is it based on, this community of affects that conditions the social life of human beings? On the very nature of these affects, which immediately appears as a common—and one might say communal—nature. On this point, it is not essential to refer to the detail of the demonstrations that interconnect the third part of the *Ethics*: it suffices to refer to the brief summary of them that Spinoza himself presents at the beginning of the *Political Treatise*, for, despite its schematic nature, it draws out quite clearly its essential spirit.

The peculiarity of human desires is that they do not develop on the basis of the singular self-relation of the individual considered as an autonomous entity, as a "subject," for the good reason that this relation is illusory and has no reality from the standpoint of nature. Instead, human desires are immediately constituted on the basis of a relation to others that provides human nature with the objective context of its development. Not only are human beings subject to a certain number of elementary passions, which make them envision for themselves a mode of life adapted to their aspirations, to the extent of their fears and hopes, but they are simultaneously driven to "desire" (*appetere*) that other human beings also live according to their own idea: whence the spirit of competition and the conflicts that, for human beings, necessarily coincide with the free realization of their desires, that is, with the manifestation, the expression of the power in each of them, in so far as they are "parts of nature."

In this sense, according to Spinoza, one can speak of a kind of spontaneous socialization of human affects, which ensures that individuals exist and become conscious of themselves only on the previously constituted basis of the reciprocal relations established between them and others, and which right away makes them communicate. The fact that these relations are imaginary in no way alters their characteristic of necessity, which is on the contrary reinforced by the fact that they are submitted to rather than wanted by virtue of a rational decision.

This relational theory of affects presents "desire" (*appetitus*), in so far as it directly derives from the natural tendency of the individual to persevere in its being (the *conatus*), as naturally having the form of desire of the other, in the two senses this expression can have. Which could be said as follows: there is not first my desire, and on the other hand the desire that the other can himself have, from which there next results their confrontation; rather, the other finds himself immediately implicated in the structure of my own desire, which is thus simultaneously mine and his, because it is in fact not the property of any particular subject, and which would remain enclosed within the limits that fix its particularity to it. For this reason Spinoza's doctrine does not at all enter into the framework of what have been called the doctrines of possessive individualism: for, according to Spinoza, the individual cannot want for himself without by the same token also wanting for others. Hence, his acts are inscribed inside a network of preestablished relations, which necessarily ties him to other human beings. These relations constitute the horizon of his subjection, inside which he must indeed find the conditions of his liberation. Thus, to act on his own idea (*ex suo ingenio*), by following inclinations which are completely governed by this system of imaginary relations, whence result all the conflicts of human beings, is not to be free, but on the contrary is to expose oneself to assume all the weight of constraint that results from the causal chain of affects and transforms the fact of living according to one's own right (*esse sui juris*) into that of being subjected—one could just as easily say alienated—to the right of the other (*esse alterius juris*). Now all this inevitably makes one think of the dialectic of *Anerkennung* that Hegel put at the basis of the relation between consciousnesses in his *Phenomenology of Spirit* (chapter 4).

This analysis is crucial, because it establishes the fundamental continuity of nature and right. Not only do human beings, from the fact that they are subjected to a right which is no longer that of nature but already also that of society, not take leave of human nature to adopt an entirely different one (TP IV/4), but one can say that the immediate forms of their existence, to the extent that they are completely determined by the laws of nature, are right away marked by right, or, if one may put it this way, in power of right, to the extent that, as we have just seen, they take place within the system of imaginary relations that spontaneously create a kind of natural society among individuals, even if this society takes the form of a savage society, a society torn by the blind conflict of the passions. This is why to enter into society, according to Spinoza, is never to abandon the state of nature once and for all, because in the last instance it is in the state of nature that are given the elements or materials on the basis of which the social life of human beings is constituted.

On this point, Spinoza remains as far removed from Rousseau's theoretical positions as from Hobbes's. Rousseau criticizes Hobbes by reproaching him for having, without even giving an account of it, projected inside his description of the state of nature the conditions of life in society which take the form of permanent competition between individuals; and so, on his side, Rousseau defines the human being in the state of nature as being completely alone and idle. But having carried out this critique, Rousseau is completely in agreement with Hobbes in maintaining a radical discontinuity between the state of nature and the state of society. He only reproaches Hobbes for having blunted the edge of this discontinuity: he himself interprets this break as the passage from a solitary to a collective mode of life, whereas Hobbes represents it through the conversion of an instinctual and conflictual sociability, practically unlivable, into a rational state, based on the calculation of interests, and supposing a strict control, indeed the bracketing, of the natural passions. Thus, despite the quite considerable divergences opposing them, Hobbes and Rousseau nonetheless agree in admitting that the social human being is not the same as the natural human being. Yet it is precisely on this point that Spinoza adopts a different position: according to Spinoza, the human being does not change nature from the fact that he lives in society; fundamentally the same causes direct his behaviour in the state of nature and in the state of society, which two it is impossible in any case to separate radically.

Having reached this point, we see that the formula "the human being is a social animal" is enriched with new meaning. It means that human beings are naturally plunged into right, which is thus not the result of an artificial construction, produced on the basis of a voluntary engagement or a rational calculation, as all contractarian doctrines represent it. One understands, then, how, in the *Political Treatise*, Spinoza ceased to refer to a social pact. When he writes that "human beings are not born but become civil" (*homines civiles non nascuntur sed fiunt*) (TP V/2), it is precisely so as to assert that human beings are fashioned by the right imposed on them, exactly in the same way that Hegel shows all the representations of individual consciousness as being immediately informed by a cultural conditioning objectively embodied in the spirit of a time, and which determines their entire historical existence. Thus, one could say, no one can leap over the right of their time: for Spinoza this means that the attempt to escape the state of society and to live in solitude is futile, because no human being, whether free or enslaved, can like or seek solitude. "But since all human beings fear solitude, because no isolated individual has enough power to defend himself and procure the necessaries of life, they desire the civil state by nature [*statum civilem natura appetere*], and can never dissolve it entirely." (TP VI/1) As has been said, one does not really escape nature in order to live in society. Reciprocally, one never entirely leaves society in order to return to nature, because the very nature of human beings, as it plays across the free chain of their affects, spontaneously inclines them toward one another, or, if one may put it this way, inclines them to one another, without ever being able to free themselves from this inclination, which is not reducible to a simple representation of their consciousness but is inscribed within the system of nature. If it is possible, according to Spinoza, to speak of a political naturalism, rather than an effort to relate politics to the natural, as a superstructure to an infrastructure, there is, on the contrary, an attempt to think both at the same level as two simultaneous and interconnected determinations, which inextricably connect their effects inside the network of the collective relations that tend to bring together all individuals inside nature defined in its totality. If the political order depends on the conditions of a nature, this is also because the order of nature is, in the most general sense, political.

Here again, one sees the positions of Spinoza and Hegel connected through the very divergence that sets them apart. No doubt one relates right to nature and the other to spirit; but in both cases it is in order to confer the maximum of objectivity and necessity on right, without thereby granting right an absolute nature, detached from its historical conditions of possibility. What does it mean to say that right is an objective and necessary system? It means that right is not reducible to the subjective intentions and decisions of individuals, who on the contrary are themselves formed only on the basis of right and within the preestablished framework that right imposes on them. It also means that the rationality of right is not reducible to the fact that human beings subordinate their behaviour to the instructions of reason, which either depends on the existence of right itself, since one no longer thinks freely in a well-ordered society, or else arises from entirely different conditions, since the problems of absolute Spirit must not be confused with the problems of objective Spirit, even if they can no longer be completely separated.

On this point, on the basis of premisses that appear fundamentally different, Spinoza and Hegel reach conclusions that seem quite close—a judgement confirmed by the fact that they are identically opposed to contractarian theories of right. For both, reason must ruse with right, that is, reason simultaneously uses right as an instrument in its struggle to secure the conditions of an authentically free life and also takes right as it already is so as to readjust its functioning, so that their respective interests may be brought into agreement and human existence may quite simply become livable. Yet this process depends neither on intentions nor even on the acts of any individual, or group of individuals, who by themselves or for themselves would decide what is good for everyone else, and who by the same token, without even managing to suppress right, would only bring right back to the conditions of its native irrationality. Spinoza and Hegel agree, then, on this fundamental point: right is a process without a subject.

Notes

1. Hegel 1991, 22.
2. Comte 1975, 54.
3. Hegel 1965a, XV, 293.
4. Hegel 1965b, 107.

V
Appendix (1964)

Georges Canguilhem's Philosophy of Science: Epistemology and History of Science

Presentation by Louis Althusser

The article you are about to read provides the first systematic overview of the works of Georges Canguilhem. The name of this philosopher and historian of the Sciences, Director of the *Institut de l'Histoire des Sciences* of the University of Paris, is well known to all those who, in philosophy and in the sciences, are interested in *new* research in the field of Epistemology and the History of Science. Canguilhem's name and work will soon know a much larger audience. It is fitting that the journal founded by Langevin should receive the first serious study that has been devoted to him in France.[1]

Epistemology (or philosophy of science), History of Science. These disciplines are not new. Why speak of *new* research, and what *radical* novelty is to be expected from a way of thinking which already has a very long past and a considerable number of works to its credit? Isn't every scientist interested, being naturally a little curious, in the *history* of his science; doesn't every scientist present, even in a simple form, certain fundamental questions about the *raison d'être* of the problems, concepts and methods of his science, philosophical (epistemological) questions about his own science? Don't there exist some excellent, quite erudite, works on the history of each science, and, for example, haven't the mathematicians themselves who, under the collective name of Bourbaki,[2] have signed the greatest mathematical work of the last twenty years, been careful to provide, in all their works, an *historical* note prior to the treatment of all problems? Regarding the philosophy of science, it arises at the origins of philosophy: from Plato to Husserl and Lenin (in *Materialism and Empirio-criticism*), by way of Cartesian philosophy, eighteenth-century rationalist philosophy, Kant, Hegel and Marx, the philosophy of science is much more than one part of philosophy among others: it is philosophy's *essential* part, to the extent that, at least since

Descartes, science, the existing sciences (mathematics with Descartes, then physics in the eighteenth century, then biology and history in the nineteenth, and since then mathematics, physics, mathematical logic and history) serve as a *guide* and a *model* for every philosophical reflection. Marxist-Leninist philosophy has taken in the best of this heritage: it requires a theory of the history of science and an epistemology referring to one another in a profound unity.

It is precisely this *unity* which today constitutes a problem and difficulty. Very rare are the works, either of the history of science, or of epistemology, which offer us this *unity*. Usually, the historian tells the "history" of a science by recounting the succession of discoveries or, better, the succession of theories, in order to show their progress, to enable us to see how every theory responds to the insoluble problems of the previous theory, etc. The implication is that the progress or "History" of a science depends either on the accidents of the discoveries or on the necessity of the responses to be given to the questions that previously remained without response. The historians of science thereby indicate to us that from the *History* about which they speak they fashion for themselves a certain (rarely stated, but real) idea, which is: either the idea of a *contingent* History (a succession of inspired accidents: discoveries); or the idea of a *logical* History, I mean moved by the *logic* that wants every science to progress by *responding* to the *questions* that have remained without response in the previous state of the science—as if on the contrary the real progress of a science did not occur quite often by *rejecting* the *questions* that remained in suspense, and by posing *entirely different* questions. The two conceptions of history just designated (contingent, logical) are idealist conceptions. It is in the eighteenth century, in the Encyclopedists d'Alembert, Diderot, Condorcet, and their disciples, that are found the purest examples of these conceptions, which are today still generally accepted.

At the foundation of the most widespread sciences are too often only simple scientific—or on the contrary (idealist) philosophical—chronicles of History, seeking in the development of the sciences the means to justify, by their "example," the ideological "values" carried by these philosophies. Similarly, quite often the essential feature of all modern (idealist) critical rationalist philosophy since Descartes, which concentrates all of philosophy on the sciences, is only the justification, in the example of the structure and the problems of a science, of the ideological theses that every idealist philosophy defends and proposes.

For some years, under the effect of a specific theoretical conjuncture (an encounter of theoretical questions posed, on the basis of real scientific problems and different but relatively convergent problematics: those of Marx–Lenin, Husserl, Hegel—indeed, paradoxically but really for those who know those "ruses" of history, of Nietzsche—without forgetting everything that proves valuable today in the linguistic model), the old conception as much of the history of science as of the philosophy of science (Epistemology) has been called into question. Some *new* paths have been opened, in epistemology by Cavaillès, Bachelard and Vuillemin, and in the History of Science by Canguilhem and Foucault.

The first novelty of these inquiries concerns this elementary—but hitherto often neglected—theoretical requirement: a scrupulous respect for the reality of real science. The new epistemologists are similar to ethnologists, who go "into the field": they want to see science up-close, and refuse to speak about what they are ignorant of, or about what they know only at second or third hand (unhappily, this was the case with Brunschvicg) or perceive from outside, that is, from afar. This simple requirement of honesty and scientific knowledge vis-à-vis the reality about which one speaks has overturned the problems of classical epistemology. The modern epistemologists have quite simply discovered that *things do not happen in science* as one used to believe, and in particular as too many philosophers used to believe.

The second novelty of these inquiries concerns this other elementary requirement: that it is impossible by right to take a simple chronicle, or a philosophy of history (that is, an ideological conception of history, of the progress of history, of the progress of Reason, etc.), for *History*. Here again the new historians of history have gone into the field. They have studied in detail, at the cost of an enormous labour of research (for they had to use properly *unknown* documents, those which their predecessors had refused to use, because they did not support their proofs ... those which had been buried in official oblivion, because they contradicted the official truths), the very reality of real history. And they, too, have discovered that in history *things no longer happen as one used to believe*. In his time, Marx had the same experience with what everyone nonetheless regarded as the most "scientific" part of history: English political economy—and of course with the ideological conceptions of History, of the "motor" of history and of the respective role of the economy, of politics and ideas. The new historians of science, who are sometimes far from calling themselves Marxists (Canguilhem knows Marx very well, but in his work he invokes quite different masters—from Comte[3] to Cavaillès and Bachelard), have had the same experience in their research work. They are beginning to offer us their results.

Some important results: which are quite simply in the process of overturning the old traditional, empiricist, positivist, idealist conceptions of epistemology and History.

The first result: the distinction between the reality of real scientific labour and its spontaneously "positivist" interpretation (this word must be understood in its ideological sense, which is fairly distinct from the term *positivism* by which Comte baptized his idealist conception of human history and the history of science). Science no longer appears as the simple established fact of a *truth*, which is naked and given, which one supposedly *discovers* or reveals, but as the production (having a history) of knowledges, a production dominated by the complex elements of which the theories, concepts, methods, and multiple internal relations organically connect these different elements. To recognize the real labour of a science presupposes the knowledge of this entire complex organic totality.

The second result: this knowledge presupposes another knowledge: that of the real becoming, of the history of this organic totality of theory-concepts-methods and of its results (acquisitions, scientific discoveries) which come to be integrated into the totality by modifying its figure or structure. History, the genuine history of science, thereby appears as inseparable from every epistemology, as its essential condition. But the history these researchers discover is also a new history, which no longer has the appearance of the previous idealist philosophies of history, which above all abandons the old idealist schema of a *continuous* mechanistic (cumulative: d'Alembert, Diderot, Condorcet, etc.) or dialectical (Hegel, Husserl, Brunschvicg) progress, without breaks, paradoxes, setbacks or leaps forward. A new history appears: that of the becoming of Reason which is scientific but stripped of this reassuring idealist simplicity which, just as kindness is never forgotten but always finds its reward, ensured that a scientific question never remains without a response but always finds *its* response. Reality has a little more imagination: there are imaginary responses which leave the real problem they evade without a true response; there are sciences which are called sciences and are only the scientific imposture of a social ideology; there are non-scientific ideologies which, in paradoxical encounters, give birth to true discoveries—just as one sees fire leap from the impact of foreign bodies. The entire complex reality of history, in all its determinations—economic, social, ideological—thereby enters into play in the intelligence of scientific history itself. Bachelard's, Canguilhem's and Foucault's *oeuvre* offers proof of it.

The most serious error to commit in the face of these sometimes quite surprising results (thus Canguilhem has *demonstrated* that the theory of the reflex was born historically at the heart of the *vitalist* ideology and not, as everyone used to believe, for the needs of the [good?] cause, in the heart of the *mechanistic* ideology of the seventeenth century) would be to believe that these results throw us into a variety of *irrationalism*. This would be a minor error of judgement, but its consequences would be heavy. In truth, this new epistemology and the new history of science that is its basis are the scientific form of a truly *rational* conception of their object. Whether rationalism could have been idealist, whether it could also have known, in its old elected domain, a mutation which carries it to the shores of materialism and the dialectic, it is certainly not Marxism which should be amazed or disturbed by it. Lenin had, in some texts which are on everyone's lips, announced it half a century ago.

Louis Althusser

*   *   *

The history of a science could not be a simple collection of biographies, and still less a chronological table . . .[4]

We must cure the history of science of such impatience, such a desire to render the moments of time transparent for one another. A well-done history, whatever its topic, is one that succeeds in making sensible the opacity and the thickness of time . . .

. . . Here is the really historical element of an inquiry, to the extent that history, without being miraculous or gratuitous, is entirely different from logic, which is capable of explaining an event that has occurred but incapable of deducing it before its moment of existence.[5]

Georges Canguilhem's epistemological and historical work is striking first of all because of its specialization.[6]

The reflection in it is so rigorously and so continuously related to precise objects that one must finally wonder about the status of a research so concrete and *focused*: for it is not only erudite but contains a general teaching; it has not only a function of knowledge of the details, it has the import of *truth*. Whence the following paradox: what is in question throughout a series of studies which seem to owe their consistency only to their objects, among which, however, is manifest an astonishing convergence? An initial inventory puts us in the presence of a radical diversity. First of all, a diversity of subjects: illness, environment, reflex, monsters, functions of the thyroid gland. Next, a diversity of themes: within each work and each article, one encounters a multiplicity of levels, to the point that it seems possible to make several readings of them at once, in order to seek and find in them a theory of science, a theory of the history of the sciences, and finally the history of the sciences itself and of techniques, in the reality of its pathways. And all of this without one level ever being substituted, as its pretext, for another: one does not find, *regarding* the reflex, or the thyroid, used as illustrations, a reflection on the history of the sciences. The different lines that one can isolate necessarily go hand in hand; and it is this *unity* that must be thought, since the relation of the different levels designates the consistency between a reflection, its objects, and its methods.

But how should this *unity* be approached? At the beginning two ways are possible: one can seek either a *common* content or a common problematic, a common object or a common question. And it is alongside the object that one is naturally drawn: because every reflection on science, whether it be historical or essential, seems to derive the coherence of its existence from the presence *in fact* of a constituted science. But if science is indeed the object sought after, one must know how to define this object: one is then referred directly to a theory of science, to the problem of the existence by right of science, of its legality, a problem that must be resolved within science itself, that is, within an epistemology. However, this problem presupposes another problem: for it is the existence *in fact* of science that poses the *question of right*, a question no longer internal to the development of science, but a different question, posed to science and no longer posed by science. One is thus led back from the problematic of the object to the problematic of the question: this is to say that one is going to describe the scientific phenomenon as an *attitude*, as *taking a position* inside a debate. And it is because science does not completely determine the conditions of this debate, because it does not entirely carry it out, remaining only *a part* in the process, that it is also possible to interrogate it from *outside*. It is because science is *the taking of a position* that it is possible, *reciprocally, to take a position in relation to science*.

In fact, in Canguilhem's books one is dealing with an essentially *polemical* work, not restricted to the description of its object, but haunted by the problematic of an evaluation, which is applied less to the *results* than to the formulation of a certain question: *what does science want?* To the extent that science, in the detail of its advent, in its discursive reality, elaborates an attitude, the forms of a problematic, to this very extent the reflection regarding science is itself the search for an attitude, the formulation of a question. In order to account for a history of science, it will thus not be a question of making the description of a description; in addition, it is only a certain *ideological parti pris* of science towards itself that leads science to be only the description of a universe of *objects*, a *parti pris* that must also be judged. Every philosophy of science consists, then, in asking a question about a question. It will not be necessary to stop at the inventory of a certain number of discoveries, but to pose for oneself at each moment, through the rigorous description of the event that constitutes their appearance, the main question of their *meaning*, of their *raison d'être*. Or again, and this vocabulary will be clarified in what follows: one will not advance a *theory about theories*, which would be only to take note of a certain number of results, but one will carry out a conceptualization about concepts, which is the very effort to account for a movement, a process, by reaching the question that clarifies it as an origin.

Such a procedure is traditionally tied to a determinate mode of investigation: *historical* exposition. Through the diversity of subjects and points of view, the object or question is never given except within the discursivity of a succession, of an unfolding. It seems, from the beginning, that phenomena take on only the meaning that is reflected in their history.[7]

Unfolding, history—these are still only names, too general and even ambiguous: whoever says unfolding seems to say development, hence, the progressive appearance of what could be enveloped in the origin as in a seed. Instead of the word "progress," affected by historical value judgements, one could settle provisionally for the word "process," without being afraid to give the word its double meaning.[8] This hesitation regarding the *word* is not arbitrary: it responds to the necessity of *naming* a *paradoxical* form. In fact, historical exposition never proceeds by itself in Canguilhem: it is rarely presented in an immediate order (chronological succession which would wind up confusing the history of the sciences with the history of a continual success); it is most often transcribed in a very elaborate way, often even more *unsuspected* than the exact opposite of its natural order. The most striking example of it is the article "Milieu" in *La connaissance de la vie* (we start from Newton in order to go on to the twentieth century; from there we are led back to Antiquity, and there resume the historical order, up to Newton); in the chapter on Comte, from the *Normal and the Pathological*, beginning with Comte, we go on to Broussais, then to Brown,[9] that is, a century back. Whether it is a question, then, of a reflexive history or a reversed history, one encounters a *paradoxical distortion of immediate succession*. Before we give the secret a meaning, this fact will first be a methodological index for us: this way of writing history suggests first of all a critical intention. The first point will be, then, to see how to criticize the ordinary way of writing the history of science.

A Critique of History as It Is Done

One will not elaborate on the historical "style" most widespread: the style of lists, censuses, inventories. One might easily demolish this style by attacking two of its determinations, which are absurdly contradictory but whose meeting is not ad hoc, since it shows the looseness of this style's intentions. As the dullness of assembled facts (but in such a context—that of a heap—the notion of scientific fact loses all its meaning), an account *in the form of a chronicle* gives the illusion that there is an accumulation of acquisitions. Here one finds only a pale line that no obstacle can ever darken, a line that canot regress or break. But, on the other hand, to the extent that this accumulation seems to proceed on its own, it implies the idea of an *accident*, instead of a *teleology* (which is still too strong a light). The narrative's line is simply the form given to a *radical discontinuity*: led one by one, the contributions that provide nothing, are aligned with nothing. This is a purely *contingent* history, which collects dates, biographies and anecdotes, but finally accounts for nothing, especially not the historical status of a constituted science.

Against so arbitrary a history, which is fundamentally only an indifferent history, it must be possible—it is necessary—to write an *interested* history. It is inside this requirement that the debate is going to begin: through the critique of a way of writing history, taken as a model, of which the *person in charge* seems the first one interested in writing a history of science—*the scientist*. One will see that the scientist has too great a stake in this operation, and that he lacks its goal. Iinstead of writing a history, he fashions legends, *his legend*, reorganizing the past by crushing its presence out of it, folding the historical element into the norms of his fundamental passion: the logic of *his* science, that is, of *current* science. What one wants to know is if it is possible to write another history which is careful to highlight a true meaning while respecting the *reality* of past events, a history that simultaneously reveals science as constitution and as discovery.

One will therefore start with the history of science as it is given in and by science. Its place is well defined inside scientific work: it is housed entirely in the introductory chapter, which is devoted to the "historical" aspect of the problem studied in the rest of the book.[10] The scientist has not so much accounts to render to history at the end of his process, as an *account to settle* with it, beforehand. Examples abound: the most striking one is that of Du Bois Reymond: the history he makes of the problem of the reflex, not in an introductory chapter but in an official discourse.[11] One sees in it fully what elements determine this *artificial* return to the past: a chronology full of holes, through which twine retrospective praises, not dispensed for nothing. This history is obviously FALSE; but what is more, *it is not even a history*. One can designate it by three of its essential features: it is analytic, regressive, and static.

Analytic: in a first sense, because it isolates a particular, and not the *historical*, line of a determinate problem (which presents other questions); it is content with a *partial* treatment of this problem. When Gley and Dastre fashion the history of the question of internal secretions, "both separate physiological experiences from the historical experiences of their establishment, cut them off and reconnect them to one another, calling on the clinic and pathology only to confirm observations or to verify the hypotheses of physiologists," whereas in this fragment of history, physiology has no primary role (it has a role "of exploitation and not foundation").[12] Narrowing the gap, the field inside which a particular problematic develops, one is prevented from understanding the logic proper to its movement.

But this is still only a first form of division: at base, one finds the will to divide the interior of history itself, by using criteria given by *the current state* of a science. The investigation of a past coincides, then, with a labour of decomposition: it is a question of retrospectively detecting pieces, germs of truth, and of extracting them from the margins of error. The invention of scientific discovery is therefore never what its conditions of appearance *made* it, but the pure appearance of what *should be*. If need be, one denounces the *missing* inventions, by reconstructing the true solution of a problem on the basis of its elements: this is what happens, for example, if one "reviews the knowledges of every species and of every origin in which it seems that J. Müller was able to find, in a unification of which he was certainly capable, the presentiments of what, sixty years later, regarding the thyroid, should be contained in an ordinary treatise of physiology."[13] Thus one *lacks* the object that must occupy the historian of sciences; there is this declaration by Müller in his *Handbuch*: "We don't know what the function of the thyroid is," not in a *confession* of ignorance, but with the will to say precisely *what he knows* which really governs the *content* of his ignorance. Scientific truths march past, *cut off from their real context*, which makes one simultaneously believe in the continuity of an illumination and in the persistence of an occultation: the bands of ignorance delay the march of knowledge; then one speaks of a "viscosity of progress."[14]

The truth of such a representation of history resides in the exact opposite of the description that one gives of it: *one shows the passage from the false to the true only provided one presupposes the true at the beginning*. One presupposes at the beginning, as unmentioned or unmentionable, a scientific *golden age*, in which the totality of science is read by right transparently, with no intervening necessity of a labour and a debate: an innocence of the true, after which history is only a fall, a rendering obscure, the chronicle of a futile struggle. The secret of this history is thus a purely mythical reflection, not for all that deprived of meaning, for the myth has a precise function: to project *the current state of science* into a beginning which renounces every temporality because it radically precedes it.

The exposition is *regressive*, since it reconstructs truths on the basis of the true (given in the present of science, reflected back into a mythical beginning). Rather than be exact, this history chooses to be reflexive. This point is important, for the other history, which Canguilhem writes and which will be built on the ruins of the latter, will also be *reflexive*: one will see that on the basis of the recursive method, another account of historical fact can be established. The regression of the history of scientists is specific, because it confuses its movement with the movement of analysis: retrospection is simultaneously *découpage*; the deployment of theories is in fact only a sudden appearance reconstructed on the basis of the final theory.

Finally, the exposition is *static*, because no duration is any longer possible for it: everything is played in the *present* of the theory that serves as a point of departure and point of reference. Once the décor (the current state of a theory) has been set up to deceive the eye, it is impossible to escape the theatre; and the intrigues played out there have all pretended to do so. Similarly, the beginning is only a mythical reflection, the time of this history is only the disguising of a logic. To borrow one of Canguilhem's images, the previous theories are only the *rehearsals* of the theory that has come last, in the *theatrical* sense of the word as in its ordinary sense of *recapitulation*.[15] Because at the beginning and at the end one must find the same thing; *between the two nothing happens*. Notions come and go, but it would not occur to anyone to ask about this parade: things only exist then because it has always been in their nature to exist, and one ends up speaking of "notions as old as the world."[16] Nothing appears, nothing is born, there is only the "development" of a transition.

One goes no further than the *presently constituted science*: history is only its inverse deployment, its mirror, its retrospective deduction. From such a perspective, it is impossible to speak of the *real formation* of a science, of a theory (but one will precisely see that it is not theories that are *"formed"*): preceding the final stage, there is only an *artificial prehistory* after which everything remains to be done. The most characteristic example of this *deformation* is given by the concept of reflex in its relations with Cartesianism.[17] Having become mature, the scientific concept of reflex allows a theory of involuntary movement to be established independently of every psychology of sensibility: it naturally seems to be inscribed within a context of *mechanistic inspiration*, and then nothing is more natural than to seek its origin in Descartes. In fact, in article 36 of the *Treatise on the Passions*, in the *Treatise on Man*, one indeed finds the *word*, or the shadow of the *word*, and an observation which corresponds to what one has since learned to designate as a reflex phenomenon. Yet an attentive study of Cartesian physiology shows first of all that he is concerned *with something other than a reflex phenomenon* in the texts used, and second, that the totality of Cartesian theory (conception of animal spirits, of the structure of the nerves, of the role of the heart) makes the formulation of the concept of the reflex *impossible*. One thus finds oneself in the presence *of a legend*, but a tenacious legend, truly constitutive and *symbolic* of a certain way of writing history, or rather of *rewriting* it. The example instead shows that it is a question of a historiography, of an oriented, apologetic science, and not always for reasons which pertain to science or theory: Du Bois Reymond only promotes Descartes in order to evade Prochaska, and if the professor from the University of Berlin erases the Czech scientist from history, *it is in order to affirm the nationalistic supremacy of a "strong" science over the science of a minority*.

Instead of a science which writes its own history, here one sees a scientist who writes his Memoirs (which happens by projecting his present into a past). But the example of the reflex is not only demonstrative, it makes us enter into the reasons for this deviation and allows its exact form to be described: for the *concept* of reflex, once completed, *seems* by full right to have its place in a mechanistic *theory*. However, one will have to see if this place is exclusive of every other place; instead, history according to the scientist transports the concept into another theory, in harmony with the first: the movement of this fictive history thus takes place between two theories, or even between two forms of the same theory. The concept is here only as a *mediation*, a screen for this operation of substitution; actually, one perceives that the concept is forgotten as such, to the point of being recognized *where it is not*. On the other hand, this historiography is not a pure phantasm, a simple phenomenon of projection; it rests on real data, which it uses or exploits as pretexts: above all it refers to certain protocols of observation judged as "sufficient"; the presence of the same *phenomenon* seems to suffice in order to confirm the permanence of the concept (for example: the palpebral reflex is seemingly found in the observations reproduced by Descartes; at least what has been later recognized as the palpebral reflex is actually observed and described by Descartes). The mechanism of deformation is thus the following: *one takes phenomena for concepts, and concepts for theories; from the beginning, there is an organized confusion of levels*. A true representation of history, on the contrary, must rigorously distinguish that which is related to the observation of phenomena, experimentation, the concept, and theory.

It is *the distinction between concept and theory* which remains the most difficult to define, because in appearance it doesn't correspond to *separate operations*. For the moment one can only provide still approximate determinations. A *concept* is a word plus its definition; a concept has a history; at one moment of this history, one says that it is formed: when it allows a protocol of observation to be established,[18] and when it passes into the practice of a society.[19] A *theory* consists in the general elaboration of what for the moment we shall call the applications of the concept. Whereas the path of real history *proceeds from the concept to the phenomenon through two closely interdependent mediations, experimentation and theory*, history as seen by scientists *is based on a hierarchical conception of levels, from observation to theory*, which simultaneously permits operations of substitution (phenomenon = concept = theory) and the conception of history as a *chain* of theories: one starts with theories—and one ends up at theories—that one links to one another because they constitute *the most finished element* of scientific practice. A typical idealist approach.

The idea of a chain implies dependence in relation to a logic, which is that of the lastest theory, since the lastest theory is the reason for all the other theories. Canguilhem substitutes *the filiation of concepts for the chain of theories*. In this way every *internal* criterion will be rejected which can only be given by a scientific theory. Canguilhem's goal is thus to give to the idea of a *history* of science all its value, by seeking to identify, behind the science that conceals its history, the real history that governs and constitutes science. It is thus a question of pursuing the history *external* to science itself, which is a way of stating that this history is in fact the passage from a "one does not know" to a "one knows." One will say again that this is the effort to think science in its real body, the concept, instead of in its ideal legality. A properly dialectical and materialist approach.

The Births and Adventures of Concepts

Before going any further into this subject, the orientation that has been proposed henceforth leads us to consider history as a succession of *real* events and not as the unfolding of *fictive* intrigues or as a dispersion of accidents. The research method will thus necessarily be empirical and critical: it is duty-bound to be open to every possibility of information, all the more as it is in the presence of an essentially distorted material. Thus, the formation of the concept must be retraced through a certain number of original, specific stages, whose observation is inspired more by a logic of biology than by a formal or philosophical logic. Every concept, then, has its own history, in which, however, one always finds two essential moments: the moment of *birth* and the one in which it receives its proper *consistency* (one no longer speaks of coherence, for all states of a concept rightly possess their own coherence). It is said then of the concept that it is *formed*: for the concept of reflex, one can say that this second stage was completed *in* 1800.[20] These two articulations are turning-points, reference points; they do not in any way constitute divisions or outcomes.

1) The theme of *birth* refers to a dual methodological requirement: concepts are not given from all eternity; the question of their *appearance* rightly precedes and thus contests that of their *prefiguration*. With birth, one also describes the appearance of a mode of thinking scientifically independent of every theoretical elaboration: theory can coincide, coexist with the concept, but theory does not determine the concept. Or again: in order to appear, a concept does not require a *predetermined theoretical background*; it turns out that the concept of reflex does not have its origin in the mechanistic context into which it was retrospectively transposed, but, with the work of Willis, it arises inside a doctrine of dynamist and vitalist inspiration. The birth of a concept is thus an *absolute commencement: the theories* which are its "consciousness" *only come after*, and several theoretical excrescences can be grafted onto the same concept. The indifference of a nascent concept to the theoretical context of this birth[21] gives the concept its first determination, which is the promise of a veritable history for it: *theoretical polyvalence*. The concept's adventure in part will be in its passage from one theoretical context to another.

The concept at its birth and the conditions of this birth must be described more precisely. As we have said, the concept begins by being only a word and its definition. A definition is what allows the concept to be *identified*: it specifies it among concepts and in so far as it is a concept. Inside the succession of levels we have already spoken about, a definition thus has a discriminatory value: "One cannot take as the equivalent of a notion either a general theory, as is the Cartesian explanation of involuntary movement, or, all the more, a reminder of observations many of which go back further than our author."[22] The scientistic conception of history, on the contrary, *eliminates the notion, or the concept, by confusing theory and observation.* But at the same time that the function that is characteristic of the concept is distinguished, the definition raises the concept above its immediate reality, valorizing the *language* by which it seems to be entirely constituted: from the word it forms a notion.[23] To discern the appearance of a notion is to bring science back to its first immediate material, *language*, without losing sight of the practical conditions of its fabrication, which enable one to know whether or not it is a question of simple *words*. Thus, one will be able to describe the invention of the concept by emphasizing its real *instruments*; and it is a question of something quite different from an intellectual psychology. These instruments are of two kinds, and they will have to be studied separately: language and the practical field.

First of all, *the practical field*: it intervenes at the level of experimentation, through the role actually driving the *techniques* that arise from sciences other than the one under construction; this role is determining without necessarily being directed. Even at the moment of observation, science can only be constituted if it is urged on by requirements it is incapable of finding in itself and which emphasize its crucial phenomena: in the history of physiology, this role is played by the clinic, through the mediation of pathology. The case of the functions of the thyroid is particularly demonstrative of this type of interference: "In this domain, physiology has been a tributary of pathology and of the clinic with respect to the significance of its first experimental results, and the clinic has been a tributary of theoretical or technical acquisitions of extramedical origin."[24] The study of these encounters is decisive: if its detail seems to arise most often from the anecdote, it is a question of the *illuminating, determinate anecdote*, since it allows the exact depth of a scientific field to be measured. This knowledge has a twofold value: the gap of the field can be appreciated as an *obstacle*, to the extent that, across it, two lines will have more difficulty encountering one another; but the depth of the field also announces a *fruitfulness*, to the extent that the lines will have the chance to intersect. One will see that, in what it unites and in what it separates, this gap allows one to account for almost all the *events* of a scientific history, which then cease to be obscure *accidents* in order to become intelligible *facts*.

Language is more than a means in the genesis of a scientific thought: it is the condition of its movement. Behind the concept, the word guarantees the transfers of meaning. It is the constituted presence of the same word that allows the passage of the concept from one domain to another. From a non-scientific domain to a scientific domain: the concept of *threshold* in a scientific psychology is borrowed from the philosophical theory of small perceptions; the concept of *tonus* in physiology comes from the Stoic theory of *pneuma*. But the transfer can also occur from one science to another: the concept of *intensity* (that one finds, after Leibniz, in the attempt at a *mathesis intensorum*) is displaced from the field of dynamics to the field of optics. The *word* itself can change at the same time as it displaces the concept, and this labour of language on itself perhaps precedes, in fact definitely aids, the mutation of meaning; an appendix to *La connaissance de la vie*, which, by staying at the level of the vocabulary, thus describes the passage from the fibrillar theory to the cellular theory, concludes:

> One sees in summary how a conjectural interpretation of the striated aspect of muscle fibre gradually led the holders of the fibrillar theory to use a terminology such that the substitution of one morphological unit for another, if it required a true intellectual conversion, was facilitated by the fact that it found much of its vocabulary of exposition already prepared: vesicle, cell.[25]

This plasticity of words, this almost "spontaneous" power they possess to move in order to welcome a new concept in advance, obviously finds its main reason in the image the concept conceals in itself only to expose it in the crucial moments of the history of ideas. The study of the *variations of language* leads, then, to a meditation about the function of the *imagination*. This function is ambiguous: a body prepared for all anticipation, the image is offered simultaneously as an obstacle and as a guide. As an obstacle: one finds here all the Bachelardian themes of the return to mythology; the recursive fiction is also a theoretical regression. This is why one can say that there are images as old as the world, *which is impossible regarding concepts*: the slope of reverie always brings one back to the same point, where history is halted.

The chapter on the "Inflamed Soul" in the *Formation du concept de réflexe* shows what this parade of pre-scientific figures can be, and poses a notion short of its real possibilities: as if the imagination had gone too far in their exploration, taking refuge in a familiar and always tempting image. However, such descriptions must not make us forget the power of *canvassing* that images hold. Willis forms the notion of the reflex within the framework of a *fantastic* doctrine. Invention appears as the will to follow his images to the end, to pursue as far as possible the logic of their dream: it is because Willis *thinks of life fully as light* that he had recourse, in order to describe movement, to *optical laws of reflection*, making between two domains the connection that Descartes had precisely *lacked*. To represent is no longer, then, to create illusion, or to remain at rest by returning to the mythical themes of an arrested reflection: the image receives its own consistency; it is no longer an evocation, seen from afar as a home base, but grasped at the beginning as a springboard for a genuine deduction.[26] The image has then become the correlate and condition of a definition.

One manages, then, to reveal a singular and especially precarious logic which is the logic of words. It is not a question of emphasizing this logic without qualification, of turning the life of language into the foundation of invention. But the history of science is not only the history of successful foundations. The reason of its movement is often, on the small scale of singular discoveries, only an unsuspected connection, or a curious flight. To return to these real conditions, which are not always flattering, to the moment of *invention*, is to give oneself the representation of a *rigorous* succession. The flight can be unhappy, the connection risky; these very difficulties are then "stimulants"[27] of invention, and this history is only the more determinate and more rational *for being missing*.[28] Chance, precisely because it is always resituated in the total field of its appearance, receives its entire function as reality: "If everything, in a sense, happens at random, that is, without premeditation, nothing happens by chance, that is, gratuitously."[29] The event is *identified*, in the very strong sense that poetry has sometimes given this word, as an *encounter*: this is what paradoxically, but not for the historian, eliminates its uncertainties. There are encounters which would happen in every way, which happen at several places at the same time, there are chains of encounters. The time of discovery is thus precisely *situated*. Against the illusion of a viscosity of progress, history marches, then, to its own real rhythm. This is what legitimates the decision to be attentive to opacity instead of transparency (the logic of science). To the decision of illuminating chance in the light of a circumstantial necessity responds the determination of a *production* in place of a *deduction*. The line of development is broken, but along this line one begins to be able to point out the "ages of knowledge."

This description of a formation essentially rests on a *problematic of the origin*: the origin is what specifies a concept from the beginning, individualizes it at its birth, independently of every relation to a theory. The origin appears as a choice which determines, *without containing it*, the particular history of the concept. The origin is thus not a neutral commencement, a degree zero of scientific practice. An unpublished course of Canguilhem's on the origins of scientific psychology (1960–61) relies on the distinction, etymologically established, between the concepts of *commencement* and *origin*: *origo-orior* means to start from, *cum-initiare* (a word of the *Basse Epoque*) means *on the contrary*: to enter into, to force a way. "It is when one ceases to be preoccupied with commencements that one discovers origins." Thus it is that these concepts do not describe two interpretations of the same moment but two historically different moments: scientific psychology *commences* in the nineteenth century, but it finds its origins in Locke and Leibniz. Thus the apprehension of the commencement and origin refers to two movements of exactly opposite appearance: *one starts from the commencement*, but *one arises at the origin*. It is this second *sense* that designates traditional recursive history, retrospective and apologetic history, as an *archaeology*, a reflexive determination of origins. Such a return does not establish for itself the goal of revealing an identity (= I interpret the concept of the reflex within a mechanistic context, and *in addition* it is indeed within the same context that it appears) but of a specificity. It is a question, inside the *inverted reflection* of history, of recognizing the true sense of a notion, not within a simple retrospective theoretical context but within *a real problematic*: "It is in the present that problems provoke reflection. And if reflection leads to a regression, the regression is necessarily related to it. Thus, the historical origin is really less important than the reflective origin."[30]

To rise to the origin of the concept is thus to bring out the permanence of a question, and to clarify its current meaning. For example, to seek the origins of the concept of norm, as Canguilhem does at the end of his book on *The Normal and the Pathological*, is to show how the idea of a physiology has been advanced on the basis of a pathology and through clinical necessities. One simultaneously determines, then, the meaning and the value of a discipline: its nature.

This approach still allows the distinction between concept and theory to be specified: a concept's continuous presence along every diachronic line that constitutes its history attests to the permanence of the same *problem*. *To define a concept is to formulate a problem*; the marking of an origin is also the identification of the problem. What is important, then, is to recognize through the succession of theories "that the problem itself persists at the heart of a solution presumably given to it."[31] Therefore, to accentuate the concept in order to write the history of a science, and to *distinguish* its particular line, is to refuse to consider the beginning of this history, and each of its stages, as a *germ* of truth, as an *element* of theory, only appreciable on the basis of the norms of the later theory; one refuses to fashion the reconstitution of imaginary premises, in order not to see, in what *initiates* in this history, only the fruitfulness of an attitude, or even the elaboration of a problem. If the concept is on the side of *questions*, theory is on the side of *responses*. To start with the concept is to choose to start with *questions* in order to write history.

The concept of *norm* offers a good example of this destitution of the theoretical level and of the privilege granted to the *opening* of a problematic. It is impossible to offer a scientific determination of the concept of norm: all attempts made in this direction (by the object of physiology, by the idea of the average . . .) escape the domain of science. These responses are attached to another level than the question: thus, the response to the "question" of Quêtelet's "average man" is given to him by God; they cannot serve, then, as a point of view on history, because they belong to *another* history as God's response shows clearly enough. It is impossible to reduce a concept to the theory that occasionally supports it, to illuminate it by the theory. Which does not mean it is impossible to define a concept, or that the question that inhabits it is meaningless; on the contrary, *it is a question in search of its meaning* and for this reason fundamentally implies a *history*. In this way the concept of norm possesses an eminently heuristic value: a norm is neither an object to be described nor a potential theory; thus, it can be used as a rule of research. "It seems to us that physiology has something better to do than seek to define the normal objectively,[32] and that is to recognize the originally normative character of life."[33]

To recognize the concept is to remain faithful to the question and to its nature as a question instead of seeking to *realize* it, hence, instead of having done with it without really having responded to it. This requirement is as important for the procedures of science as for the history of science, without their being reduced in this way to a common measurement or a point of view. "What matters to us is less to furnish a provisional solution than to show that a problem deserves to be posed."[34] It is in this way, astonishingly, that the formula that turns philosophy into "the science of resolved problems,"[35] in a sense that Brunschwicg never meant the expression to have, is retrieved: philosophy—and it must immediately be said, although this can only be made entirely clear in what follows, that philosophy is history—is *the science of problems* independent of their solution. It is the science that is not preoccupied with solutions, because in a certain way there are always solutions, the problems are always resolved at their level; *and the history of solutions is only a partial history*, an obscure history, and obscuring everything it touches, by giving the illusion that one can dissolve—and forget— problems. Passing behind the accumulation of theories and responses, history is really *in search of forgotten problems, up to their solutions*.

What distinguishes Canguilhem's 1943 *thèse de médecine* (on the Normal) from his other books is that it precisely does not carry this methodological requirement as far as they do, to the extent that, in numerous passages, it seems to offer the "solution": *life*. In Canguilhem's *oeuvre*, in which fidelity to the "spirit of vitalism" is regularly recalled, one could distinguish *two vitalisms*: the first, without a doubt, would contain the response to the question of physiology, and would establish it by the same occasion. It would contain this response, because, this vitalism is immediately criticized by the interpretation given of the spirit of vitalism, which confers on it a privileged place in relation to all possible theories: the place of being theoretical only in appearance, being basically only the preservation of a concept, *the will to perpetuate a problematic.* The response is then only a transposition of the question, and it is the means found in order to *conserve* it. "Animism or vitalism, that is, doctrines which respond to a question by lodging the question in the response."[36] There are two possible ways of conserving it: the one that takes the question for a response, which is paid with a word, and hastens to forget the question by tirelessly repeating the word. The other way, more secret and difficult, retrieves the question, rediscovers it, recognizes it, and admits vitalism against other theories *only because it is not a theory*; not because it critiques *them*, but because *in them* it criticizes theory (or rather its illusion), and thus restores to science, in this case physiology, both a history and a future.

One thus touches on one of the greatest difficulties in the labour of disengaging a concept: if the presence of the concept envelops the permanence of a question, it usually does so only in an *obscure* way, presenting the question as a response, dressing up the concept as a theory. Yet *the question is never forgotten*: transposed, it remains, and it is what in the last analysis is reflected by the one who *uses* the concept, even if he is ignorant of what he is reflecting.

In sum: to return to a concept is to exhibit *the original question*, and it is the meaning of the enterprise of an *archaeology*. To the extent that the question is not attached to its responses by a relation of necessity—a concept remaining independent of a theoretical context—history describes a veritable becoming which is determinate but *open*, being applied to restore its true mutations; and the latter can be spotted only through their relation to a birth which has value as a measurement only in that it is not the index of something immutable.

2) To constitute a concept's history after its birth is to account for a movement while one possesses the secret of its *consistency*, which is defined originally by a *polyvalence*. There will be no question, then, of a line which is reflexive in itself, but of a trajectory which only exists through its changes in meaning, its distortions. Only then is the theme of the origin demystified, for one has separated it from the representation of a golden age of truth, realized positively by simple projection, and negatively as the non-existence of an inconsistency. To escape the golden age is to accentuate what was really rejected in myth: the chaos of error.

One finds here the Bachelardian idea of the *epistemological value of the false*, which alone allows the *passage from non-knowledge to knowledge* to be expressed. As for the principle of method, one finds, then, the *decision to distinguish the problematic of true/not true from the problematic of knowledge/ non-knowledge, and to attach oneself exclusively to the second*. To use a Marxist vocabulary which isn't Canguilhem's, one will say that the first is an *ideological* problematic—and the scientist is actually engaged in the ideology of his science—in opposition to the second, which is a *scientific* problematic: one sees the epistemological revolution implied by this particular way of writing history. By the same token one recognizes the significance of *a teratology of concepts*, as a rigorous description of non-knowledge: for example, a retrospectively viable concept, because one knows how to appreciate its fruitfulness, can appear at the moment of its birth as *aberrant*; it doesn't rest on anything; it has not yet constituted its theoretical background. It is then that one can understand how the concept evolves for non-theoretical reasons, in particular by the *intervention of a practice which is non-scientific or governed on the basis of another science: the false then reveals itself to be most often only the non-codified interaction of two distant domains*; its truth is to be disproportion, but it then attains simultaneously the condition of appearance of a science.

The history that refuses to be translated in terms of a logic given at the start, independently of it, can occasionally find and think the *logic of the unanticipated*. Is there any need to specify it? This is a theory of historical rationality itself, and not an ideology of irrationality, or irrationalism.[37]

An Epistemology of History: Science and Philosophy

The encounter of history and its object has been indicated several times: it must now be *justified*. On the path of a history of biology is elaborated, not a biology of knowledge in the traditional sense of the word, that is, a mechanistic explanation of the process of production of knowledges, but a reflection on the knowledge of biology precisely illuminated by biology. There is a relationship between the method and content of the research, a homogeneity between the concepts that does not only derive from the necessity, for the historian, of passing where science has already passed. Through this relationship is indicated a thought which is perpetually reflected in its objects: immediately, the choice of these objects is profoundly significant; behind the apparent diversity of interests—it is from here that one began—there is revealed *a unity of structure*, a determinate aim. The project of treating the history of science in the field of biology is profoundly *consistent*: one understands the value of the precision that can be drawn from it.

The means of formulation for the method of science and for the observation of this method are not common but parallel, incessantly *borrowed* from one another. The language of history is full of theoretical resonances. Thus, at the limit it would be possible to transpose certain passages, however purely engaged by the movement of the scientific history they describe and, at the cost of slight transformations, to give them *another* significance, of a more general import: in a word, to make them reflect on themselves in order to make them express out loud the philosophy that speaks in them silently.

We will take as an example, in this regard, a passage from Canguilhem's article on Darwinian psychology. *What is said about Darwinian theory could also be said about the way we account for theories; what is said about a science could also be said about the history of science.* Contrary to custom, we put only the *modified* passages between quotation marks:

> In the genealogical tree of "science"—substituted for the linear series that proceeds from "truth to error"—ramifications mark stages and not outlines, and the stages are not the effects and the testimonies of a plastic power aiming beyond them; they are the causes and agents of a history with no anticipated resolution.
>
> Yet at the same time that "established science" ceases to be taken for the initial—and for certain "historians" inaccessible—promise of "ignorance," "ignorance" ceases to be taken for the permanent threat to "science," for the image of a risk of decline and fall present at the very heart of apotheosis. "Ignorance" is the memory of the prescientific state of "science," it is its "epistemological" prehistory and not its metaphysical anti-nature."[38]

Obviously, this is a game that one wouldn't have to push too far. And it would be tempting to say that there is here after all only an encounter of *words*, if one had not been prepared to attach so much importance to the means of the formulation of an idea, never to separate a meaning from the process of its figuration and formulation. The persistence of a *language*—there is no "epistemological intersection" in Canguilhem—is therefore significant: in fact, it leads us—and could serve only as an introduction—to a deeper connection. The article "Expérimentation" in *La connaissance de la vie* already shows how the methods of science can themselves be considered objects of science (in this precise case, of the same science), and even that they take on their true meaning only in this possible transposition into the world of objects: in biology experimentation receives a privileged value because an exerpiment about functions is itself a function. "This is because there is for us a kind of fundamental kinship between the notions of experiment and function. We learn our functions in experiments, and our functions are then formalized experiments."[39] The heuristic nature of experimentation in biology has to do, then, with its function of *reconstituting* the reality of functions: the history of experimentation could be the history of the constitution of a function. History is not, then, the simple *application* or superposition of a gaze upon an object; this gaze extends to another gaze, constitutes a harmonious series with it. One knows that in biology the object of knowledge agrees precisely with the subject of knowledge: independent of a parallelism or an adequation, there is elaborated a history *inscribed* within the movement of what it aims at.

Thus, the concepts of history, its epistemological means, are profoundly inspired by the "knowledge of life." One concept in particular seems capable of being transposed to the theory of history : the concept of the norm.[40] Such a transposition would bring together the following levels:

physiology/actual state of a science
pathology/teratology of concepts
clinic/insertion into a universe of technical instruments.

In the biological sense, which it is necessary to begin by giving in its most general terms, the presence of the norm implies the possibility of establishing a *margin of tolerance* enjoyed; it is therefore an essentially *dynamic* concept, which does not describe arrested forms but the conditions for the invention of new forms. The concept of the norm therefore contains the following question: how can one describe a movement, in the sense of adaptation to new conditions, of organized response to unanticipated conditions? The labour of the concept coincides with a refusal to *found* the representation of this movement on the metaphysical idea of power or of life as pure invention, as essential plasticity. On the contrary, the concept helps to resituate the question within a new context, to include it within another question, that of the relations of the living and the environment. Organic movements are themselves conditioned by a fundamental movement, which is the history of the environment. "Because the qualified living being lives in a world of qualified objects, it lives in a world of possible accidents. Nothing happens by chance, everything happens in the form of events. Here is how the environment is inconstant. Its inconstancy is simply its becoming, its history."[41] The living being is not related to a nature in exteriority, radically frozen, but to an environment inhabited by a history, which is also that of the organism to the extent that it contributes to constituting it. The fact that the environment *poses problems* for the organism within an order, in theory unpredictable, is expressed in the biological notion of *discussion*. This way of circumscribing the fundamental question of biology does not throw it back on an indeterminism—on the contrary. "Science explains experience but it does not for all that annul it."[42] One finds, then, as an experience of a rationality, the thematic of the unpredictable. Biology and its history agree on two concepts: *the question* and *the event*.

Now one might wonder, then, to pursue this philosophical reflection, what would be a history *systematically* constructed on the basis of the idea of the norm. It would meet three requirements.

First of all, *the representation of science as a discussion with a context* (see everything that has been said about the importance of the methodological notion of *field*: a technical field, an imaginary field, the interaction of scientific fields or of a scientific field with non-scientific fields, whether they be practical, technical, or ideological). It is only from the perspective of a *gap* that the movement of history can be justified (the passage from an "it isn't known" to an "it is known"). Likewise, the current state of a question receives all its meaning only from the possibility of a diachronic putting into perspective. As an illustration of this theme, one can propose a new transposition: "Hence we cannot clearly understand how the same man with the same organs feels normal or abnormal at different times in environments suited to man unless we understand how organic vitality flourishes in man in the form of technical plasticity and the desire to dominate the environment."[43] It suffices to replace "man" by "science," "with the same organs" by "with the same value of consistency," "organic vitality" by "search for a scientific rationality."

Secondly, *the refusal of a pure, speculative logic*. Movement cannot be described on the basis of the ideal presence of the true, but only on the basis of its real absence. Now the idea of the norm truly offers the means to describe this absence (it doesn't exist, it cannot be determined scientifically). Then one understands how the movement of scientific history is not reducible *to the elimination of the false but implies a resumption of error inside the movement itself*; likewise, illness is also a physiological term. "It is the abnormal which arouses theoretical interest in the normal."[44]

Thirdly, *the highlighting of a question of principle*: the question of the "value" of *science*. In the same way, physiology must be considered as an evaluation of the living being, a study of its requirements and its possibilities: on both sides, the main objective is in *the highlighting of questions*. But to this very extent, history, and the rational intelligence of the essence of "historicity," the essence characteristic of history, that is, philosophy, *is a question about the questions of science*. It is therefore externally situated in relation to it, *it poses to it* its own questions: "The history of science can be written only with leading ideas without relation to those of science. . . . It is therefore not astonishing to see the historical being of the reflex composed little by little as one has seen it to have been done, since it is non-scientific motives which lead to the sources of the history of science."[45] One sees that the harmony between the methods of history and what history describes has *a discontinuity* for a necessary correlate, which would then allow one to criticize the idea of a biology of knowledge in the strict sense after having used, as a philosophical guide, the very model of biology in order to attain the concept of a history of science.

Philosophy therefore asks the following: What does science want? Or rather: What does each science want? What philosophy reflects, and science practises without reflecting, is the *determination, the limitation of a domain*, hence, of a real essence. This domain is not given as a world of objects presented before the scientific gaze; it depends on the constitution of an objectivity:

> The characteristic unity of the concept of a science has traditionally been taken as deriving from the object of that science: the object has been thought of as

itself dictating the method to be used in the study of its properties. But in the last analysis this amounted to limiting science to the study of a given, to the exploration of a domain. When it became apparent that every science more or less gives itself its given, and thereby appropriates what is called its domain, the concept of a science began to place more emphasis on method than on object. Or, to be more precise, the expression "the object of the science" acquired a new meaning. The object of a science is no longer simply the specific field in which problems are to be resolved and obstacles removed, it is also the intentions and ambitions of the subject of the science, the specific project that informs a theoretical consciousness.[46]

It is only then that one possesses the meaning of the reflection on origins. The object of *The Normal and the Pathological* is finally revealed, in the final chapters, to be to show on what terrain physiology, "the spirit of nascent physiology," is correctly constituted (see the reference to Sigerist, regarding Harvey's *oeuvre*): a science of the conditions of health. Thus it is that a historical line is freed, studied on the basis of a central concept, which sketches an *appearance* instead of exploring an object. Thus, research recovers a recognized form by thematizing it: the history of a *scientific problem*. One comes to determine the subject instead of the object of physiology (see the conclusion of *The Normal and the Pathological*, 227–9).

After having characterized *conceptual origin* in this way, it is possible to study science as it exists in fact and to connect science to *its* determination: what science wants. It can happen that one detects a disproportion, a displacement, not between intentions and actions—a vocabulary which is psychological *only in appearance*, but which is really theoretical, and theoretical precisely as revealing the *theory of a real history*—but between the *real meaning*, as it is inscribed in history, *and its expressions*. The most illuminating case is that of *scientific psychology*, which at the moment that it has finished being born enters into decline; *it is then found that it does something other than what it intends, that it is at the service of interests other than its own*. It is applied to a domain which does not belong to it, but which has been given to it: man as tool. It is at this moment that the question of philosophy is put to science, which is only possible when philosophy has become profoundly what it is: *history* (thus it is that it knows origins). The question can then be posed very directly, all the more as one has taken as a point of departure, as a support, a history whose rules are external to the practice of science. Recall how Canguilhem's lecture "Qu'est-ce que la psychologie?" concludes:

> But equally, philosophy cannot be prevented from continuing to question the scientifically and technically ill-defined status of psychology. As it does so, philosophy conducts itself with its inherent naïveté (not at all the same as simple-mindedness, and not exclusive of a certain working cynicism) and thus goes back once again onto the side of the people and of the born non-specialists.

Thus it is with a degree of vulgarity that philosophy confronts psychology with the question "Tell me what you are up to and I'll know what you are." But once in a while, at least, the philosopher must be allowed to approach the psychologist as a counsellor and to say: if you leave the Sorbonne by the exit in the Rue Saint-Jacques, you can either turn up the hill or go down towards the river; if you go up, you will get to the Pantheon which is the resting place of a few great men, but if you go downhill then you're bound to end up at the *Préfecture de Police.*[47]

We could have considered another example: the article on scientific diffusion, which also concludes with a *warning*, whose possibility is found established in the rational epistemology of history. To the extent that the *means* enlisted to describe an object imply a conception of the object itself, so the conditions of a possible questioning of this object are created.

Instead of fashioning a theory of science, one must formulate *the concept of science*, or the concept of *each* science; and this concept is expressed nowhere else than in the history of its formulations. At the limit it can only with difficulty be *extracted* from it. This concept characterizes science as a function which must be rediscovered at each step, by following the backward path of an archaeology: this function cannot be described in itself, apart from its modalities of appearance. Far from giving a general idea of science, the concept *specifies* the notion of science. Thus, in a very Freudian sense, archaeology is the elucidation of a present specificity. It would be out of place to borrow from a different discipline—let us recall: there is no "epistemological intersection"—the term that characterizes this representation. One will therefore reject the word of psychoanalysis, taken up again, however, by Bachelard, in a sense that is further removed from its original sense than it would be here. But perhaps it is permissible to say that with Georges Canguilhem's *oeuvre* one possesses, in the very strong and non-specialized sense given by Freud to this word, that is, in the objective and rational sense, *the analysis of a history.*

Notes

1. Paul Langevin (1872–1946) was an important French physicist who participated in the Resistance and in 1940 was briefly imprisoned for his political activities. In 1939 Langevin, psychologist Henri Wallon, and the French Communist Party leader Georges Cogniot co-founded the Marxist theoretical journal *La Pensée*, the journal in which Althusser's introduction and Macherey's article appeared in 1964. (Trans.)
2. Nicolas Bourbaki is the pseudonym adopted by a group of mostly French mathematicians, centered at the École Normale Supérieure in Paris, who began to publish collectively and anonymously in the late 1930s. (Trans.)
3. Canguilhem would not disown this admirable text of Comte's:

"For not only have the various parts of each science been simultaneously developed under the influence of one another, while they must be separated in the dogmatic order—a fact which would tend to make us prefer the historic order, but the different sciences, as becomes more and more apparent, have mutually and simultaneously perfected one another, even the progress of the sciences and the arts has been interdependent, through innumerable mutual influences, and finally all have been linked to the general development of human society. This vast interdependence is so real that often in order to understand how a scientific theory came to be generated, one is led to consider the improvement of some art which has no rational link whatsoever with it; or even some social advance, without which the discovery could not have taken place. Thus the true history of any science, that is, the emergence of the discoveries of which it is composed, cannot be known except by the study of the history of humanity. That is why all the facts and proofs collected up till now on the history of mathematics, astronomy, medicine, etc., however valuable, can only be regarded as raw material." (Comte 1974, 50–1)

4. Canguilhem 1963c, 18.
5. Canguilhem 1958a, 78, 91.
6. To the two titles cited above should be added three books: *Essai sur quelques problèmes concernant le normal et le pathologique* (*thèse de médecine*, 1943); *La connaissance de la vie* (1952); *La formation du concept de réflexe aux XVIIe et XVIIIe siècles* (1955). Then, several articles, among which the most important are: "Note sur la situation faite à la philosophie biologique en France" (1947); "Qu'est-ce que la psychologie?" (1958b); "Sur une épistémologie concordataire" (1957); "L'histoire des sciences dans l'oeuvre épisté-mologique de Gaston Bachelard" (1963b); "L'homme et l'animal au point de vue psychologique selon Darwin" (1960); "Nécessité de la 'diffusion scientifique'" (1961); "Gaston Bachelard et les philosophes" (1963a); "Scientific change" (Symposium on the History of Science, Oxford, 1961); participation in an issue of *Thalès* on *L'histoire de l'idée d'évolution* (1962) and in the *Histoire générale des sciences* directed by René Taton.
7. See, for example, Canguilhem 1955, in which it is shown that epistemological problems always amount to historical problems. And also in Canguilhem (1952, 16–17): only history provides the meaning of an "experimental fact" (the laboratory version of muscular contraction); by way of Swammerdam, a demonstration set in its pedagogical presentation refers back as far as Galen.
8. *Procès* can mean both "process" and "trial." (Trans.)
9. John Brown (1735–1788), a Scottish physician. (Trans.)
10. One must insist, then, on the break with an old tradition represented by Kayser's treatise: its introduction is considered in its own right by a *historian of science* and not a physiologist.
11. Given to commemorate the death of Johannes Müller in 1858; cited in Canguilhem 1955, 139.
12. Canguilhem 1958a, 87.
13. Ibid., 78.
14. Ibid.
15. Canguilhem 1960, 85.
16. Canguilhem 1955, 148.
17. This is one of the central themes of Canguilhem 1955.
18. See Canguilhem 1955, 161: "In 1850 the concept of reflex was inscribed in books and the laboratory in the form of apparatuses of exploration and demonstration having arisen for it and which would not have existed without it. The reflex ceases to be only a concept in order to become a percept . . . ."
19. At the same as the hammer appears that detects the knee-jerk reflex, the word passes into current language: the diffusion of the concept coincides with its popularization. And at this moment another part of its history commences, which is less that of its deformation than the established fact of its growing inadaptation to what one wants to make it say: this is the beginning of its revision (the opposite of formation).
20. It then carries its complete definition, in which one can find, as in stratifications, the entire history that separates it from its birth. See Canguilhem 1955, 131: "A reflex movement (Willis) is one whose immediate cause is an antecedent sensation (Willis), the effect of which is determined by physical laws (Willis, Astruc, Unzer, Prochaska)—in conjunction with the instincts (Whytt, Prochaska)—by reflection (Willis, Astruc,

Unzer, Prochaska) in the spinal cord (Whytt, Prochaska, Legallois), with or or without concomitant consciousness (Prochaska)."

21. See Canguilhem 1963c, 18–20: "the problems themselves that are not born necessarily on the terrain in which they find their solution."

22. Canguilhem 1955, 41.

23. On the importance of the word and the analysis it must undergo in order to see if it really supports a concept, hence on the dual attitude towards the role of language (interest and warning), there are two quotations which complement one another: "Certainly, words are not the concepts that they carry, and one knows nothing more about the functions of the thyroid when one has, in a correct etymology, restored the meaning of a morphologist's comparison. But it is not indifferent to the history of physiology to know that when in 1905 Starling first launched the term *Hormone*, at W. Hardy's suggestion, it was after consultation with their colleague, a philologist at Cambridge, W. Vesey." (Canguilhem 1958a, 80) "The same words are not the same concepts. It is necessary to reconstruct the synthesis into which the concept is found inserted, that is, simultaneously the conceptual context and the guiding intention of experiences or observations." (Canguilhem 1963a)

24. Canguilhem 1958a, 78–9.

25. Canguilhem 1952, 215.

26. This movement can surpass its goal, leave behind the concept itself, by preferring the shadow it casts before it in the *élan* of a racing diffusion: see the late history of the reflex, its popularization, which ends by no longer retaining anything but the image of which it makes an abstraction.

27. See the chapter on experimentation in Canguilhem 1952.

28. See Canguilhem 1963c, 18–20: "it is only at this cost that one can situate according to their true value of significance the accidents that prohibit a peaceful development for every research, the obstacles to exploration, the crises of methods, the technical shortcomings, sometimes happily converted by way of success, into new unpremeditated beginnings."

29. Canguilhem 1958a, 85.

30. Canguilhem 1989, 63.

31. Ibid., 76.

32. I.e. as an object.

33. Canguilhem 1989, 178. (Translation modified.)

34. Ibid., 177.

35. See Canguilhem 1955.

36. Canguilhem 1963c, 16.

37. And this without being present, or only named, contains the intention of erecting a *model* for all history on the basis of the type of rationality thus revealed. A rigorous analysis can be rightfully considered *exemplary*: one is right to elicit its lessons. Canguilhem's *oeuvre* does not serve only to reflect on certain episodes in the history of physiology. But this would be to take it in the opposite way—and not only excessive— that of representing it as multipliable to infinity, that is, to believe that one can *transpose it as such* to other domains: the transposition, or so to speak the usage, of a theoretical *result* obeys rules of a very precise variation, of an intentional manipulation. In other words, it would be necessary, before going on to explain a method, *to reflect on what it is to apply it*: method does not carry, in the adventure of its formation, the rules of its value; this is precisely what Canguilhem teaches us about *a particular case*. It is necessary, then, to *commence by describing the precise nature of a method*: this is what we are doing here, then, in another moment, to study *the conditions of its transfer*, which implies a knowledge, if not complete then at least coherent (possessing its own *coherence*), of the terrain of its transplantation. The method one starts with *helps* to formulate this recognition, but it does not suffice to abolish the gap in principle between two domains. There is not enough time to develop this point. However, it must be pointed out that most epistemologists *reflect on an object they privilege, without saying so, or even without reflecting on this privilege*; and those who read and use them act as if they had carried out this labour of reflection, and then generalize descriptions which perhaps owe their rigour and their value only to their profoundly *adapted* nature.

One would not have to give the impression that this is the case here. And it is indeed in order to help it that it will not allude, for example—not that this would be without interest—to the possible confrontation with other labours of what Canguilhem has obtained: one will not wonder what place the notion of *break* would have in his history of physiology. This is because there is no question of saying that he agrees with others, or that he distinguishes himself from them, before having understood what his *attitude* specifies.

38. Here is the text in its original form, which is given in its entirety in order the better to bring out the *variation on its meaning*:

"In the genealogical tree of man—substituted for the linear animal series—ramifications mark stages and not outlines, and the stages are not the effects and the testimonies of a plastic power aiming beyond them; they are the causes and agents of a history with no anticipated resolution.

"Yet at the same time that humanity ceases to be taken for the initial—and for certain naturalists, inaccessible—promise of animality, animality itself ceases to be taken for the permanent threat to humanity, for the image of a risk of decline and fall present at the very heart of apotheosis. Animality is the memory of the prescientific state of humanity, it is its organic prehistory and not its metaphysical anti-nature." (Canguilhem 1960, 85)

39. See the article "Expérimentation" in Canguilhem 1952.
40. Reflection about the concept of the norm frames Canguilhem's *oeuvre*; it is the subject of his first book (1943), and also of the course he taught at the Sorbonne in 1962–3.
41. Canguilhem 1989, 198.
42. Ibid.
43. Ibid., 201.
44. Ibid., 209.
45. Canguilhem 1955, 158–9.
46. Canguilhem 1980, 38.
47. Ibid., 49.

Bibliography

Adorno, Theodor et al. 1976. *The Positivist Dispute in German Sociology*. Trans. Glyn Adey and David Frisby. New York, NY: Harper and Row.

Althusser, Louis. 1976. *Essays in Self-Criticism*. Trans. Grahame Lock. London: New Left Books.

Althusser, Louis, and Etienne Balibar. 1970. *Reading Capital*. Trans. Ben Brewster. London: New Left Books.

———. 1995. *Ecrits philosophiques et politiques*, tome II. Paris: Stock/IMEC.

Aristotle. 1985. *Nicomachean Ethics*. Trans. Terence Irwin. Indianapolis, IN: Hackett Publishing Company.

Audouard, Xavier. 1959. "Pourquoi Hegel? Lettre au Dr. Charles Durand en réponse à sa question par Xavier Audouard." *La Psychanalyse* 5, 235–56.

Bergson, Henri. 1946. "Philosophical Intuition." In *The Creative Mind*, 126–52. Trans. Mabelle L. Andison. New York: Philosophical Library.

Borges, Jorge Luis. 1993. *Ficciones*. Edited by Anthony Kerrigan. New York, NY: Knopf.

Canguilhem, Georges. 1943. *Essai sur quelques problèmes concernant le normal et le pathologique*. Publications de la Faculté des Lettres de l'Université de Strasbourg, Fascicule 100. Clermont-Ferrand: Imprimerie "La Montaigne."

———. 1947. "Note sur la situation faite à la philosophie biologique en France." *Revue de métaphysique et de morale* 52, 322–32.

———. 1952. *La connaissance de la vie*. Paris: Hachette.

———. 1955. *La formation du concept de réflexe aux XVIIe et XVIIIe siècles*. Paris: Presses Universitaires de France.

———. 1957. "Sur une épistémologie concordataire." In *Hommage à Gaston Bachelard: Etudes de philosophie et d'histoire des sciences*, 3–12. Ed. G. Bouligand et al. Paris: Presses Universitaires de France.

———. 1958a. "Pathologie et physiologie de la thyroïde au XIXe siècle." *Thalès* 9, 77–97.

——. 1958b. "Qu'est-ce que la psychologie?" *Revue de métaphysique et de morale* 63, 12–25.

——. 1960. "L'homme et l'animal au point de vue psychologique selon Darwin." *Revue d'histoire des sciences* 13, 81–94.

——. 1961. "Nécessité de la 'diffusion scientifique.'" *Revue de l'enseignement supérieur* 3, 5–15.

——(with G. Lapassade, J. Piquemal, and J. Uhlmann). 1962. "Du développement à l'évolution au XIXᵉ siècle." *Thalès* 11, 1–65.

——. 1963a. "Gaston Bachelard et les philosophes." *Sciences* 24, 7–10.

——. 1963b. "L'histoire des sciences dans l'oeuvre épistémologique de Gaston Bachelard." *Annales de l'Université de Paris* 1, 24–39.

——. 1963c. "Introduction. La constitution de la physiologie comme science." In *Physiologie*, vol. 1, 1–48. Ed. Charles Kayser. Paris: Editions médicales Flammarion.

——. 1980. "What is Psychology?" *I & C* 7, 37–50.

——. 1989. *The Normal and the Pathological*. Trans. Carolyn R. Fawcett in collaboration with Robert S. Cohen. New York, NY: Zone Books.

——. 1994. *A Vital Rationalist: Selected Writings from Georges Canguilhem*. Trans. Arthur Goldhammer. Ed. François Delaporte. New York, NY: Zone Books.

Comte, Auguste. 1974 "Course in Positive Philosophy." In *The Essential Comte*. Edited by Stanislav Andreski. Translated by Margaret Clarke. New York, NY: Barnes and Noble Books.

——. 1975. "Plan of the Scientific Operations Necesary for Reorganizing Society." In *Auguste Comte and Positivism: The Essential Writings*. Edited and translated by Gertrud Lenzer. New York, NY: Harper Torchbooks.

Deleuze, Gilles. 1988a. *Foucault*. Trans. Seán Hand. Minneapolis, MN: University of Minnesota Press.

——. 1988b. *Spinoza: Practical Philosophy*. Trans. Robert Hurley. San Francisco, CA: City Lights Books.

——. 1990a. *Expressionism in Philosophy: Spinoza*. Trans. Martin Joughin. New York, NY: Zone Books.

——. 1990b. *The Logic of Sense*. Trans. Mark Lester with Charles Stivale. Ed. Constantin V. Boundas. New York, NY: Columbia University Press.

Deleuze, Gilles, and Claire Parnet. 1987. *Dialogues*. Trans. Hugh Tomlinson and Barbara Habberjam. New York, NY: Columbia University Press.

Diogenes Laertius. 1958. *Lives of Eminent Philosophers*, vol. 2. Trans. R.D. Hicks. Cambridge, MA: Harvard University Press.

Duras, Marguerite. 1984. *Outside*. Paris: P.O.L.

Eagleton, Terry. 1982. "Macherey and Marxist Literary Theory." In *Marx and Marxisms*. Ed. G.H.R. Parkinson. Cambridge: Cambridge University Press.

Foucault, Michel. 1954. *Maladie mentale et personnalité*. Paris: Presses Universitaires de France.

———. 1962. *Maladie mentale et psychologie*. Paris: Presses Universitaires de France.

———. 1963. *Naissance de la clinique*. Paris: Presses Universitaires de France.

———. 1972. *Histoire de la folie à l'âge classique*. Paris: Gallimard.

———. 1973. *The Birth of the Clinic: An Archaeology of Medical Perception*. Trans. A.M. Sheridan Smith. New York, NY: Pantheon Books.

———. 1982. "Pierre Boulez ou l'écran traversé." *Le Nouvel Observateur* 934, 51–2.

———. 1983. "The Subject and Power." In *Michel Foucault: Beyond Structuralism and Hermeneutics*, 2nd ed., 208–26. Ed. Hubert Dreyfus and Paul Rabinow. Chicago: The University of Chicago Press.

———. 1984. "What is Enlightenment?" In *The Foucault Reader*. Ed. Paul Rabinow. New York, NY: Pantheon Books.

———. 1985. *The Use of Pleasure*. Trans. Robert Hurley. New York, NY: Pantheon Books.

———. 1986. *Death and the Labyrinth: The World of Raymond Roussel*. Trans. Charles Ruas. New York, NY: Doubleday.

———. 1987 (1976). *Mental Illness and Psychology*. Trans. Alan Sheridan. Berkeley, CA: University of California Press.

———. 1988. "The Art of Telling the Truth." In *Politics, Philosophy, Culture: Interviews and Other Writings 1977–1984*, 86–95. Ed. Lawrence D. Kritzman New York, NY: Routledge.

———. 1992. "Is It Really Important to Think?" *Philosophy and Social Criticism* IX, 1, Spring 1992.

Freud, Sigmund. 1959. "From the History of an Infantile Neurosis." In *Collected Papers, Volume III: Case Histories*, 471–607. Trans. Alix and James Strachey. New York, NY: Basic Books.

———. 1962. *Three Essays on the Theory of Sexuality*. Trans. James Strachey. New York, NY: Basic Books.

Gallagher, Catherine. 1989. "Marxism and the New Historicism." In *The New Historicism*. Ed. H. Aram Veeger. New York: Routledge.

Giancotti, Emilia. 1970. *Lexicon Spinozanum*, two volumes. The Hague: Martinus Nijhoff.

Hegel, Georg Wilhelm Friedrich. 1965a. *Sämtliche Werke*. Stuttgart.

———. 1965b. *La raison dans l'histoire: introduction àlaphilosophie de l'histoire*. Trans. Kostas Papaioannou. Paris : Union Générale d'Editions.

———. 1977. *Phenomenology of Spirit*. Trans. A.V. Miller. Oxford: Oxford University Press.

———. 1991. *Elements of the Philosophy of Right*. Trans. H.B. Nisbet. Ed. Allen W. Wood. New York, NY: Cambridge University Press.

Heidegger, Martin. 1962. *Being and Time*. Trans. John Macquarrie and Edward Robinson. New York, NY: HarperCollins.

——. 1969. *Identity and Difference*. Trans. Joan Stambaugh. New York, NY: Harper and Row.

——. 1985. *Schelling's Treatise on the Essence of Human Freedom*. Trans. Joan Stambaugh. Athens, OH: Ohio University Press.

——. 1987 (1959). *An Introduction to Metaphysics*. Trans. Ralph Manheim. New Haven, CT: Yale University Press.

——. 1991. *The Principle of Reason*. Trans. Reginald Lilly. Bloomington, IN: Indiana University Press.

——. 1993 (1977). "Letter on Humanism." In *Basic Writings*, revised and expanded edition, 213–65. Ed. David Farrell Krell. New York, NY: HarperCollins.

Hollier, Denis. 1986. *The Politics of Prose: Essay on Sartre*. Trans. Jeffrey Mehlman. Minneapolis, MN: The University of Minnesota Press.

Horkheimer and Adorno. 1989. *Dialectic of Enlightenment*. Trans. John Cumming. New York, NY: Continuum.

Hyppolite, Jean. 1957. "Phénoménologie de Hegel et psychanalyse." *La Psychanalyse* 3.

——. 1988. "A Spoken Commentary on Freud's *Verneinung*." In Lacan 1988, 289–97.

Kant, Immanuel. 1992. "Attempt to Introduce the Concept of Negative Magnitudes into Philosophy." In *Theoretical Philosophy, 1750–1770*, 203–41. Trans. and ed. David Walford in collaboration with Ralf Meerbote. New York, NY: Cambridge University Press.

Lacan, Jacques. 1966. *Ecrits*. Paris: Seuil.

——. 1978. *The Seminar of Jacques Lacan, Book XI: The Four Fundamental Concepts of Psychoanalysis*. New York, NY: Norton.

——. 1988. *The Seminar of Jacques Lacan, Book I: Freud's Papers on Technique 1953–1954*. New York, NY: Norton.

Lebrun, Gérard. 1970. *Kant et la fin de la métaphysique: essai sur la critique de la faculté de juger*. Paris: Armand Colin.

Macherey, Pierre. 1978. *A Theory of Literary Production*. London: Routledge.

——. 1979. *Hegel ou Spinoza*. Paris: François Maspero.

——. 1992. *Avec Spinoza: Etudes sur la doctrine et l'histoire du spinozisme*. Paris: Presses Universitaires de France.

——. 1995. *The Object of Literature*. Trans. David Macey. New York, NY: Cambridge University Press.

Marx, Karl. 1973. *Grundrisse*. Trans. Martin Nicolaus. New York, NY: Vintage Books.

Marx, Karl, and Friedrich Engels. 1976. *Collected Works*, vol. 5. New York, NY: International Publishers.

Negri, Antonio. 1982. *L'anomalie sauvage: puissance et pouvoir chez Spinoza*. Trans. François Matheron. Paris: Presses Universitaires de France.

——. 1991. *The Savage Anomaly: The Power of Spinoza's Metaphysics and*

Politics. Trans. Michael Hardt. Minneapolis, MN: University of Minnesota Press.

Pascal, Blaise. 1966. *Pensées*. Trans. A. J. Krailsheimer. New York, NY: Penguin Books.

Rey, J.M. 1974. "De la dénegation." In *Parcours de Freud*. Paris: Galilée.

Sartre, Jean-Paul. 1977. "Self-Portrait at Seventy." In *Life/Situations: Essays Written and Spoken*. Trans. Paul Auster and Lydia Davis. New York, NY: Pantheon Books.

——. 1988. *"What is Literature?" and Other Essays*. Cambridge, MA: Harvard University Press.

Spinoza, Baruch. 1958. *The Political Works*. Trans. and ed. A.G. Wernham. Oxford: Oxford University Press.

——. 1985. *The Collected Works of Spinoza*. Trans. and ed. Edwin Curley. Princeton, NJ: Princeton University Press.

——. 1991 (1989). *Tractatus Theologico-Politicus*, 2nd ed. Trans. Samuel Shirley. New York, NY: E.J. Brill.

——. 1995. *The Letters*. Trans. Samuel Shirley. Indianapolis, IN: Hackett.

Index